T0330451

Intellectual Property Enforcement

International Perspectives

Edited by

Xuan Li

Programme Coordinator, Innovation, Access to Knowledge and Intellectual Property Programme (IAKP), South Centre, Switzerland

Carlos M. Correa

Director of the Centre for Interdisciplinary Studies of Industrial Property Law and Economics, University of Buenos Aires, Argentina

SOUTH CENTRE

Edward Elgar
Cheltenham, UK • Northampton, MA, USA

Published by
Edward Elgar Publishing Limited
The Lypiatts
15 Lansdown Road
Cheltenham
Glos GL50 2JA
UK

Edward Elgar Publishing, Inc.
William Pratt House
9 Dewey Court
Northampton
Massachusetts 01060
USA

A catalogue record for this book is available from the British Library

Library of Congress Control Number: 2009925931

Mixed Sources
Product group from well-managed
forests and other controlled sources
www.fsc.org Cert no. SA-COC-1565
© 1996 Forest Stewardship Council

ISBN 978 1 84844 652 6 (cased)
ISBN 978 1 84844 663 2 (paperback)

Printed and bound by MPG Books Group, UK

Contents

Contributors

Yusong Chen is currently a diplomat at the Permanent Mission of China to the WTO. Previously, he was a legal affairs officer in the Department of Treaties & Laws of China's Ministry of Commerce (MOFCOM). He participated in many Chinese legislative activities, including the drafting of China's Foreign Trade law, antidumping/CVD/safeguard regulations, and so on. As a negotiator, he participated in the WTO Doha negotiations, mainly focused on the issues of TRIPS (GIs and CBD) and rules (anti-dumping, subsidy and fisheries subsidies), as well as many bilateral trade negotiations, including China's FTA negotiations. He was also involved in the WTO dispute settlement proceedings on behalf of China. He holds an LLB in International Economic Law with magna cum laude from the Law School of Peking University (PKU) and a Diploma in Public Administration from China's National School of Administration (CNSA). He also has an LLM with distinction in EU and International Trade Law from Amsterdam Law School, Universiteit van Amsterdam (UvA). He has published various articles in the field of international economic law.

Henrique Choer Moraes is a career diplomat currently posted at the Permanent Mission of Brazil to the European Communities (Brussels), where he is in charge of following intellectual property issues as well as the work of the World Customs Organization (WCO). Prior to that, he worked at the Intellectual Property Division of Brazil's Ministry of External Relations, where he served from 2004 to 2007. In that capacity he took part in negotiations on patents, copyrights and intellectual property–biodiversity issues at the World Trade Organization, and the Convention on Biological Diversity. From 2000 to 2004 he worked as Professor of Public International Law at the University Ritter dos Reis, Porto Alegre (Brazil). He holds a Master's degree in integration and business international law from the Universidade Federal do Rio Grande do Sul (Porto Alegre).

Carlos M. Correa is Director of the Centre for Interdisciplinary Studies of Industrial Property Law and Economics of the University of Buenos Aires and of the Postgraduate Courses on Intellectual Property of the same university. From 1991 to 2004 he was the Director of the Master's Programme on Science and Technology Policy and Management. He is member of the Permanent Court of Review of MERCOSUR and has been a consultant to UNCTAD, UNIDO, WHO, FAO, Inter-American Development Bank and its unit INTAL, World Bank, SELA, ECLAC, UNDP and various other regional and international organizations as well as governments in different areas of law and economics, including investment, science and technology and intellectual property. He was a member of the UK International Commission on Intellectual Property, established in 2001. In 2004 he was appointed as member of the Commission on Intellectual Property Rights, Innovation and Public Health created by the World Health Assembly, as well as the FAO Panel of Eminent Experts on Ethics in Food and Agriculture. He currently chairs the Genetics Resources Policy Committee of the CGIAR. He is the author of several books and numerous articles on law and economics, particularly on investment, technology and intellectual property.

Henning Grosse Ruse-Khan is a Research Fellow at the Max Planck Institute for Intellectual Property, Competition and Tax Law in Munich since 2007. His research focuses on new approaches for balancing private rights and public interests in international economic law, in particular intellectual property protection. Formerly, he was a Lecturer in International Trade Law at the University of Leicester (United Kingdom) and a research fellow at the Institute for Information, Telecommunication and Media Law (ITM) of the University of Münster on intellectual property and information technology law. He has also acted as a visiting scholar on WTO, International Trade and Intellectual Property Law at the International Islamic University in Islamabad (2004–05) and at the University of Frankfurt (2007). He has several publications on international trade and intellectual property law to his credit.

Xuan Li is Programme Coordinator of the Innovation, Access to Knowledge and Intellectual Property Programme (IAKP) at South Centre in Switzerland, an intergovernmental organization and think tank of developing countries. She is the Director of the

South Centre Distance Learning Course on 'Intellectual Property Policy and Development', jointly implemented with the United Nations Institute for Training and Research (UNITAR), and a member of the Editorial Committee of *South Bulletin: Reflections and Foresights*. She has been a consultant to a number of national and intergovernmental organizations, including the World Health Organization, the Food and Agriculture Organization, the Chinese Ministry of Commerce, the Chinese State Intellectual Property Office, the State Administration of Traditional Chinese Medicine, and the World Trade Institute, among others. She has worked on international trade, intellectual property and development issues for the Asian Development Bank and ICTSD, and was Lead Economist of the South Centre. She has also been actively involved in the Chinese National Strategic Formulation on Intellectual Property Rights. She is the author of several books and numerous articles on intellectual property, law and economics, particularly on innovation, enforcement, technology, traditional knowledge, IP standardization, philosophy and literature.

Viviana Muñoz Tellez is a Programme Officer at the South Centre. She conducts policy-oriented research on innovation, access to knowledge and intellectual property policy. Previously she worked at the Queen Mary Intellectual Property Research Institute, London. She has also worked as a consultant to the United Nations Industrial Development Organization and various non-governmental organizations. Viviana received a Master's degree in Development Management from the London School of Economics. She has several publications on intellectual property and development issues to her credit.

Joshua D. Sarnoff is the Assistant Director of the Glushko-Samuelson Intellectual Property Law Clinic and a practitioner-in-residence at the Washington College of Law, American University, where he supervises law students in the practice of intellectual property law. He is also a registered patent attorney and a member of the Board of Directors of the Federal Circuit Bar Association, and has been involved in a wide range of intellectual property legal and policy disputes. He has published several articles on patent law and has received the Emalee C. Godsey Award for his scholarship, submitted testimony to and coordinated an academics' position statement for the US Congress on patent law reform bills, filed numerous amicus briefs in the US Supreme Court and the Court of Appeals for the Federal Circuit on important patent law issues, has been a pro bono mediator for the Federal Circuit, and has been a consultant to the UNCTAD on intellectual property, trade and environmental issues. Mr Sarnoff was formerly in private practice in Washington, DC, and previously taught at the University of Arizona College of Law.

Hong Xue is a Professor of Law at Beijing Normal University and Research Fellow of the Information Society Project of Yale Law School. Previously, she was the Associate Professor of the Faculty of Law, University of Hong Kong. Dr Xue specializes in intellectual property law, information technology law and the Internet governance. Dr Xue was elected as one of the Ten Nationally Distinguished Young Jurists by the China Law Society and granted the Special Governmental Allowance for prominent contribution to social science by the State Council of the People's Republic of China. She was also the awardee of the Outstanding Young Researcher Award of the University of Hong Kong. She has published widely in both Chinese and international journals. She works in many governmental and non-governmental organizations. She is the only Asian Scholar in the Executive Committee of the International Association for Promotion of the Advanced Teaching and Research of Intellectual Property (ATRIP) and the Editorial Board of *The Journal of World Intellectual Property*. She was a founding member of the ICANN At-Large Advisory Committee from 2003 to 2007, and she is now a member of the ICANN Nomination Committee and the President's Advisory Committee on Internationalized Domain Names. She is also one of the founders of the Internet Users Organization in the Asia-Pacific Region.

Abbreviations

ACE	Advisory Committee on Enforcement
ACP	African, Caribbean and Pacific countries
ACTA	Anti-Counterfeiting Trade Agreement
ACWL	Advisory Centre on WTO Law
ADB	Asian Development Bank
AMA	Anti-Monopoly Act
BIRPI	Bureaux Internationaux Réunis pour la Protection de la Propriété Intellectuelle
BITs	Bilateral Investment Treaties
BSA	Business Software Alliance
CAFTA	Central African Free Trade Agreement
CARIFORUM	Caribbean Forum of African, Caribbean and Pacific States
CBD	Convention on Biological Diversity
CDIP	Committee on Development and Intellectual Property
CEBR	Centre for Economics and Business Research
CFI	Court of First Instance
CGIAR	Consultative Group on International Agricultural Research
CIEL	Centre for International Environmental Law
CIPIH	Commission on Intellectual Property Rights, Innovation and Public Health
CIPR	Commission for Intellectual Property Rights
CMPI	Center for Medicine in the Public Interest
CVD	Countervailing duty
DMCA	Digital Millennium Copyright Act
DNA	Deoxyribonucleic acid
DOJ	Department of Justice
DRM	Digital Rights Management
DSB	Dispute Settlement Body

EC	European Commission
ECLAC	UN Economic Commission for Latin America and the Caribbean
ECJ	European Court of Justice
EFPIA	European Federation of Pharmaceutical Industries and Associations
EPA	Economic Partnership Agreement
EPSPS	Glyphosate-tolerant 5-enolpyruvylshikimate-3-phosphate synthase
EU	European Union
FAO	Food and Agriculture Organization
FTA	Free trade agreement
FTC	Federal Trade Commission
G8	Group of Eight countries
GATS	General Agreement on Trade in Services
GATT	General Agreement on Tariffs and Trade
GDP	Gross domestic product
GI	Geographical indication
GM	Genetically modified
GMO	Genetically modified organism
IAKP	Innovation, Access to Knowledge and Intellectual Property Programme
ICANN	Internet Corporation for Assigned Names and Numbers
ICN	International Competition Network
ICTSD	International Centre for Trade and Sustainable Development
IFPI	International Federation of Phonogram & Videogram Producers
IMPACT	International Medical Products Anti-Counterfeiting Taskforce
INTERPOL	International Criminal Police Organization
IP	Intellectual property
IPR	Intellectual property right
ISP	Internet service provider
IT	Information technology
LDC	Least developed country
MERCOSUR	Southern Common Market
MFN	Most favoured nation
MPAA	Motion Picture Association of America

OECD	Organisation for Economic Co-operation and Development
R&D	Research and development
RIAA	Recording Industry Association of America
RR	Round-Up Ready
RTA	Regional trade agreement
SAFE	Framework of Standards to Secure and Facilitate Global Trade
SECURE	Provisional Standards Employed by Customs for Uniform Rights Enforcement
SELA	Latin American and Caribbean Economic System
TNC	Transnational corporation
TPM	Technological protection measures
TRIMS	Trade-Related Investment Measures Agreement
TRIPS	Trade-Related Aspects of Intellectual Property Rights
TWN	Third World Network
UN	United Nations
UNCTAD	United Nations Conference on Trade and Development
UNDP	United Nations Development Programme
UNESCO	United Nations Educational, Scientific and Cultural Organization
UNIDO	United Nations Industrial Development Organization
UPOV	Union Internationale pour la Protection des Obtentions Végétales (Union for the Protection of New Varieties of Plants)
UPU	Universal Postal Union
USD	United States dollar
USPTO	United States Patent and Trademark Office
USTR	United States Trade Representative
WCO	World Customs Organization
WCT	WIPO Copyright Treaty
WGTCP	Working Group on Trade and Competition Policy
WGTTT	Working Group on Trade and Transfer of Technology (WTO)
WHO	World Health Organization
WIPO	World Intellectual Property Organization
WPPT	WIPO Performances and Phonograms Treaty
WTO	World Trade Organization

Preface

This book draws on two international symposiums on enforcement of intellectual property (IP) and development held by the South Centre[1] in October 2007 and September 2008 in Geneva, regarding recent trends at the national and regional level and new developments in such forums as the World Trade Organization (WTO), the World Intellectual Property Organization (WIPO), World Health Organization (WHO), the World Customs Organization (WCO), the Universal Postal Union (UPU), Group of Eight developed countries (G8), and the Anti-Counterfeiting Trade Agreement (ACTA), among others.

The book analyses the IP enforcement debate in three parts. Part I presents an explanation of the evolving IP enforcement debate and its challenges through an analysis of shifting trends in global governance on IP, the general misunderstanding that informs the IP enforcement discourse, the challenges posed by the discourse for multiple stakeholders, and the current status of IP enforcement standards negotiations. Chapter 1 on 'The changing global governance of intellectual property enforcement: a new challenge for developing countries' by Viviana Muñoz Tellez discusses in brief the relationship between intellectual property and development and traces the historical evolution of international intellectual property law and policy-making up to the present. The chapter finds that the strategies pursued by developed countries and industry lobbies today to exert pressure on developing country governments to increase the enforcement of intellectual property rights and establish TRIPS-plus enforcement standards are not dissimilar from those employed in the 1970s to mid-1990s to bring about TRIPS minimum global standards on intellectual property protection and enforcement. It finds that significant changes are taking place in the global governance of the current international rules for the effective enforcement of intellectual property rights. Finally, the chapter advances two policy recommendations aimed at developing countries and least developed countries. First, these countries should avoid adopting TRIPS-plus standards for the enforcement of intellectual property rights by coordinating at the multilateral level to resist and proactively counter the TRIPS-plus enforcement agenda. Second, they should zealously maintain and make use of the flexibilities still available in the international intellectual property system to tailor their national systems for the protection and enforcement of intellectual property rights in line with their national development goals.

Chapter 2 on 'Ten general misconceptions about the enforcement of intellectual property rights' by Xuan Li is intended to assist the developing and least developed countries' public authorities and academia in correcting the misconceptions on enforcement of intellectual property rights (IPRs) under the TRIPS Agreement. Currently, the arguments from developed countries tend to oversimplify the discourse on IP enforcement by offering a misleading interpretation of IP enforcement obligations of states under international law or by over-exaggerating a particular aspect of the counterfeit and piracy problem. Such oversimplification is dangerous, for it creates misconceptions that not only confuses the public as to the cause and extent of the problem, but also misleads policy-makers into finding solutions that fail to address the crux of the enforcement of IPRs. In this context, this chapter gives an account of a series of misunderstandings that inform the discourse, including substantive issues such as definition and scope of enforcement, and procedural issues such as administrative and judicial enforcement. It attempts to reconfigure ten general misconceptions about enforcement of IPRs, namely (1) counterfeiting and piracy includes patent infringement; (2) product falsification, counterfeiting and IP-infringed goods are identical; (3) IP infringement poses a consumer threat; (4) the magnitude of claimed IP infringement is enormous; (5) governments should take the primary responsibility of enforcement; (6) governments should bear the cost of IP enforcement; (7) WTO members are bound to provide border measures for all IPR infringement including patent infringement; (8) WTO members are bound to provide a special judicial system for IPR enforcement; (9) criminal procedures must be established for IP-infringing products; and (10) customs administrations have the authority to determine IP infringement.

The notion to strengthen regimes for the enforcement of intellectual property currently takes centre stage in various international, regional and national forums. In general, developed countries are demanding stronger enforcement, while developing countries take a defensive stand aiming to prevent further obligations beyond those found in Part III of the TRIPS Agreement. Against this background, enforcement of intellectual property is generally connoted with the enforcement of the right-holders' exclusive entitlements – thus neglecting other elements of the intellectual property system such as exceptions and limitations to exclusive rights and their 'enforcement'. This prevents a holistic view on the issue of IP enforcement where all stakeholders and their role and interests in the IP system are examined. Chapter 3 on 'Re-delineation of the role of stakeholders: IP enforcement beyond exclusive rights' by Henning Grosse Ruse-Khan identifies the relevant actors in IP enforcement on the basis of such a holistic approach to IP enforcement. This allows a more comprehensive perspective on the issue of enforcement where developing countries not only have defensive interests in preventing further reductions in the policy space available under TRIPS, but also have significant offensive interests in giving effect to those elements of the intellectual property system that suit their domestic innovation and technology policies and recognize other public interests. The chapter concludes that the current enforcement debate not only suffers from a disproportionate bias towards the interests of right-holders, but at the same time marginalizes the offensive interests of developing countries. Hence, the developing countries should assess the interests of their domestic stakeholders and establish a comprehensive IP strategy that focuses on enforcing these interests.

In the area of IP protection, the latest attempts to dictate TRIP-plus standards by developed countries is clearly aimed at establishing a new international trade order that will serve their own interests at the expense of developing countries. Since the negotiating capacity of developing countries at the World Trade Organization (WTO) and the World Intellectual Property Organization (WIPO) is relatively strong, the developed countries have not been able to fully realize their objective of ratcheting up TRIPS-plus standards on IP enforcement in these forums. Hence, the developed countries launched simultaneous initiatives in other international or regional forums such as the World Customs Organization (WCO), Universal Postal Union (UPU), World Health Organization (WHO), as well as the Group of Eight developed countries (G8), bypassing the WTO and WIPO process in order to impose TRIPS-plus-plus standards. In particular, developed countries have made the WCO one of the key battlefields with a proposal to expand the authorities of national customs administrations through negotiations on the Provisional Standards Employed by Customs for Uniform Rights Enforcement (SECURE). Xuan Li analyses the SECURE negotiations process in the WCO in Chapter 4 titled 'WCO SECURE: legal and economic assessments of TRIPS-plus-plus IP enforcement'.

Part II of the book provides an account of three recent disputes pertaining to IP enforcement, which depicts the challenges for developing countries and offers insights into lessons that can be drawn from these disputes. In Chapter 5 on 'Enforcing border measures: importation of GMO soybean meal from Argentina', Carlos M. Correa gives an account of the recent cases filed by the US multinational corporation Monsanto in the courts in Denmark, the Netherlands, Spain and the United Kingdom against European importers of Argentine soymeal shipments, seeking that the shipments be detained in the ports in those countries on the grounds that the Argentine soymeal shipments contained the RR gene, which is patented by Monsanto in Europe, and thus the shipments infringed Monsanto's IPR over the same. This case shows the possible implications that a TRIPS-plus IP enforcement regime can have for developing countries. While the case is primarily between Monsanto and European importers, it actually targets the government and soybean producers in Argentina. Moreover, Monsanto relies on its European patent and its enforcement in Europe by producers in Argentina, though Monsanto did not patent the RR gene in Argentina. Thus, through enforcement proceedings in Europe, Monsanto attempted to effectively extend the enforceability of its patent to Argentina, where it did not have a patent over the RR gene. This chapter explains the reasons as well as the possible consequences of this transnational litigation and illustrates its possible impact of broad border measures on legitimate trade, particularly when applied to alleged patent infringements.

While developed countries have been vehemently advocating for a strong TRIPS-plus IP enforcement regime globally that overwhelmingly advances the interests of right-holders, there have been developments within the developed countries that point to a contrarian emerging trend. A very prominent example of this is the US Supreme Court's 2006 decision *eBay, Inc.* v. *MercExchange, L.L.C.*, which reversed a long prevailing general rule in US jurisprudence that courts will issue permanent injunctions against patent infringement absent exceptional circumstances, and held that the existence of an IP infringement itself did not necessarily entitle the right-holder to an injunction. In Chapter 6 on 'Flexible application of injunctive relief in intellectual property enforcement (with reference to lessons from the emerging US jurisprudence)', Joshua D. Sarnoff examines the developing law in the United States applicable to judicial decisions to grant or to deny various forms of equitable injunctive relief as a tool for intellectual property rights enforcement in the context of the *eBay* decision and points to the possible lessons in terms of policy choices that US jurisprudence may offer the law-makers and the judiciary in developing countries in balancing the right-holders' interest and public interest when deciding on granting an injunction, which is a major tool for IP enforcement.

Developing countries are also being pushed to change their IP enforcement systems through litigation before the WTO DSB (Dispute Settlement Body). A most prominent example of this is the ongoing dispute between the United States and China at the WTO on 'Measures Affecting the Protection and Enforcement of IP Rights'. Chapter 7 on 'Enforcement for development: why not an agenda for the developing world?', by Hong Xue analyses the US–China dispute as a telling example of how developed countries intervene in the IP law-making and enforcement systems of developing countries and regards the dispute as a case that will test the cornerstones of international IP law and answer whether the developmental values that underpin the international IP regime are still cherished. The chapter argues that to resist the pressures exerted on them by developed countries, developing countries must take an aggressive strategy to inform the global IP enforcement discourse with a pro-development perspective that will make global IP enforcement norms flexible and diversified.

Part III of the book seeks to advance the strategic considerations that should inform the developing countries in addressing the challenges thrown up by the aggressive TRIPS-plus IP enforcement agenda being pushed forward by developed countries. A forum of immediate concern in this regard is the WCO. Chapter 8 by Henrique Choer Moraes on 'Dealing with forum shopping: some lessons from the SECURE negotiations at the World Customs Organization' analyses the WCO as a shopped forum by developed

countries to advance a TRIPS-plus agenda in the area of enforcement of IPRs. Despite the important role that customs might play
in the fight against piracy and counterfeiting, the chapter argues that
the work of the WCO in the field of IPRs should not be promoted
without due consideration to the negative impacts many of the
remedies proposed can produce over trade in generic medicines and
access to culture. Developing countries' participation in defence of
their interests is made difficult by the murky or non-existing rules of
procedures in place at the WCO as well as by the highly unbalanced
and non-transparent institutional arrangements that govern the
functioning of the organization. The chapter elaborates on the many
examples that show why the WCO is a unique case of forum shopping and seeks to draw some lessons that can be useful for developing countries. One of the most prominent lessons is the need to
ensure strengthened coordination at the domestic level between officials in charge of intellectual property policy-making and customs
administrations.

In Chapter 9 on 'Ensuring the benefits of intellectual property
rights to development: a competition policy perspective', Yusong
Chen suggests that developing countries should accord great importance to competition policy aspects in their IP enforcement systems
in order to derive benefits from the IP system. The chapter argues
that current WIPO treaties and the TRIPS Agreement provide sufficient policy space to the developing countries for formulating and
implementing appropriate competition policy for controlling abuse
of IPRs.

Chapter 10 briefly presents the main conclusions drawn from the
previous chapters.

The authors of the various chapters in this book are experts
renowned in the international IP circles, officials from international
organizations and diplomats who have directly participated in
WTO/WCO negotiations. They provide analytical frameworks to
understand the complex issues raised by enforcement of IPRs and
rich first-hand experience of recent negotiations on the subject,
adding a special appeal to the book.

It is hoped that the legal analysis, case studies, conclusions and
recommendations presented in this book will contribute to a better
understanding of the implications of IP enforcement measures,
particularly in connection with development policies. The book is
intended for a broad reach of readers, including scholars, experts and

students of international relations in general and IP rules-making in particular, government officials and negotiators and companies engaged in offensive or defensive enforcement actions.

Xuan Li
Carlos M. Correa

NOTE

1. The South Centre is an international organization that operates as a think tank for developing countries in relation to various areas of international debates and negotiations, such as international trade, intellectual property and global governance (see Appendix).

Acknowledgements

We are immensely grateful to those who have contributed in various ways to the publication of this book. The development of the book has been a long process, involving many strategic discussions with Geneva-based and Brussels-based developing country delegates dealing with IP enforcement negotiations; intensive interactions with capital-based policy-makers; high-level meetings with board members of the South Centre; series of dialogues with the officials and professionals of several international organizations, such as the WTO, UNCTAD, WIPO, WHO, WCO, UPU, ACWL; and in-depth interactions with colleagues from non-governmental organizations, including TWN, CIEL, ICTSD, and so on.

We would like to acknowledge the valuable contributions from the participants who attended the first and the second South Centre International Symposiums on 'Examining IP Enforcement from a Development Perspective', held in Geneva on 9 October 2007 and 16 September 2008, respectively. In particular, we would like to express our sincere appreciation to H.E. Mr Zhenyu Sun, Ambassador of the People's Republic of China to the WTO, and H.E. Dr Makarim Wibisono, Ambassador of the Republic of Indonesia to the UN, for their substantive support and strategic vision. We would like to acknowledge the valuable views and steadfast support from many developing countries' delegates, particularly Guilherme de Aguiar Patriota, Sunjay Sudhir, Boumediene Mahi, Johan van Wyk, Ali Asad, Luis Vayas Valdivieso, Mohamed Omar Gad, Maximiliano Santa Cruz, Ines Fastame, Deny Kurnia, Maigari Buba, Cristiano Berbert, Mohamed A. Bdioui, Zhihua Dong, Yan Huo, Xiangchen Zhang, Susanna Chung, Simon Z. Qobo, Judha Nugraha and Peter Aumane.

This book also benefits from the concrete and insightful inputs by many experts. In this regard, we are especially grateful to Martin Khor, German Velásquez, Jian Liu, Christoph Spennemann, Roger Kampf, Ermias Biadgleng, Fernando Piérola, Hui Fu, Konstantinos Karachalios, Joost Pauwelyn, Carsten Fink, Qin Zhang, Sean

Flynn, Weiwei Li, Yueshi Wu, Pedro Roffe, Sangeeta Shashikant, Dalindyebo Shabalala and Ahmed Abdel Latif.

This project would not be possible without the support of the Ford Foundation, the Rockefeller Foundation, the Swedish International Development Cooperation Agency, the Open Society Institute Zug Foundation, and John D. and Catherine T. MacArthur Foundation. We, therefore, express our sincere indebtedness to all the funders of this very important book project.

It is our great pride to acknowledge that we are blessed with the strong leadership of the Executive Director of the South Centre, and the enormous support and assistance from our dedicated colleagues at the Secretariat, in particular Nirmalya Syam, Viviana Muñoz Tellez, Caroline Ngome Eneme, Vikas Nath, Vasanthan Pushparaj and Xin Cui, among others. We are especially grateful to Nirmalya Syam who assisted in editing the draft manuscripts and providing his intellectual inputs on the book.

Disclaimer: The views expressed is this book are the personal opinions of the authors, and do not reflect the position of the South Centre and its Member States. All errors and omissions in this study are the authors' sole responsibility.

PART I

THE IP ENFORCEMENT DEBATE

1. The changing global governance of intellectual property enforcement: a new challenge for developing countries

Viviana Muñoz Tellez

INTRODUCTION

Over the past decade, the understanding on the relationship between intellectual property and development has increased significantly. This is largely due to the expansion of research conducted across multiple disciplines – law, economics, political science, international relations, development studies – and the consolidation of intellectual property systems in developing countries. Groundbreaking works (CIPR, 2002; CIPIH, 2006) have shown that the relationship is complex, multifaceted and dynamic. Empirical and historical evidence reveal mixed outcomes regarding the impact of strong intellectual property protection among countries at different levels of economic and technological development and economic sectors. In terms of policy, it means that intellectual property rules should be designed, implemented and adjusted to balance the various effects of intellectual property protection, in line with national development priorities.

The ability of developing countries, including least developed countries, to integrate development concerns into their intellectual property systems is constrained by the growing number of multilateral, regional and bilateral commitments they continue to make in the area of intellectual property. Accordingly, it is ever more important today that developing countries maintain and make use of the flexibilities that are available in the international intellectual property regime, rather than strengthen intellectual property protection without making a thorough assessment beforehand of the needs, risks and impact of increasing protection.

One of the major challenges facing developing country governments today is how to deal with the growing number of demands from intellectual property right-holders and developed country governments, to reform their systems for the enforcement of intellectual property rights.

Despite the enormous concessions already made by developing countries in the area of intellectual property, developed countries are placing increased pressure on developing countries to increase their efforts at the national level to strengthen the enforcement of intellectual property rights. In parallel, they are pursuing an active agenda to establish new global TRIPS-plus intellectual property enforcement standards. The strategies pursued by developed countries and industry lobbies today to exert pressure on developing country governments to increase the enforcement of intellectual property rights and establish TRIPS-plus enforcement standards are not dissimilar from those employed in the 1970s to mid-1990s to bring about TRIPS minimum global standards on intellectual property protection and enforcement.

THE EVOLUTION OF INTERNATIONAL INTELLECTUAL PROPERTY LAW AND POLICY-MAKING

Intellectual property systems assign, protect and place limits on the use of intellectual property rights. In their design, policy-makers must strike a delicate balance between the interests of right-holders and the broader public interest. In the case of developed countries, intellectual property systems and their legal enforcement has evolved over time in accordance with national economic interests. Levels of protection and enforcement of intellectual property rights were strengthened with the pace of technological change and advancement in the pharmaceutical, software, audiovisual, chemical and other industries. The historical trajectory of intellectual property systems in developing countries is remarkably different. While developed countries took over two centuries to design, experiment with and progressively institute national intellectual property systems, developing countries for the most part adsorbed foreign-imposed intellectual property systems due to colonial rule. The post-colonial era offered developing countries greater freedom to tailor their intellectual property systems, but increasing globalization and inter-national trade over the past decade has brought new external press-ures on developing countries to reform their intellectual property systems.

The main source of pressure can be traced to European, Japanese and United States-owned multinational companies seeking to increase the value of their exports and expand their global market revenues. The monopoly of intellectual property rights was regarded as an instrument to avoid further catching up based on imitative paths of industrialization (Correa, 2000, p. 4). Governments in developed countries have responded to these demands by pressur-ing developing country governments to strengthen national stand-ards of intellectual property protection, utilizing a carrot-and-stick approach and idealization of the benefits derived from strong intel-lectual property protection, and by advancing treaties for the global protection of intellectual property rights.

The first major intellectual property treaties date back to the 1880s (the Paris Convention, 1883, the Berne Convention, 1886). Most of the nations classified today as developing countries did not become parties to these treaties until after the 1950s and therefore had no say in the standards these treaties set. Most international treaties were subsequently negotiated and concluded under the auspice of the Bureaux Internationaux Réunis pour la Protection de la Propriété Intellectuelle (BIRPI), established in 1893 to administer the Paris and Berne Conventions. The World Intellectual Property Organization (WIPO) replaced the BIRPI in 1967, and in 1974 became part of the United Nations system as a specialized agency. WIPO now admin-isters 24 treaties. The growing number of developing countries that have joined WIPO since the 1970s and their increased participation in the norm-setting processes in the organization has increased their influence in the organization. Evidence of their growing influence is the establishment of a WIPO Development Agenda as of September 2007.

Forum Shifting: From the WIPO to the WTO

Historically, developing countries have not played a prominent role at the WIPO in terms of standard-setting. This may be explained by a variety of factors. The first is the historical leadership of developed countries in advancing international intellectual property standards.

It is also partly explained by the fact that developing countries have only recently begun to devise and implement national intellectual property systems that closely model foreign standards, and thus have taken longer to articulate their demands for international standard-setting in the area of intellectual property. Technical assistance to implement intellectual property treaties remained the main demand of developing countries at the WIPO.

Other important factors that explain the historically limited role of developing countries in standard-setting at WIPO relate to the internal organizational and political dynamics of WIPO. Industry and groups representing private right-holders' interests at WIPO have historically held significant influence in the organization. Over 85 per cent of the income of the organization derives from the fees paid in by the private users of the systems of global intellectual property protection administered by WIPO. The Secretariat or International Bureau has also played a very significant role in WIPO, defining the vision for the organization, shaping the nature and final outcome of the treaty negotiations and discussions and advancing soft-law recommendations (Dutfield and Musungu, 2003, p. 8). By the 1980s, developing countries were playing an increasingly active role at WIPO, including in opposing and rebutting developed country proposals.

The continuation of WIPO as the main multilateral forum for negotiations on intellectual property posed a dilemma for industry players, particularly in the areas of pharmaceuticals and software, seeking to advance stronger and harmonized global standards of intellectual property protection and enforcement. WIPO treaties were considered to offer only minimal standards of protection and the organization lacked a mechanism for the enforcement of intellectual property rights. Developing countries were also gaining new ground in the organization. Such considerations led developed countries to strategically move negotiations for a new far-reaching international intellectual property treaty away from WIPO to a new forum where industry would achieve more favourable outcomes (Correa and Musungu, 2002).

The role of multinational companies, particularly from the United States in bringing about the historic shift is well documented (Correa, 2000; Matthews, 2002; May and Sell, 2005). By convincing the United States and other developed countries of the need to link intellectual property and trade, industry players were able to push their agenda and include intellectual property as an integral part of the Uruguay Round of trade negotiations under the General Agreement on Tariffs and Trade (GATT). The GATT was replaced by the World Trade Organization (WTO) as an international organization on 1 January 1995. The outcome of the Uruguay Round was a package deal that included the Agreement on Trade-Related Aspects of Intellectual Property Rights (TRIPS).

While developing countries resisted the inclusion of so-called 'trade-related intellectual property' in the trade negotiations, the agreement was part of the trade-offs made for concessions in other areas, particularly market access for agricultural goods. It also stemmed from the notion that if developing countries agreed to multilateral negotiations in the GATT framework, developed countries, in particular the United States, would stop threatening them with unilateral trade sanctions under the United States Trade Representative 'Special 301' Report and mandating high standards of intellectual property protection as part of bilateral and regional trade agreements (Drahos, 2002). This notion, however, soon proved to be false as the use of such measures by developed countries actually multiplied rather than declined after the TRIPS Agreement was concluded as part of the active and to date very effective strategy to pursue upward global standards for intellectual property protection and enforcement via multilateral, regional, bilateral and unilateral avenues.

The main perceived advantage of the WTO was that it was an agreement with teeth that could bite hard, which the WIPO lacked. By bringing intellectual property rules into the multilateral trade framework, it would oblige all WTO members to meet minimum standards of intellectual property and enforcement. Given that the TRIPS Agreement is subject to the WTO dispute settlement system, trade remedies and sanctions can be used as a mechanism to enforce the obligations contained in the agreement between all WTO members (Dutfield and Musungu, 2003).

The TRIPS Agreement: The Globalization of Minimum Standards for the Protection and Enforcement of Intellectual Property Rights

The TRIPS Agreement is the most comprehensive international intellectual property treaty concluded to date. For developing countries, the TRIPS Agreement meant that significant changes with profound effects had to be introduced in their international systems for the protection and enforcement of intellectual property rights (Correa, 2000). Building up on previous agreements, the TRIPS Agreement introduced minimum standards for the protection of nearly all forms of intellectual property rights, including patents, copyrights and related rights, trademarks, geographical indications, industrial designs, undisclosed information and integrated circuits. In addition, the TRIPS Agreement introduced minimum standards for the enforcement of intellectual property rights, a major novelty in international intellectual property law. No international intellectual property treaty had ever included detailed provisions setting out general principles and detailed provisions regarding procedures and measures for the enforcement of intellectual property rights.

The priority of developed countries in the negotiations of the TRIPS Agreement in the WTO was twofold. First, to assist their national intellectual property right-holders to gain recognition and protection of their intellectual property rights in other WTO member countries to the same extent as granted in their national jurisdictions. Second, to make it easier for national right-holders to enforce their intellectual property rights in foreign markets. Although developing countries were able to introduce some public interest safeguards and flexibilities in the TRIPS Agreement, the agreement is mainly concerned with the granting and enforcement of intellectual property rights. The TRIPS Agreement does not set out comprehensive multilateral rules to ensure that national intellectual property systems function in a manner that strikes an adequate balance between the interests of right-holders and the public interest. Rather, the exercise of the flexibilities, limitations and safeguards contained or otherwise not explicitly prohibited in the TRIPS Agreement is left to national discretion.

A thorough analysis of the TRIPS Agreement indeed reveals that the Agreement leaves ample room for developing countries to tailor their national intellectual property systems and measures to ensure its enforcement in accordance with their developmental priorities (UNCTAD-ICTSD, 2005). However, in practice, developing countries are often unable to do so for lack of technical knowledge or resources, or choose otherwise. Various political economy factors are at play. A significant deterrent is the ever-present threat of potential multilateral trade sanctions through the WTO Dispute Settlement System and unilateral retaliatory sanctions from developed countries with which some developing countries still maintain a relationship of economic or other form of dependence. This has meant that developing countries have given priority to meeting their TRIPS Agreement obligations, rather than to experimenting with the policy space that is still available to balance within their national intellectual property systems the competing interests in and mixed effects of strong protection and enforcement of intellectual property rights.

THE CHANGING GLOBAL GOVERNANCE OF INTELLECTUAL PROPERTY STANDARD-SETTING

Significant changes are taking place in the global governance of intellectual property law and policy-making in the post-TRIPS era. One of them is the agenda being pursued by developed countries and global industry players to set new global 'TRIPS-plus' standards for the enforcement of intellectual property rights and the discourse on the global threats of 'counterfeiting and piracy' (Biadgleng and Muñoz Tellez, 2008a; Sell, 2008).

This new agenda is comparable in terms of strategy and goals with the agenda pursued in the 1970s to mid-1990s that culminated in the establishment of the TRIPS Agreement. It differs significantly in that the current strategy involves a much more sophisticated form of forum shifting and a new element that can be called 'multiple forum capture'. Forum shifting for TRIPS-plus intellectual property enforcement measures is being pursued by developed countries and industry lobbies. The strategy is to bring the TRIPS-plus agenda simultaneously and co-ordinatedly at various forums, including by establishing initiatives in forums that lie outside the regular multilateral institutional framework for intellectual property norm-setting. When faced with strong opposition from developing countries in one forum, the agenda is continuously pursued in other forums. The strategy is proving effective partly because developing countries are less likely to participate or able to oppose the TRIPS-plus enforcement agenda in forums in which intellectual property discussions appear to fall outside of the organizations' mandate.

Examples of TRIPS-plus initiatives in non-traditional intellectual property forums include the following:

- The Global Congress on Combating Counterfeiting and Piracy. It is held annually each time at different locations to produce recommendations mainly aimed at government authorities to step up enforcement mechanism and actions.
- The SECURE Working Group of the World Customs Organization (WCO). This working group is negotiating TRIPS-plus standards that would increase the role of customs administrations in the enforcement of intellectual property rights without the WCO membership having even given the working group any terms of reference.
- The International Medical Products Anti-Counterfeiting Taskforce (IMPACT) on counterfeit medicines. The WHO acts as Secretariat to the taskforce even though it has not been endorsed by the member states of the WHO.

The dangers of the increasing power of such initiatives to influence international intellectual property policy-making and their lack of legitimacy has yet to be widely exposed and condemned. What is most troubling is that the Secretariat of some multilateral forums such as the WCO, WIPO and WHO are directly participating, providing finance and helping coordinate such initiatives together with groups representing industry interests without having received an express mandate from or requested the consent of their full membership, including a large number of developing country and least developed country members, to do so.

The overall picture that emerges is a web of numerous multilateral forums, regional and bilateral agreements and unilateral institutions being captured to pursue a global TRIPS-plus enforcement agenda (Biadgleng and Muñoz Tellez, 2008a). Figure 1.1 below summarizes the changing governance on intellectual property enforcement and growing web of institutions involved.

Many factors may help to explain the shift led by developed countries towards a TRIPS-plus agenda on enforcement. One factor may be the fact that most countries are now required to comply in full with the TRIPS Agreement. This means that developed countries and global industry players have all but achieved the goal of establishing TRIPS-compliant global minimum standards on the protection of intellectual property rights and their enforcement. In consequence, there is now a greater window of opportunity to pursue global TRIPS-plus enforcement standards as a means to

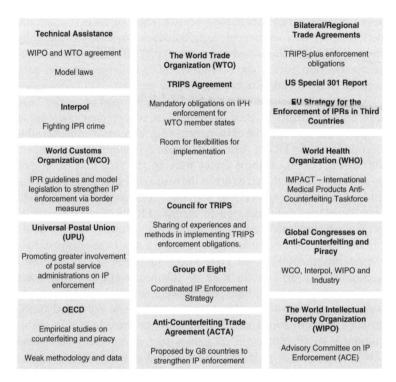

Technical Assistance	The World Trade Organization (WTO)	Bilateral/Regional Trade Agreements
WIPO and WTO agreement Model laws	TRIPS Agreement	TRIPS-plus enforcement obligations
		US Special 301 Report
Interpol Fighting IPR crime	Mandatory obligations on IPR enforcement for WTO member states	EU Strategy for the Enforcement of IPRs in Third Countries
World Customs Organization (WCO)	Room for flexibilities for implementation	World Health Organization (WHO)
IPR guidelines and model legislation to strengthen IP enforcement via border measures	Council for TRIPS	IMPACT – International Medical Products Anti-Counterfeiting Taskforce
Universal Postal Union (UPU)	Sharing of experiences and methods in implementing TRIPS enforcement obligations.	Global Congresses on Anti-Counterfeiting and Piracy
Promoting greater involvement of postal service administrations on IP enforcement	Group of Eight	WCO, Interpol, WIPO and Industry
OECD	Coordinated IP Enforcement Strategy	The World Intellectual Property Organization (WIPO)
Empirical studies on counterfeiting and piracy	Anti-Counterfeiting Trade Agreement (ACTA)	Advisory Committee on IP Enforcement (ACE)
Weak methodology and data	Proposed by G8 countries to strengthen IP enforcement	

Figure 1.1   The changing global governance of intellectual property enforcement

achieve greater protection of intellectual property rights. While the TRIPS Agreement entered into force on 1 January 1995, developing countries and least developed countries could choose to avail themselves of certain transitional periods before complying with the agreement. The only provisions that all countries had to comply with as of 1 January 1996 were those of national treatment and most favoured nation treatment (MFN). All countries were provided with a one-year transition period from the date of entry into force of the agreement. An additional four-year transition period was available for developing countries, which expired on 1 January 2000.

Least developed countries, however, may still benefit from a transition period that is set to expire on 1 July 2013, or until such a date on which they cease to be a least developed country, whichever date is earlier. This is because the TRIPS Agreement stipulates that least developed countries can request an extension of their transitional period upon duly motivated requests. Such request was made by least developed countries before the expiry of their original ten-year transition period on 1 January 2005, and was granted with conditions for an additional period of 7.5 years.

A second factor is the fact that many developed countries have introduced reforms in their domestic law enforcement systems to facilitate and increase the enforcement of intellectual property rights beyond what the TRIPS Agreement requires (Biadgleng and Muñoz, 2008a, pp. 11–19). A third factor may be the fact that developed countries have concluded or are in the process of negotiating regional and bilateral trade agreements with many developing countries and least developed countries, which include TRIPS-plus standards of protection and enforcement of intellectual property rights (ibid., pp. 29–35). These countries may constitute a new base of support for the establishment of global TRIPS-plus standards.

Finally, a fourth factor may be the new resistance that some developing countries and least developed countries have been able to build at certain multilateral institutions such as the WTO and WIPO to backstop developed country attempts to introduce new global standards of IP protection. Processes such as international patent law harmonization at the WIPO are stalled as developing countries have introduced their own demands for topics to be included in the negotiations as a condition for advancing such discussions. These frustrated attempts may partly explain why developed countries are now focusing more on establishing new global standards for the enforcement of intellectual property rights. Intellectual property enforcement is an area in which most developing countries lack expertise and are thus less prepared to find off demands for TRIPS-plus enforcement standards in multilateral institutions and regional and bilateral agreements with developed countries.

CONCLUSION

One of the major challenges facing developing country governments today is how to deal with the growing number of demands from intellectual property right-holders, national and foreign, and developed country governments, to reform their systems for the enforcement of intellectual property rights. The pressures for developing country governments to step up their efforts to enforce intellectual property rights is not dissimilar from the conceptual basis and strategies employed by industry lobbies in the 1970s to mid-1990s to bring about minimum global standards on the protection and enforcement of intellectual property rights. But the challenge is more complex today as the new global governance structure for intellectual property standard-setting now comprises a deeper web of multilateral, regional, bilateral and unilateral institutions.

Developing countries that adopt TRIPS-plus standards for the enforcement of intellectual property rights further hinder their ability to tailor their intellectual property systems in accordance with their national development priorities. Coordination among developing countries and the crafting of an alternative agenda on international intellectual property standard-setting may serve as a mechanism to resist the pressure to adopt TRIPS-plus enforcement standards, particularly at multilateral forums where developing countries are more powerful compared with regional and bilateral negotiations with developed countries.

2. Ten general misconceptions about the enforcement of intellectual property rights
Xuan Li

INTRODUCTION

Thirteen years after the entry into force of the Agreement on Trade-Related Aspects of Intellectual Property Rights (TRIPS Agreement), strengthening enforcement of intellectual property rights (IPRs) has become a central issue in most international, regional and bilateral negotiations. Strengthening the international legal framework on the enforcement of IPRs is one of the priorities on the agenda of the G8, as expressed at its summit held in June 2007. Japan, the European Union and the United States announced in October 2007 their plans to negotiate an Anti-Counterfeiting Trade Agreement (ACTA). The submissions of developed countries to the TRIPS Council demonstrate that most of the technical assistance provided to developing countries is now aimed at strengthening their capacity to enforce the protection of intellectual property rights.

Although IP enforcement has been extensively discussed, commentators hardly provide a rational economic theory and sound legal analysis on this highly contentious global issue. Rather, the criticism from developed countries often oversimplifies the complicated issues by over-exaggerating a particular aspect of the counterfeit and piracy problem or by offering an abbreviated, easy-to-understand, yet somewhat misleading version of the story. For instance, the Fourth Global Congress on Combating Counterfeiting and Piracy held in Dubai on 3–5 February 2008, hosted by the World Customs Organization (WCO), Dubai Customs, the International Criminal Police Organization (INTERPOL) and the World Intellectual Property Organization (WIPO), largely reflected the simplistic views, rather than present a holistic picture of the

Table 2.1   Ten misconceptions on IP enforcement

	Misconceptions	Characteristics
1	Counterfeiting and piracy includes patent infringement	Definition
2	Counterfeit medicine equates IP infringed medicine	Definition
3	IP infringement poses health threat	Effect
4	Magnitude of claimed IP infringement is enormous	Methodology
5	Government should take the primary responsibility of enforcement	Responsibility
6	Government should bear the cost of IP enforcement	Responsibility
7	WTO Members are obliged to provide border procedures for all types of transactions and all forms of IPRs	Responsibility
8	WTO Members are bound to provide judicial system for IPR	Responsibility
9	Criminal procedures are obligatory to establish for IP-infringing products	Responsibility
10	Customs administrations have authority to determine IP infringement	Authority

issue. Such oversimplification is dangerous, because it creates misconceptions that confuse the public not only with regard to the definitions, cause and magnitude of the problem, but also the obligations of the IP enforcement on governments, and misleads policy-makers into finding solutions that fail to address the crux of the piracy problem.

In this context, this chapter discusses ten general misconceptions about enforcement of IPRs including both legal and economic issues (Table 2.1). In particular, the chapter attempts to reconfigure the misguided public debate on IP enforcement by underscoring the necessity to focus on the obligations and rights of developing countries' governments specified in the TRIPS Agreement. Out of ten misconceptions, the first two are about the definition, the third is about the effect, the fourth is about the methodology of calculation of the scale of claimed IP infringement, the fifth to ninth are about the responsibility of right-holders and governments, and the last one is about the authority of customs administrations.

TEN MISCONCEPTIONS ON ENFORCEMENT OF INTELLECTUAL PROPERTY RIGHTS

Misconception 1: Counterfeiting and Piracy Includes Patent Infringement

Complaints over excessive damages as a result of patent infringement can often be heard in the international arena. A first misconception occurs as to whether the scope of counterfeiting and piracy includes patent infringement. A proper understanding of the boundary of counterfeit and piracy is crucial not only to determine the responsibility of governments under TRIPS, but also in terms of measuring the magnitude of the infringement. This is because the definition determines the nature of the IP infringement, the measurement of the loss and the obligation under international agreements such as TRIPS. WTO Members have different obligations of enforcement for different IPRs under TRIPS. It should be noted that patents, trademarks and copyrights are regarded as distinct IPRs under TRIPS, with specific disciplines applicable for each category of IPRs under the TRIPS Agreement itself.

To better understand the terms of counterfeit and piracy defined under TRIPS, it is important to track the *travaux préparatoires* (negotiating history), which is a key interpretative tool in reflecting the mind of the negotiators at the time they agreed to the TRIPS text. During the 1973–79 Tokyo Round, the United States had pushed for an anti-counterfeiting code to deal with cross-border movements of counterfeit goods, but, despite some support from the European Community, Japan and Canada, was not successful. Developing countries argued that WIPO, the specialist UN organization for intellectual property, had primary jurisdiction over intellectual property matters, not the General Agreement on Tariffs and Trade (GATT) (Drahos and Braithwaite, 2004). From the outset of the Uruguay Round negotiations in 1986, the developed countries, led by the United States, supported by the European Community and Japan, pressed for an initiative in the GATT on counterfeiting and making a general intellectual property code a much longer-term priority. The negotiations on IP began in the Negotiating Group on Trade-Related Aspects of Intellectual Property Rights, including Trade in Counterfeit Goods (the Negotiating Group). Its original mandate under the terms of the Punta del Este Ministerial

Declaration of 1986 stated that 'negotiations shall aim to develop a multilateral framework of principles, rules and disciplines dealing with international trade in counterfeit goods'. At the mid-term review of the negotiations of the Uruguay Round, the Trade Negotiation Committee expanded the mandate of the Negotiating Group to a broad coverage. Later, this broad IPR protection initiative had been restricted to an understanding of trademarks counterfeit and copyright piracy under Article 51 (Roffe, 2008). Under TRIPS, as defined in footnote 14 to Article 51, the definition of 'counterfeit trademark goods' only refers to registered marks as counterfeit trademark goods, that is:

> any goods, including packaging, bearing without authorization a trademark which is identical to the trademark validly registered in respect of such goods, or which cannot be distinguished in its essential aspects from such a trademark, and which thereby infringes the rights of the owner of the trademark in question under the law of the country of importation. (Li, 2008a)

Figure 2.1 presents the obligations of enforcement for copyright and trademark under the TRIPS.

However, developed countries have intentionally extended the boundaries of counterfeit and piracy beyond the contours of TRIPS to all other types of IPR, including patents. For instance, the OECD defined counterfeiting and piracy as 'terms used to describe a range

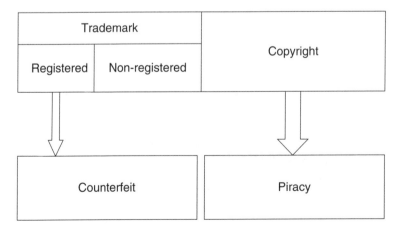

Figure 2.1   IP enforcement under the WTO TRIPS

of illicit activities linked to intellectual property rights (IPR) infringement' (OECD, 2007). The work that the OECD is conducting focuses on the infringement of IPRs described in the TRIPS Agreement, including trademarks, copyrights, patents, design rights, as well as a number of related rights (EU, 2005). Similarly, the EU's 'Strategy for Enforcement of IPR in Third Countries' covers 'all kinds of IP (copyrights, trademarks, geographical indications, patents, designs, etc)'.[1] All these statements rely on similar methods to develop an understanding that deliberately misconstrues counterfeit and piracy with patent infringement in particular. Thus, developed countries are trying to revive what they could not get at the Uruguay Round.

This misconception substantially enlarges the limited obligations of IP enforcement under the TRIPS to all types of IPRs. In the case of OECD, it extends the scope of border measures not only from registered marks to all trademarks, including a trademark in question under the law of the country of importation, but also extends the protection from trademark and copyrights to all other types of intellectual property rights, for example, goods that infringe a patent, plant variety rights, geographical indicators, and so on. By mixing up concepts of counterfeit, piracy and patent as well other forms of IPRs, developed countries discretely confuse the public about the scope and obligations of IP enforcement under TRIPS.

Expanding the definition of counterfeit and piracy to include all forms of IPR infringement on the basis of this misconception can have multiple implications. First, the victim of an alleged counterfeit IP infringement may claim more damage for such IP infringement. Second, this will expand the obligation of governments to enforce necessary civil, criminal and administrative measures to deal with this situation at immense cost implications for the public treasury. Third, it will deter competitors from resorting to using the flexibilities of IP laws under the threat of abuse of the right of enforcement by the right-holders.

Misconception 2: Product Falsification, Counterfeiting and IP-Infringed Goods are Identical

The terms 'counterfeiting', 'IP-infringed goods' and 'product falsification' are frequently confused and misused. For instance, the EU cites 'danger of health threats from counterfeit food and pharmaceuticals drugs' as a way to contribute to fighting counterfeiting.

Australia has expressly listed counterfeit medicines as one of the impacts of counterfeits on consumers (Australian Government, 2007). Canada intends to include the pharmaceutical industry in ACTA consultations whereas other industry groups were excluded (Geist, 2008). Do product falsification or fake goods equate to counterfeit or IP-infringed goods?

By definition alone, these terms are distinct. Falsification is the act of producing something that lacks authenticity with the intent to commit fraud or deception. Counterfeiting is an imitation that is made usually with the intent to deceptively represent its content or origins. 'IP-infringed goods' is a broader term of IP violation, which does not distinguish between counterfeiting, piracy, patent infringement, and so on. It should be highlighted that product falsification does not necessarily mean a counterfeit or IP-infringed good. Moreover, no matter whether it constitutes an IPR violation, product falsification that creates danger for the consumers is prohibited.

However, the conflation is widespread particularly in the field of medicine. Counterfeit medicines range from random mixtures of harmful toxic substances to inactive, useless preparations. Occasionally, there can be 'high quality' fakes that do contain the declared active ingredient. According to WHO, a counterfeit medicine is defined as one that is:

> deliberately and fraudulently mislabeled with respect to identity and/or source. Counterfeiting can apply to both branded and generic products and counterfeit medicines may include products with the correct ingredients but fake packaging, with the wrong ingredients, without active ingredients or with insufficient active ingredients or with fake packing. (WHO, 1992)

In practice, counterfeit medicines are defined in different ways in different countries. For instance, in the United States, it is directly related to a trademark violation,[2] while some countries focus on the active pharmaceutical ingredients contained in the drug instead.

Simply put, the misconception lies in the confusion between quality control and IP violation. Product falsification is the matter of a low-quality product, which is deliberately mislabeled in order to deceive consumers. In contrast, a counterfeit good is an issue of trademark violation, which is one among various types of IPR infringements. Precise differentiation of the above terms could help better grasp the essence of the problem.

Misconception 3: Counterfeit and Piracy Pose a Consumer Threat

Counterfeiting and piracy are identified as having a damaging effect upon the public health and safety of consumers. The damage generally involves consumer deception about the quality of the counterfeit product, with the consequential risk to health and safety (Blakeney, 2005). For instance, some tend to emphasize that consumers are victimized by the fact that while some consumers are defrauded into mistakenly buying counterfeits, other consumers who purchase authentic goods pay higher prices. The G8 asserted that 'fake products are often substandard and can be dangerous, posing health and safety risks' (G8, 2008). It stressed that 'the proliferation of pirated and counterfeit goods continues to pose a grave threat to the global economy, health and welfare'. At the WCO, in the 'Introduction' to its proposed 'Provisional Standards Employed by Customs for Uniform Rights Enforcement' (SECURE), reference was made to the G8 Summit and its wording on 'the health hazards of IP infringed goods and parts', though it was highly controversial. Likewise, the EU stressed that pirated and counterfeit goods are usually produced by anonymous entities that pay no heed to health, safety and quality requirements and provide no after-sales assistance, guarantees, operating instructions, and so on. Illustrating this problem are growing seizures of fake medications, food (and even bottled water), car and plane parts, electrical appliances and toys (EU, 2005). Not surprisingly, the International Chamber of Commerce supported this misconception with much conflating evidence, for example, dozens of people died in Cambodia through taking ineffective, counterfeit malaria medicines; counterfeit drugs were used to fight antibodies in RhD negative mothers, and so forth, thereby attempting to demonstrate damaging consequences of IP infringement (Blakeney, 2005).

However, it is misleading to label IP infringement with consumer threat. Such misconception originates from the confusion between product falsification and IP violation. As pointed out in the previous section, these distinct terms 'counterfeiting', 'piracy' and 'product falsification' are frequently misused. Indeed, fake products may involve health and food security issues; however, it does not necessarily mean that threat is originating from IP violation, and vice versa. For instance, product falsification or fake drugs can cause harm to patients and sometimes lead to death; however, a medicine with trademark violation may or may not be harmful as it does not contain active ingredients, an insufficient quantity of active ingredients, or entirely incorrect active ingredients. In addition, many methodologies have been employed to inflate or misrepresent the damage, which will be revealed in detail later in this chapter.

The real intention of developed countries is to prepare the ground to legitimize the initiatives on advancement of IP enforcement by establishing strong causation between IP infringement and health or consumer threat. This misconception also creates a moral justification for TRIPS-plus standards of IP enforcement, by co-opting the language of morality and public health and consumer rights. For instance, based on the assertion that the proliferation of pirated and counterfeit goods continues to pose a grave threat to the global economy, health and welfare, the G8 decided to advance existing anti-counterfeiting and piracy initiatives as well as lay the groundwork for the concrete proposals on outstanding themes and issues that need to be addressed.

Misconception 4: Magnitude of Claimed IP Infringement is Enormous

Numerous reports suggest that there are enormous losses resulting from counterfeiting and piracy in terms of total volume, quantity and value of counterfeit and pirated products. According to developed countries, the so-called 'proliferation of infringements of intellectual property rights', particularly counterfeiting and piracy, poses an ever-increasing threat to the sustainable development of the world economy. Some figures on piracy rates are frequently cited as proof to support this statement. For instance, an analysis carried out by OECD indicated that the volume of tangible counterfeit and pirated products in international trade could be up to USD200 billion in 2005 (OECD, 2007). WCO estimated that around 5 per cent of all world trade is falsified (WIPO, 2003).[3] The Business Software Alliance (BSA) *Global Software Piracy Study*, a frequently quoted report, posited that the Chinese software piracy rate was 90 per cent in 2005 (BSA, 2005). It reported that the countries with the highest piracy rates were Vietnam (92 per cent), Ukraine (91 per cent), China (90 per cent), Zimbabwe (90 per cent) and Indonesia (87 per cent), and so on. The US-based Center for Medicine in the

Public Interest (CMPI) predicts that counterfeit drug sales will reach USD75 billion globally in 2010, an increase of more than 90 per cent from 2005, while recognizing that 'although precise and detailed data on counterfeit medicines is difficult to obtain, estimates range from around 1% of sales in developed countries to over 10% in developing countries, depending on the geographical area' (WHO, 2006). Based on these reports, developed countries make IP enforcement a top priority agenda and press developing countries to strengthen the IP enforcement in the international negotiations.

Developed countries attempt to further establish the causation between the regulatory and legal framework and the number of piracy cases by highlighting that counterfeiting is greatest in those regions where the regulatory and legal oversight is weakest. For instance, according to a WHO report:

> most industrialized countries with effective regulatory systems and market control (e.g. USA, most of EU, Australia, Canada, Japan, New Zealand) have a low proportion of counterfeit products, i.e. less than 1% of market value. Many countries in Africa and parts of Asia and Latin America have areas where more that 30% of the medicines on sale can be counterfeit, while other developing markets have less than 10%; overall, a usual range is between 10% and 30%. Many of the former Soviet republics have a proportion of counterfeit medicines which is above 20% of market value – this falls into the developing country's range. Medicines purchased over the Internet from sites that conceal their physical address are counterfeit in over 50% of cases.

Such an observation then leads to the policy recommendation that governments should strengthen their IP enforcement systems.

The above-mentioned reports and figures on the counterfeiting activities reflect the joint effort of the governments and interested groups in developed countries. Some industrial and commercial associations in developed countries regularly produce statistics on counterfeit and piracy that are used by their governments. These include the music industry (for example, IFPI, International Federation of Phonogram & Videogram Producers; RIAA, Recording Industry Association of America), the pharmaceuticals industry (EFPIA, European Federation of Pharmaceutical Industries and Associations), and the software industry (BSA). 'Public–private partnerships' dealing with IP enforcement were created by the European Commission (EC) to produce public information that suits their commons needs (EU, 2005). Strategically speaking, a supra-large scale of losses on counterfeit and piracy would contribute to putting tremendous pressure on developing countries during international, regional and bilateral negotiations for more vigorous IPR enforcement. In other words, whether or not supported by facts, these statistics suit the negotiating strategy of developed countries.

Since the true objectives of these reports are to highlight the extent of counterfeiting and piracy, the methodology used and the results thus derived are biased and of doubtful nature (Bosworth, 2006). Take the piracy rate of software stated in the BSA report, for example. Let us assume the piracy rate of China as stated in the report was 90 per cent. In that case, Chinese pirated software would be nearly ten times that of real copies. If that were the case, the market turnover of the software in China would be close to 4000 billion yuan (as the output of the software industry was 390 billion yuan), or nearly 25 per cent of China's GDP in 2005, and the software market itself would be far larger than the entire Chinese IT market. In fact, a more authoritative survey on the Chinese software piracy rate commissioned by the Chinese State Intellectual Property Office shows that on the basis of newly installed software market in 2006, the piracy rate in China was 20 per cent (down from 25 per cent in 2005), considering the market value of pirated software (Li, 2008a).

Further, let us take the OECD report (2007) as another example. If as stated in the report, USD200 billion of internationally traded products could have been counterfeit or pirated in 2005, the amount is even larger than the combined national GDPs of about 150 developing economies. However, OECD itself recognized the 'lack of indicative data and the difficulty in detecting counterfeit and pirated products'. The question is, with such difficulty in detecting counterfeit and pirated products and without solid data sources, how were the OECD reports able to draw the striking conclusion that 'the volume of tangible counterfeit and pirated products in international trade could be up to USD200 billion'?

Measurement of counterfeit and pirated products is at the heart of the problem. How are statistics like border seizure exaggerated and biased? Methodologically, the exaggeration arises from four major factors: (1) inclusion of IP infringements that are outside the obligation under the TRIPS Agreement within the ambit of the definition of IP infringement, for example, patent; (2) lack of valid data; (3)

the adoption of different units of measurement; (4) valuation: using misleading unit prices.

Extending the definition beyond the scope defined under the TRIPS

As discussed above, under TRIPS, counterfeit and piracy refer to trademarks and copyrights only. However, developed countries tend to expand the definition much beyond the scope defined under the TRIPS, for example, OECD subtly included patents in the definition. By doing so, the figures of IPR infringement are increased substantively.

Validity of data

Most figures cited in various reports are hypothetical assumptions without reliable data sources. In this regard, the Centre for Economics and Business Research (CEBR) rightly indicated that:

> From the research we have undertaken it has become apparent that there is only limited reliable data on the counterfeiting phenomenon currently in existence. We have been surprised by the lack of information – and by the lack of transparency regarding the basis for the information that does exist. Although interest in the causes and consequences of counterfeiting is significant, very little in the way of robust or even credible numerical data exists. (CEBR, 2002, p. 23)

Unit of measurement

The unit of measurement of IP infringement that is chosen is also a source of exaggeration of the volume of counterfeit and piracy losses. In the EC annual seizure statistics, the total number of seizure cases and the total number of articles confiscated are reported. A seizure case refers to an event where some quantity of counterfeit goods is found and the number of articles appears to be a simple count of the number of items seized. Depending on the unit used, the same seizure can be reported as either a big number or a smaller one in terms of the quantities of articles seized. For instance, a single cigarette was reported as *a* unit of seizure, and therefore, seizures of boxes containing 20 cigarettes in packets of 20 was calculated as $20 \times 20 = 400$ cases. In this way, the reported number of articles seized was 75733068 in 2005.[4] The EC's admission of the error made it necessary to revise the figures relating to the total amount of items seized to ensure consistency in the method of calculating the quantities of articles. The issue of unit of measurement is only an example of how the losses may be quantified by developed countries.

Valuation
Where a valuation takes place, the unit price of measurement is another convenient tool to inflate the total losses. The industrial and commercial associations tend to use the price of the branded goods to measure the value of the counterfeit and pirated goods. In other words, the value of the seized goods according to their reported price tends to be the same as the price at which the branded goods are sold in normal retail outlets. Therefore, the lost benefits resulting from pirated goods are calculated on potential revenues that the right-holders would have earned. In the BSA report, the valuation of the losses is based on the assumption that each piece of copied software represents a direct loss of sale for software companies. As such, the total losses were estimated to be USD29 billion in 2003. However, even the author of the BSA report, John Gantz, Director of Research for International Data Corporation admitted that perhaps only one out of ten unauthorized copies might be a lost sale as many users in developing countries cannot afford software imported from the West. Instead of describing the USD29 billion as sales lost to piracy, he suggested that 'I would have preferred to call it the retail value of pirated software' (Locklear, 2004). These statistics were described by a draft report of the Australian government as a 'self-serving hyperbole', 'unverified and epistemologically unreliable'.[5] In the cases of Internet piracy, since no payment is made for the product, the price of the official product is the only measure available. In sum, these valuation methods lack reasonable foundation as lost benefits should be calculated on the basis of legitimate expectations and not on potential revenues that the right-holders would have earned based on the market value without taking price elasticity into consideration.

Therefore, the claimed losses on counterfeit and piracy that are frequently cited have been exaggerated to a great extent without any proper foundation, reflecting the views of powerful interest groups. Such exaggeration is the result of a close tie of 'public–private partnership' between business sectors and government in the developed world. Consequently, motivated reports commissioned by industries are promoted by developed countries' governments in various international forums.

Misconception 5: Government Should Take the Primary Responsibility for Enforcing IPRs

Multinationals as well as governments of developed countries frequently criticize developing countries' governments for not enforcing their IPRs effectively. Consequently, they attribute the responsibility for weak enforcement of IP solely on the governments of developing countries. For instance, in its annual review of countries' IPR practices (the 'Special 301' Report), the United States Trade Representative lists many countries under categories of 'priority watch list' and 'watch list' according to their level of IP enforcement as perceived by the United States. Many developing countries such as China, Pakistan, India and Venezuela are on the 2008 list. In 2007 the EU sought to introduce wide IP enforcement as a condition for Economic Partnership Agreements (EPAs) that it was entering into with African, Caribbean and Pacific (ACP) countries. These examples suggest that the EU and the United States assume that the responsibility to enforce IPRs lies with the governments of the developing countries. Some international organizations such as WIPO also asserted that 'In countries where there is a significant risk of intellectual property infringement at street level, it will be for the government to take the initiative in bringing criminal cases and thereby committing its authority to the elimination of widespread infringement' (WIPO, 1999).

Under the misconception that governments should take primary responsibility to enforce IPRs, developing countries are spending enormous public resources for enforcement of private rights. Some developing countries, for example, Thailand, conduct police raids to enforce IPRs against infringers (Ariyanuntaka, 2005). A similar practice has been widely applied in China, which has introduced administrative procedures apart from civil judicial procedures concerning the enforcement of IPRs (China National Intellectual Property Protection Working Group, 2007). The administrative protection is triggered by right-holders who believe their rights have been infringed. However, the public authorities can also initiate administrative protection and impose sanctions on the infringing enterprises. There were a significant number of cases involving administrative protection in 2003 and 2004 in China (ibid.). In this context, the real questions are: what are the responsibilities of governments on IP enforcement and who should take the primary responsibility for enforcing IPRs?

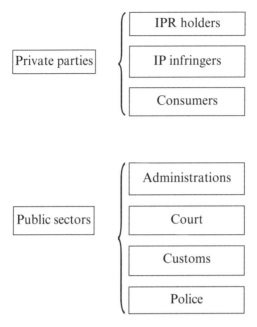

Figure 2.2   Who are the stakeholders of IP enforcement?

The confusion lies in the delineation of responsibility for enforc-ing IPRs. A proper delineation of responsibility among various stakeholders is of utmost importance. Overall, there are (1) private parties and (2) public sectors that are involved in IP enforcement. Private parties include right-holders, infringers, consumers; and public sectors include the IP office, judicial bodies, customs, and so on (Figure 2.2). The responsibility depends on the nature of enforce-able subject matter. The fundamental fact that IPRs are statutorily granted private rights, in the absence of which innovators cannot claim any rights on their creations, must be noted here. As with any other kind of private rights, the enforcement of IP rights is primarily a matter concerning the individual owners of these rights. It is the primary obligation of right-holders and not governments to enforce their claimed rights and take necessary legal actions for protecting their own IPRs.

Article 41 of TRIPS defines the responsibility of governments for IP enforcement, and states that Members should: 'ensure that enforcement procedures . . . are available under their law so as to permit effective action against any act of infringement of intellectual property rights covered by this Agreement'. It is clear that the obligation for the state is to ensure availability of enforcement procedures, instead of enforcing IPRs per se. Member States would have fulfilled their obligation under TRIPS as long as there are enforcement procedures in place. Under Article 41(5), countries are not bound to make additional judicial mechanisms available for IP enforcement in addition to those available for the enforcement of their other laws.

In most jurisdictions, judicial protection is triggered when right-holders file lawsuits in civil courts for protection of their intellectual property rights based on patent, trademark, and copyright laws. For instance, in Anglo-American jurisdictions, most claimants of IP enforcement resort to civil remedies, partly because the process is appropriate to the assertion of private property amongst businesspeople, and partly because the types of remedy, particularly injunction and damages, are more useful than punishment in the name of the state (Cornish, 1999). As confessed by the EC in its strategy report, 'It is clear that the first steps to protect and enforce IPRs must be taken by the right-holders themselves' (EC, 2005). In the United States, according to the *Manual of Patent Examining Procedure*, patents are enforced by bringing a civil law suit and lawsuits for patent infringement may only be brought in a Federal Court (USPTO, 2008).

It is pertinent to wonder why developed countries and their agents devote so much effort to pressurizing developing countries' governments to take responsibility for IP enforcement. It is because responsibility of enforcement has cost implications. The interest lies in the fact that, by shifting responsibility, it would shift the cost of enforcement from private parties to the government and ensure right-holders are beneficiaries without taking responsibility. The next section will discuss who should bear the cost of IP enforcement in further detail.

Misconception 6: Government Should Bear the Cost of Enforcing IPRs

Establishing and strengthening the enforcement of intellectual property rights is a costly exercise both in terms of scarce financial resources and the employment of skilled human resources. Developed countries often claim that it is the obligation of the government to direct resources on enforcement of IPRs. Consequently, many developing nations have spent their limited resources on endeavours related to the enforcement of IPRs when actually more should have been spent on poverty reduction, subsistence improvement and provision of better health and educational services. Currently, some developing countries are increasingly redirecting resources to strengthen the enforcement of intellectual property rights at a time when global investment in areas of poverty, hunger, health and education is less than half of what is needed to reach the Millennium Development Goals. The welfare of a state is sacrificed to ensure a more robust enforcement of IPRs. It is particularly expensive for most developing countries, as these economic benefits will go largely to foreign firms. The immediate benefits for wide enforcement mostly accrue to the companies that hold the rights, often at great costs to developing countries.

Before analysing who should bear the enforcement cost, the first questions are what is the cost of enforcing IPRs and what is the optimal level of enforcement? Identifying the type of costs that the TRIPS Agreement imposes is important for advocating measures for finding a right balance and to provide policy guidance. The costs of IP enforcement that TRIPS mandates can be essentially divided into two categories: one is the direct cost of enforcement of specific rights (in terms of costs arising out of providing administrative remedies, judicial costs, establishing special infrastructure, and so on).[6] Increasingly, it is seen that governments of developing countries are voluntarily engaged in providing strong state apparatus and compliance mechanisms for fighting piracy and counterfeiting. This direct cost of TRIPS enforcement includes: (1) judicial cost; (2) administrative cost; (3) litigation cost; and (4) cost of litigation error. The second category of costs is indirect cost, which may have deeper implications than the first category of costs. These costs are duly associated with static losses that developing countries have to face due to TRIPS or TRIPS-plus compliance and the ensuing static consumer welfare losses, impediments to informal and formal modes of anti-competitive effects, and so on. Such costs arise out of the intrinsic nature of substantive rights granted to IP holders as such, but are borne by the technology users and consumers at large instead (South Centre, 2008). From a broader society point of view, the cost of enforcement of IPRs must be calculated on the weight of the cost

Cost	Static loss	Consumer welfare loss	
		Deadweight loss	
		Enforcement cost	Judicial cost
			Administrative cost
			Litigation cost
			Cost of litigation error
	Dynamic loss	Anti-competitive effect to follow-on innovation	
Benefit	Dynamic gain	Additional provision of innovative product	

Figure 2.3   Optimal level of IP enforcement

and benefit of enforcing IPRs. If the cost to the society, including private and public resources dedicated to IP enforcement, is higher than the benefit for the society as a whole, the IP regime is unhealthy and must be examined for improvement (Figure 2.3).

So the question is, who should bear the cost of enforcing IPRs? As IPRs are private rights, logically, enforcing cost should be borne primarily by the private party. In other words, the right-holders should be fully responsible for any legal actions and bear their enforcement costs, instead of governments (South Centre, 2008).

In addition, according to Article 41(5) of the TRIPS Agreement: 'Nothing in this Part [Part III Enforcement of Intellectual Property Rights] creates any obligation with respect to the distribution of resources as between enforcement of intellectual property rights and the enforcement of law in general'. Therefore, no obligation is hereby established that requires Member States to prioritize and allocate scarce resources for the enforcement of intellectual property rights before enforcing other laws in general. IP enforcement could be prioritized based on constraints that affect a Member's capacity to enforce its law in general, for example, specific resource allocation for IP enforcement that may affect enforcement of Member States' general laws.

Furthermore, under Article 8, Member States are allowed to 'adopt measures necessary to promote the public interest in sectors of vital importance to their socio-economic and technological development'.

This article should be interpreted as to enable Member States to organize their spending in such a way as to ensure the protection of the public interest. Therefore, as long as there is a mechanism in place for the general enforcement of rights, Member States are not obliged to allocate additional or specific funds for IP enforcement.

In short, the enforcement cost shall be borne by private parties as IPR is in the nature of a private right, and enforcement activities ought to be planned on a cost–benefit basis from a socially optimal perspective. It is advisable that developing countries should not bear undue costs in respect of providing these measures beyond TRIPS requirements, such as border measures beyond the requirements of Article 51, criminal actions, the creation of special policy units or tribunals to combat piracy and counterfeiting and ex-officio measures.

Misconception 7: WTO Members are Obliged to Provide Border Procedures for all Types of Transactions and all Forms of IPRs

As customs administrations lead enforcement activities at the border, there are misconceptions regarding border measures for dealing with infringed goods, notably the types of transactions and forms of IPRs that should be enforced by customs. Currently, developing countries are under pressure to provide border procedures for IP enforcement against all IP infringement at the border, and those border measures are supposed to apply to all transactions including import, export, transit, and so on.

The World Customs Organization is the primary forum through which the developed countries and right-holders are pursuing an agenda of international harmonization of TRIPS-plus standards on border measures. Though there is no consensus on the mandate of the WCO SECURE Working Group, SECURE proposes in its Standard 1 that 'Customs Administrations have the legal authority to enforce IPR laws against goods which are suspected of violating IPR laws whenever such goods are deemed under national law to be under Customs control, including, but not limited to: import, export, transit, warehouses, transshipment, free zones, duty-free shops'. In addition, SECURE also proposes in its Standard 2 that 'National legislation may extend the scope of Customs IPR legislation from trademark and copyright to other intellectual property rights' under the Provisional Standards Employed by Customs for Uniform

Rights Enforcement (SECURE).[7] Thus, the border measures are to extend from counterfeiting and piracy to all IPR infringement.

Similarly, in the recently signed Economic Partnership Agreement between the CARIFORUM States and the European Community and its Member States, under Article 163 (Border Measure, Section 3), it is required that

> the EC [European Community] Party and the Signatory CARIFORUM States shall adopt procedures . . . to enable a right holder, who has valid grounds for suspecting that the *importation, exportation, re-exportation, entry or exit* of the customs territory, placement under a suspensive procedure or placement under a customs free zone or a customs free warehouse of goods infringing *an intellectual property right* may take place. (emphasis added; EPA, 2008)

In the footnote to Article 163 of the EPA, 'goods infringing an intellectual property right' is defined as 'counterfeit goods', 'pirated goods' *and* 'goods which, according to the law of the EC [European Community] Party *or* Signatory CARIFORUM State in which the application for Customs action is made, infringe: *(i) a design*; and *(ii) a geographical indication*' (emphasis added). The question is, are WTO Members bound to provide border measures for all types of transactions and all IPRs?

As explicitly defined in Article 51 of the TRIPS Agreement, border procedures are only compulsory with regard to 'counterfeit trademark or pirated copyright goods'. A definition of such goods under footnote 14 to Article 51 provides four basic factors of what constitutes 'counterfeit trademark goods' and 'copyright piracy': (1) identical or close similarity to intellectual property protected locally, (2) unauthorized use, (3) infringement in a country of importation, and (4) traded internationally (Biadgleng and Muñoz Tellez, 2008). Members may extend application to goods that involve the infringement of other IPRs, but this is not mandatory. Hence, it is not obligatory to establish border measures for infringement of patent, design, GI (geographical indication), and so on, other than counterfeit and piracy under the TRIPS Agreement.

It is further noticed that no comprehensive border measures are required for IP-infringing products for exportation, transit, warehouses, transhipment, free zones, duty-free shops, and so on, under the TRIPS Agreement, contrary to what has been proposed in Standard 1 of SECURE at the WCO. Under Article 51 of the

TRIPs Agreement, WTO Members are not required to make border measures available for various transactions including exportation, transit, and so on, other than for imports. Nevertheless, some developing countries seem to have adopted TRIPS-plus border measures, for example, China extends border measures from importation to exportation and transit of infringing products.

Therefore, the extension of the scope of border measures for IP enforcement under the EPA text has two meanings: first, the transaction has been extended from import to *exportation, re-exportation, entry or exit*; and second, the IPRs have been extended from counterfeit and pirated goods to 'design' and 'geographical indication'. Furthermore, as indicated in the footnote to Article 163, the EC [European Community] Party and the Signatory CARIFORUM States agree to collaborate to 'expand the scope of this definition to cover goods infringing *all intellectual property rights*' (emphasis added).

Misconception 8: WTO Members are Required to Establish a Judicial System for the Enforcement of IPRs

Technical assistance from developed countries through various international organizations has misguided developing countries in understanding their obligations under TRIPS, including the interpretation that WTO Members are required to perform a judicial review function through a mechanism to be set up in the court. For instance, technical assistance was provided by the Asian Development Bank, which advised China to establish a judicial system on IP enforcement to be WTO compliant (ADB, 2002). Reference was made to Articles 42 to 50 of TRIPS, which set out the civil and administrative procedures and remedies to be offered to intellectual property rightholders. Consequently, China has established specific administrative and judicial mechanisms for IP protection in a bid to 'comply' with its obligations under TRIPS. The question is, are Member States required under TRIPS to establish parallel judicial mechanisms to cater for IP enforcement?

Article 41(5) of the TRIPS Agreement states: 'this Part [Part III Enforcement of Intellectual Property Rights] does not create any obligation to put in place a judicial system for the enforcement of intellectual property rights distinct from that for the enforcement of law in general, nor does it affect the capacity of Members to enforce their law in general'. Recognizing the institutional limitations existing in many developing countries, Article 41(5) contains a general understanding that the enforcement of intellectual property rights in a Member State should be in no better position than the enforcement of any other rights. Therefore, not only no obligation is required to establish a separate court system for the enforcement of intellectual property rights, but also this article provides no 'obligation with respect to the distribution of resources as between the enforcement of intellectual property rights and the enforcement of law in general'.

Under Article 44(1), members are not required to grant injunctions in respect of intellectual property rights acquired by a person prior to knowing or having reasonable grounds to know that dealing in such subject matter would entail the infringement of an intellectual property right.

Further, according to Article 44(2), where the remedies against infringements stipulated under the TRIPS Agreement are inconsistent with a Member's law, the remedies shall be limited to declaratory judgments and payment of adequate compensation. Members also have significant leeway in determining what amount of compensation is 'adequate'.

Therefore, Members are not required to create a parallel judicial mechanism for enforcement of IPRs. The relevant national authorities can exercise discretion in applying the mandated rules.

Misconception 9: WTO Members are Required to Provide Criminal Procedures for all IPRs under the TRIPS

Article 61 (Section 5: Criminal Procedures, Part III: Enforcement of Intellectual Property Rights) of the TRIPS Agreement has been often misconstrued as laying down the obligation to provide criminal procedures for all IP-infringed products. Consequently, there has been a growing trend of designating various types of IP infringement as criminal offences in domestic laws worldwide for purposes of TRIPS compliance or under the TRIPS-plus initiatives.

For instance, the Russian Federation, which is currently negotiating its accession to the WTO, included in its Criminal Code of 13 June 1996 three articles specifically laying down criminal sanctions for IP infringement, that is, Article 146 (Copyright and Related Rights Infringements); Article 147 (Patents Infringement); and

Article 180 (Trademark Infringement). Currently, the legislators are continuing their work on the Criminal Code with a general intention of 'establishing an even wider scope of liability and a more efficient criminal procedure' (Russian Federation, 2004).

The Andean Community, comprising four Member States – Bolivia, Colombia, Ecuador and Peru approved Decision 486, currently in force, containing the following chapters: general provisions; patents; industrial designs; marks; layout designs of integrated circuits; commercial slogans; collective marks; certification marks; notices or signs; geographical indications; well-known distinctive signs; claims; actions for infringement and unfair competition related to industrial property. Article 257 of Decision 486 states, with legal certainty, that 'the Member Countries shall establish procedures and criminal sanctions for the cases of counterfeiting of marks' (Mantilla, 2007).

> In Ecuador, the sanctions for infringement of intellectual property rights are established in Chapter III 'On Offenses and Penalties' of the Law on Intellectual Property. In accordance with this standard, the penalty is imprisonment of three months to three years in the case of infringement of patents and marks; a similar penalty is imposed for the infringement of commercial and industrial secrets and geographical indications, and the sale, import or export of counterfeit goods and the unlawful alteration or reproduction of works; by contrast, the unlawful manufacture or use of labels, stamps or packaging, the illegal reproduction of works or use of codifiers and the failure to comply with precautionary measures is sanctioned by imprisonment of one month to two years; and the sale, import or export of counterfeit goods by imprisonment of three months to three years. In each of these cases, the sanction includes a fine ranging from 657.22 to 6572.25 dollars equivalent or from 1314.45 to 13 144.50 dollars according to the subject matter of the infringement. (Mantilla, 2007)

In the EU, on 12 July 2005, the EC proposed a second directive on criminal measures aimed at ensuring the enforcement of intellectual property rights, which is often called IPRED2 (Second Intellectual Property Rights Enforcement Directive), to supplement the first Directive 2004/48/EC of 29 April 2004 on the enforcement of intellectual property rights (Civil Enforcement).[8] The second directive incriminates infringements of intellectual property rights. It deals with intentional infringements on a commercial scale or aiding, abetting or inciting the infringements. IPRED2 does not seem to be a well-drafted directive, as is evident from the unfinished drafting process as well as an unusual number of amendments on this second directive, which was passed and adopted in subsequent readings. This second draft contains provisions on criminal penalties proposed by the Commission under Article 95 EC (document (a)), which would require Member States to ensure that 'all intentional infringements of an intellectual property right on a commercial scale, and attempting, aiding or abetting and inciting such infringements' were treated as criminal offences, and obliged Member States to provide for sentences of imprisonment, with fines and confiscation of the infringing goods also applying to both natural and legal persons (European Scrutiny Committee, 2006). Further, the draft Framework Decision (document (a)) supplementing the draft directive required Member States to provide for a sentence of at least four years' imprisonment where an intellectual property offence was committed 'under the aegis of a criminal organization' or where such offences 'carry a health or safety risk'. Moreover, the proposal also obliged Member States to ensure that holders of intellectual property rights, or their representatives, and experts, were allowed to assist the investigations carried out by joint investigation teams. The draft Framework Decision also contained rules on criminal jurisdiction (European Scrutiny Committee, 2006).

These attempts at criminal enforcement of IPRs are based on Article 61 of TRIPS, which states:

> Members shall provide for criminal procedures and penalties to be applied at least in cases of wilful trademark counterfeiting or copyright piracy on a commercial scale. Remedies available shall include imprisonment and/or monetary fines sufficient to provide a deterrent, consistently with the level of penalties applied for crimes of a corresponding gravity. In appropriate cases, remedies available shall also include the seizure, forfeiture and destruction of the infringing goods and of any materials and implements the predominant use of which has been in the commission of the offence. Members may provide for criminal procedures and penalties to be applied in other cases of infringement of intellectual property rights, in particular where they are committed wilfully and on a commercial scale.

However, the interpretation of Article 61 should be confined to harnessing the general availability of the specific criminal procedures and relevant remedies. Note that criminal actions are not applied to all IP infringements under Article 61 of TRIPS. The relevance of the procedures for criminal sanctions under Articles 61 relates only to 'counterfeit trademark or pirated copyright goods'. In addition, members are only required to provide for criminal procedures and penalties for wilful trademark counterfeiting or copyright piracy 'on a commercial scale'.

In fact, criminal action has neither been provided for in most developed countries themselves, nor have they been of serious concern within developed countries. For instance, the UK government, in its Explanatory Memorandum of 16 May 2006 in response to Directive 2004/48/EC, states that 'there is no evidence to justify any extension of the scope of criminal remedies as defined under TRIPS', that the government strongly believes that 'patent rights should not be included within the scope of the proposal' and that 'the validation of patent rights and the resolution of disputes relating to alleged infringements is a particularly complex area of the law which does not . . . lend itself to the certainty required of good criminal law. We will be looking at this very closely' (European Scrutiny Committee, 2006). In the Intellectual Property Rights Enforcement Directive (Draft) (2007) in the EU, patent infringement has been excluded because 'treating patent infringements as criminal offences could deter inventors and academics from developing innovations' (European Parliament, 2007). In short, it will be misleading to say that governments are obliged to pursue criminal actions against all IP infringement under the TRIPS.

Misconception 10: Customs Administrations Have the Authority to Determine IP Infringement

Developed countries claim that Member States of WTO are free to give authorities like customs administrations the power to determine IP infringement, or even the duty to act ex officio, so as to suspend the release of the goods suspected to be infringing, even in the absence of any request by the right-holders. For example, WIPO claims that Member States are free to give the competent authority the power, or even duty, to act ex officio, so as to suspend release of the goods suspected to be infringing, even in the absence of any request by the right-holders. It has been proposed in Resolution 40 of the Universal Postal Union (UPU), entitled 'Counterfeit and Pirated Items Sent through the Post', based on a joint study by WCO and UPU, to endorse customs to take primary responsibility to determine IPR infringement at the border.

However, under Article 51 of the TRIPS Agreement, Members are only obliged to adopt procedures to enable a right-holder with valid grounds for suspicion, to lodge a written application that the importation of counterfeit trademark or pirated copyright or other goods that infringe IPRs may take place and to have the release of the goods in question suspended by customs authorities. One problem with this provision is that of definition of what would constitute 'valid grounds for suspicion'. An application by the right-holder presupposes that there are valid grounds for suspicion. While the application should be submitted to the appropriate authority, it would appear from the provision that the customs officials are responsible for determining the existence or not of valid grounds. The question is whether customs have the authority or legal competence to determine whether an item is an IP-infringed good. A related question is, are associated trade barriers resulting from such border measures legitimate under the WTO agreement?

Patent infringement determination is a highly sophisticated process. A patent contains several parts – a specification, drawings and claims. No matter how much a questioned machine, manufacture, composition of matter or process may look like the specification and drawings of a patent, it is only the claims of the patent that can be infringed (Blenko, 1990). Determination of infringement requires a construction of the meaning of the claim language and then application of the claims so construed to the accused product or process. The determination of patent infringement is a two-step process: (1) derivation of the meaning of the claims 'by a study of all relevant patent documents' and interpreting the language of the claims, and (2) reading of the claims on the accused product or process, that is, whether the claimed invention is being made, used or sold by the alleged infringer. Whether an alleged equivalent to an element of a patent claim must have been in existence and known in the relevant art as an equivalent is a long-standing problem with the Doctrine of Equivalents (Holzmann, 1995). The Doctrine of Equivalents considers the literal meaning of the claims and several other factors including the scope and content of the prior art and the prosecution history. Under the Doctrine of Equivalents, an accused device that is not literally described by the claims of a patent may still be found to infringe if the accused device performs substantially the same function, in substantially the same way, to achieve substantially the same result as the claimed invention.

There are several stages of a patent infringement litigation process. A simplified overview of the patent litigation process includes: (1) The Complainant patent infringement files a Complaint, (2) the Defendant (accused infringer) files an Answer, (3) patent infringement trial, and (4) determination of patent infringement damages. Neither does customs administrations have the mandate nor competence to determine what constitutes IP infringement. Even in the United States, US customs has no authority to make patent infringement determinations, according to US Customs and Section 337 Investigations. In the United States, the complaint is filed in the Federal District Court. A decision by a Federal District Court can be appealed to the US Court of Appeals for the Federal Circuit (Washington, DC). A decision from the Court of Appeals for the Federal District may be appealed to the Supreme Court of the United States. Most cases are not accepted for review by the Supreme Court but many are appealed to the Federal Circuit.

It is obvious that it is beyond the authority and competence of customs to determine an IP infringement. Authorizing customs to determine IP infringement may result in unpredictability and constitutes barriers to legitimate trade. If customs were to exercise such powers, the process of determining IP infringement at the border may not be 'fair and equitable' as required by Article 41(3) of TRIPS. These measures can be challenged as non-compliant according to Article 41 of the TRIPS, which states:

> Members shall ensure that enforcement procedures as specified in this Part are available under their law so as to permit effective action against any act of infringement of intellectual property rights covered by this Agreement, including expeditious remedies to prevent infringements and remedies which constitute a deterrent to further infringements. These procedures shall be applied in such a manner as to avoid the creation of barriers to legitimate trade and to provide for safeguards against their abuse.

In short, the misconception that customs has the authority to determine IP infringement must be corrected. By shifting the state's responsibility on determination of IP infringement from the judiciary to an administrative body like customs, such border measures beyond the TRIPS may constitute barriers to legitimate trade, which can be challenged as non-compliant of WTO rule according to

Article 41 of the TRIPS. Border measures that put undue burden on imported goods are not legitimate.

CONCLUSIONS

Complaints over weak IP enforcement in developing countries can often be heard in the international arena. These complaints originate from a fundamental conceptual confusion, namely, the public sector (government) instead of private sector (right-holders) should take responsibility of enforcement of IPR. Starting from this fundamental misconception, a series of other misconceptions have been purposely promoted by developed countries driven by the enormous interests of private sectors, generating detrimental implications for developing countries. Not only have public resources been misallocated to enforcing private IP right, but also innovation space in developing countries has been diminished due to abuse of IPR enforcement. Overall, ten misconceptions on IP enforcement can be highlighted: (1) counterfeiting and piracy includes patent infringement. (2) Product falsification, counterfeiting and IP infringed goods are identical. (3) IP infringement poses a consumer threat. (4) Magnitude of claimed IP infringement is enormous. (5) Government should take the primary responsibility of enforcement. (6) Government should bear the cost of IP enforcement. (7) WTO Members are obliged to provide border procedures for all types of transactions and all form of IPRs. (8) WTO Members are bound to provide a judicial system for IPRs. (9) Criminal procedures are obligatory to establish for IP-infringing products. (10) Customs administrations have the authority to determine IP infringement. As a consequence, the effect of IP infringement has been overstated due to expanded definition of IPRs, losses from counterfeit and piracy have been exaggerated since there are no robust methods of quantifying them, public resources on IP enforcement have been overspent due to misunderstanding of government's responsibilities, border and criminal measures have been over-applied due to incorrect grasp of definition and responsibilities, and customs administrations have been wrongfully granted authority on determination of IP infringement. As IP enforcement and development are intertwined, these adverse effects on developing countries must be corrected. It should be emphasized that there are clear guidelines and flexibilities under the TRIPS Agreement regarding the government obligations on IP enforcement. Developing countries should be able to maintain legitimate balance on enforcement measures between the rights of intellectual property holders and the public interest. developing countries should avoid being trapped in the conceptual framework introduced by developed countries on IP enforcement and giving up the policy space allowed under the TRIPS Agreement. In this context, this chapter serves only as the first step away from the intangible conceptual domination of developed countries. Maximizing the existing TRIPS flexibilities and formulating development-friendly strategy on IP enforcement require further methodological reflections and concrete actions.

NOTES

1. EU Strategy for the Enforcement of Intellectual Property Rights in Third Countries, http://trade.ec.europa.eu/doclib/docs/2005/april/tradoc_122636.pdf.
2. 'The term "counterfeit drug" means a drug which, or the container or labelling of which, without authorization, bears the trademark, trade name, or other identifying mark, imprint, or device, or any likeness thereof, of a drug manufacturer, processor, packer, or distributor other than the person or persons who in fact manufactured, processed, packed, or distributed such drug and which thereby falsely purports or is represented to be the product of, or to have been packed or distributed by, such other drug manufacturer, processor, packer, or distributor', United States Federal Food, Drug, and Cosmetic Act, Section 201. [21 U.S.C. 321], G(2). *IP Quarterly Update*, Issue No. 3, South Centre and CIEL (2008).
3. http://www.wipo.int/about-wipo/en/dgo/wipo_pub_888/wipo_pub_888_1.htm.
4. Revised figures: following publication by the Commission of the 2006 statistics on counterfeit and piracy, certain corrections were required to the figures, following feedback from the national customs administrations. In particular, it was necessary to revise the figures relating to the total amount of items seized, to ensure consistency in the method of calculating the quantities of articles. In previous years, in order to avoid distorting the overall statistics, it was decided to calculate the seizures of cigarettes by packets of 20 (or their equivalent). It has come to light that some of the figures notified to the Commission for 2006, referred to seizures of single cigarettes. The total amount of articles seized has been revised. The number of articles seized is 128 631 295, compared to 75 733 068 in 2005. The number of cases registered by customs is 37 334. This figure was also revised following an increase in the number of cases notified to the Commission and represents a significant increase on last year's total of around 26 000 cases. http://ec.europa.eu/taxation_customs/customs/customs_controls/counterfeit_piracy/statistics/index_en.htm, Community-wide statistics for 2006.
5. 'Australian draft report casts doubt on piracy stats', http://www.afterdawn.com/news/archive/8110.cfm.

6. Although the TRIPS Agreement does not specify in detail the enforcement measures and mechanisms to be adopted, it does impose minimum standards that generate costs for the Member Countries. The devil lies in the modalities of implementation of Part III as whole.

7. SECURE, World Customs Organization, as of 25 April 2008.

8. The first directive on the enforcement of IP rights, Directive 2004/48/EC deals with civil enforcement of intellectual property rights. It was hastily passed before the Fifth Enlargement of the European Union of 1 May 2004. It originally included criminal sanctions provisions, but this rather controversial part was omitted in order to be able to meet the deadline of 1 May 2004, http://en.wikipedia. org/wiki/Proposed_directive_on_criminal_measures_aimed_at_ensuring_the_ enforcement_of_intellectual_property_rights.

3. Re-delineation of the role of stakeholders: IP enforcement beyond exclusive rights

Henning Grosse Ruse-Khan[1]

INTRODUCTION

The enforcement of intellectual property (IP) has been at the centre of the debate in various international forums,[2] regional or bilateral negotiations on economic partnership or free trade agreements[3] as well as in developed and developing countries.[4] In the international context, developed countries are generally the demanders of stronger IP protection and enforcement in all relevant markets abroad, while developing countries take a defensive stand aiming to prevent further obligations that surpass the enforcement obligations in the TRIPS Agreement.[5] On this basis, IP enforcement is generally connoted with the enforcement of right-holders' exclusive entitlements to prevent others from (commercially) using the IP-protected subject matter – thus neglecting exceptions and limitations to IP and their 'enforcement'. This current political reality blurs a holistic view on the issue of IP enforcement where all stakeholders and their role and interests in the IP system are examined. In this chapter, I plan to identify the relevant stakeholders in IP enforcement on the basis of such a holistic approach to IP enforcement. After setting out the parameters for a wider understanding of IP enforcement in the remainder of this section, the next section delineates the main groups of stakeholders. Against this background, the third section sets out some ideas on a developing country agenda on IP enforcement, which includes not only the well-known defensive interests but also positive, offensive interests in IP enforcement.

My principal starting point for a wider understanding of IP enforcement is that – next to enforcement specific actors[6] – the relevant stakeholder groupings and their IP enforcement interests depend very much on their role and interests in the IP system in general. It is the interest and function in the overall IP system that determines the position each stakeholder will take towards IP enforcement and how it perceives IP enforcement. For example, IP users often benefit from certain exceptions to IP protection[7] and therefore have a specific interest that these exceptions can be given effect. IP enforcement here may require offering remedies against a contractual curtailment of these exceptions[8] or against the use of technological protection measures that frustrate the exercise of exceptions in copyright.[9] Right-holders in turn primarily benefit from the exclusive rights granted by IP protection and thus have the natural interest of enforcing these IP rights. Other actors have an enforcement-specific role, such as the judiciary, whose main function is to serve as an impartial and independent body judging on claims and counterclaims brought by the different actors.

This approach therefore necessitates a wide understanding of the term enforcement, which not only covers various ways of giving effect to the rights granted to right-holders but inter alia also enforcing limitations and exceptions to IP rights and ensuring that the requirements for and the scope of IP protection are upheld. Based on the diversity of interests involved in the system, it also includes upholding fairness and due process as well as public policy goals such as free competition, public health, environmental protection and other values external to the IP system.[10] While these issues are not part of the main IP enforcement debate (which focuses purely on giving effect to right-holders' interests), they are often of greater interest for developing countries and indicate the bias in the current debate on further strengthening IP enforcement.

Is there any further normative basis for such a wide understanding of IP enforcement, reaching out to general public interests as far as they potentially conflict with the exclusivity IP protection entails? Justification comes from one of the key development-oriented provisions of the TRIPS Agreement. Art. 7 on the objectives of the TRIPS Agreement prescribes that:

> The protection and *enforcement* of intellectual property rights should contribute to the promotion of technological innovation and to the transfer and dissemination of technology, to the mutual advantage of producers and users of technological knowledge and in a manner

conducive to social and economic welfare, and to a balance of rights and obligations.[11]

While a full discussion of Art. 7 goes well beyond the scope of this chapter (Gervais, 2003; Correa, 2007; UNCTAD-ICTSD, 2005; Grosse Ruse-Khan, 2008a),[12] it explicitly refers also to IP enforcement as a tool to achieve the public policy goals of promotion of technological innovation as well as the dissemination of technology. While the first goal should usually be achieved by ensuring that exclusive IP rights, arguably serving as main incentives for new innovations, are adequately enforced (Okediji, 2005, pp. x–xi, 4–8; Geiger, 2007, p. 707; Geiger, 2008, pp. 459–67);[13] the second aim requires a proper enforcement of exceptions and limitations to the exclusive rights as these generally ensure the dissemination of technology or other protected subject matter (Bently and Sherman, 2004, pp. 190–92).[14] Apart from the innovation–dissemination paradigm, the other elements in Art. 7 further support such a wide understanding of IP enforcement: it should be mutually advantageous to producers and users, balance rights and obligations and, overall, promote social and economic welfare. These and other overarching public policy goals are further emphasized in Art. 8:1 of TRIPS (Grosse Ruse-Khan, 2008b).[15] Taken together, this not only requires taking account of all stakeholders affected by the IP system and giving effect to their interests but arguably calls for sufficient policy space to tailor IP enforcement to the needs of the individual stakeholders and the domestic societal, economic and cultural environment in general (World Bank, 2001, p. 129; CIPR, 2002, pp. 18–20; Trebilcock and Howse, 2005, pp. 397–401; UNCTAD, 2007, pp. 105–7).[16]

DELINEATING THE MAIN GROUPS OF STAKEHOLDERS

A first and general delineation can differentiate between *right-holders, users and state authorities* – all of which can be distinguished further. A fourth grouping would be *intermediaries* involved in the (physical or digital) transfer or dissemination of IP-protected material, most prominently Internet service providers (ISPs). As the further analysis of their respective roles and interests in IP enforcement will show, this division, however, is not specific enough.

Right-holders

Probably the most obvious stakeholders in IP enforcement are
right-holders. Generally speaking, their main interests will be to give
proper effect to the rights and benefits IP laws provide them. As IP
rights are 'private rights'[17] right-holders are chiefly responsible for
enforcing their rights (Mathew, 2008, p. 25; Biadgleng and Muñoz-
Tellez, 2008a, p. 3). While the general approach to the law enforcement of private rights as well as Part III of the TRIPS Agreement
provide evidence that the state must provide tools such as civil remedies for damages and provisional measures under certain procedural
and substantive conditions, it is up to the right-holders to take on
the initiative and costs of IP enforcement (CIPR, 2002, pp. 146–8).[18]
Recent international initiatives, however, often try to change this
status quo by shifting the burden of IP enforcement more and more
towards specific state authorities.[19]

Although a common interest relates to effective enforcement
of the entitlements IP laws provide to all types of right-holders,
certain subgroups should be distinguished due to their specific role
and interests as they warrant special treatment in the enforcement
debate. Depending further on the domestic legal setting and overall
IP system, relevant subgroups may include authors and other creators, exploiters and investors as well as collection societies. In the
following, I will take a closer look at these subgroups.

First, right-holders may be initial right-holders such as authors or
performers of certain copyrighted works or inventors. The relevant
common denominator is that they are often ordinary people who are
employed or commissioned to create or invent. Generally they will not
be those who further exploit the IP-protected material – be it music,
films, software or technical inventions. Since these stakeholders often
transfer their IP rights or at least all relevant economic entitlements,
they may have less direct interests in optimization of enforcement
options for exclusive rights.[20] Instead, authors and other creators
will have interests in regulations and respective enforcement of rules
guaranteeing fairness in rights transfer and employment contracts
(Hugenholtz and Guibault, 2002).[21] More importantly, they have
a specific interest in statutory licensing schemes and upfront royalties or fees to be paid on any devices commonly used for mass-scale
copying – examples here are levies on photocopying machines, PCs
or scanners as well as video-tapes, recordable CD ROMs or DVDs.[22]

Such statutory remuneration is collected by state authorities or collection societies and often offers the author a reliable source of income, which usually cannot be signed away to others by contract. Effective statutory licensing mechanisms thus not only offer greater access to the protected subject matter on reasonable terms but are also likely to offer direct benefits to authors/performers.[23] Representing authors and performers in the exercise of certain (or all) of their IP rights, collection societies can play a vital role in the enforcement of those entitlements that are directly beneficial to the creative individuals.

The authors and other creators should be distinguished from those who *exploit* IP-protected subject matter, be it in the form of licensing or direct exploitation by means of producing, distributing and selling or otherwise commercializing IP-protected products or services. Amongst these exploiters of IP-protected content, investors can play a special role due to the specific legal regimes and protection that operate under (bilateral) investment protection treaties.[24] As those who take the initiative and carry the risk of investments, exploiters have the main interest of recouping their investments and making a profit by exploiting IP-protected subject matter. Their interest in IP enforcement is thus focused on enhancing and perfecting any law enforcement mechanism that applies to IP-protected material and provides options to give effect to the rights at their disposal. They further strongly press to shift the burden of taking enforcement action towards various state authorities, which are often neither designed to, nor have the resources for such additional tasks.[25] Since virtually all international initiatives currently focus on strengthening enforcement options for these exclusive entitlements, it is no wonder that the IP enforcement debate is predominantly perceived as an agenda pursuing the interests of multinational right-holder corporations.

In various industries, however, exploiters of one or even a portfolio of IP-protected material are often IP users at the same time. In the software and IT industry, for example, one product may be covered by a vast amount of patents or copyrights, which then forces exploiters into cross-licensing schemes or patent pools where they are reliant on the ability to use the other exploiters' IP (Reichman, 2008a, pp. 28–31). Here, overly strong enforcement of the exclusive rights available can serve as an inhibitor to follow-on innovation, the marketing of comprehensive products with various layers of IP rights and competitive market conditions in general.[26]

Users

The second major group, the users, can again be divided into several
subgroups with related, but not necessarily overlapping interests in
IP enforcement. First of all, consumers – understood as persons or
entities that engage in non-commercial use of IP-protected material
– form one subgroup. They include specific groups within society,
which often benefit from certain exceptions to IP protection, for
example for disabled persons, students or researchers.

On the one hand, consumers have a *defensive interest* against the
prevailing pro-right-holder bias towards rigorously enforcing exclusive rights; in particular when it disregards safeguarding privacy or
other fundamental rights of individuals.[27] Against the background
of recent trends, this entails the concern to be free from criminalization or exorbitant civil damage claims in cases of non-commercial
conduct such as downloading a music file.[28] On the other hand, consumers also have *offensive interests* in effective enforcement mechanisms for exceptions and limitations of IP rights that benefit users at
large or specific user groups. For example, in countries with specific
research or educational exceptions to copyright, students need to
be able to exercise their legal entitlements to use excerpts from text-
books for educational purposes. Here, 'digital locks' on protected
content via Technological Protection Measures (TPMs) or Digital
Rights Management systems (DRMs) should not frustrate utilizing
an exception and the legal protection of TPMs and DRMs against
circumvention must be drafted accordingly (Parliament of Australia,
2006).[29] In order to allow consumers (such as students) to continue
to benefit from their exceptions, they need effective means to force
right-holders to make the protected content available insofar as
mandated by the exception or to provide ways for consumers to
circumvent such digital locks.

Another subgroup comprises users such as competitors[30] or
those who otherwise build on or further utilize IP-protected subject
matter[31] and thus – as a unifying factor – aim for a commercial use
of the IP-protected subject matter. Again, one can identify defensive interests as users against unreasonable strong emphasis on the
enforcement of exclusive rights. Here, the broad and easy availability of provisional measures to prevent alleged infringements[32] such
as interlocutory (that is, interim) injunctions can result in significant
limitations on competition and the availability of value-added

products.[33] Requirements on right-holder applicants to offer 'reasonable available evidence' and to provide 'security or equivalent assurance sufficient to protect the defendant and to prevent abuse'[34] should be enacted in order to safeguard the interests not only of commercial users but also competitive markets and consumers.

Offensive interests of commercial users lie in upholding the inherent limitations to IP protection, whether in the form of requirements for the granting of IP rights,[35] delineations of their scope[36] or interfaces with other areas of law such as competition law.[37] On the international level, an overly broad definition of 'counterfeiting' or 'piracy' may limit (via extensive measures to combat the former) legitimate generic competition, for example in the pharmaceutical sector (Mathew, 2008; Narendranath, 2008).[38] Commercial users thus have an interest in appropriate safeguards in legitimate trade and competition when adopting enforcement measures tailored to prevent infringements of exclusive entitlements of right-holders.

Amongst these, commercial users licensees[39] probably deserve specific mention as their contractual relation with the right-holders regarding the use of IP raises specific legal issues that also impact on their IP enforcement interests. Art. 40:2 of TRIPS allows measures against licensing practices that abuse IP rights. An interesting further development can be seen in Art. 142:2 of the recent EU–CARIFORUM EPA, which contains a binding obligation that requires the contracting parties to prevent licensing practices and conditions pertaining to IP rights as soon as they (1) have the potential to affect international technology transfer and (2) either constitute an abuse of IP rights by right-holders or an abuse of obvious information asymmetries in the negotiation of licences.[40] This provision could be understood in the way that EU competition authorities have an obligation to monitor the technology transfer impact in the CARIFORUM States of IP licensing practices and other IP strategies of EU companies.[41] Licensees have an interest in effective implementation of such measures by competition authorities, which in turn should be sufficiently staffed and able to act against the abuse of IP rights.

One should finally consider the general public as another relevant stakeholder. In that sense, it probably fits best as a subgroup of users – although the lack of homogeneity may to some extent blur the view on the specific interests in IP enforcement at stake for the 'general public' (which of course in its broader meaning contains all groups discussed here). When I list it here as a specific stakeholder within the group of users, I understand it as representative of the general public interests of a society as they relate to IP enforcement. A core interest then is the need for IP enforcement to be responsive to public policies and recognition of important societal values and interests.[42] Cases of injunctive relief against the allegedly patent-infringing products in the United States and India indicate that judges are willing to consider and give effect to public interests when determining the (permanent or temporary) prohibition to market goods for which there is a strong public policy demand. In India, the Delhi High Court rejected an injunction against producing and selling allegedly patent-infringing drugs due to the 'right of the general public to access to life saving drugs'.[43] In the United States, the landmark decision of the US Supreme Court in *eBay Inc.* v. *MercExchange, LLC*, denied a permanent injunction even though it found a patent infringement on the basis of general equity considerations – thereby effectively allowing a compulsory-licensing type of use of a patented invention against compensatory payments.[44] Lower courts have taken up these equity considerations – for example, to impose a compulsory licence allowing the production of a generic drug against the payment of adequate compensation instead of issuing a permanent injunction (Correa, forthcoming 2009, pp. 30–31).[45] Overall, sufficient procedural[46] and substantive[47] checks and balances should be inserted in the IP enforcement system in order to safeguard the recognition of and if necessary giving effect to public interest concerns.

State Authorities

The third major group of stakeholders are state authorities including IP offices, the judiciary, public law enforcement bodies and customs authorities as a specifically relevant subgroup. On a general law enforcement level, the state has a legitimate interest in sufficient autonomy to determine its own enforcement priorities.[48] Indeed, given the multitude and often grave law enforcement problems developing countries face and coupled with the scarcity in resources, IP enforcement even in its broader understanding advocated here may not be a priority for most developing countries (Correa, forthcoming 2009, p. 51).[49] If resources are devoted to IP enforcement in developing countries, they should be focused on facilitating domestic innovation, aligned with a national IP strategy and proportionally addressing the concerns of all stakeholders involved.

Looking at the subgroups, IP offices such as patent or trademark offices that perform important functions in the registration or application procedures with regard to some IP rights[50] can also play enforcement-related roles. They are not only involved in granting procedures that include enforcement elements such as pre-registration trademark opposition procedures, but can also offer the appropriate forum for post-grant revocation of registered IP rights.[51] Options for pre- or post-grant administrative review proceedings allow third parties to raise concerns over the (potential) validity of an IP right and so supplement the enforcement function of granting requirements as well as limitations in scope of IP rights.[52]

Another subgroup within the cluster of state authorities is the judiciary – understood here as an (impartial and independent) authority that judges on private law claims relating to the enforcement of IP brought by private parties. IP enforcement proceedings in front of the judiciary should give due regard to the positions of both parties and implement the general need for fair and equitable procedures in private claims proceedings as well as minimum rights of parties in front of a court.[53] Nevertheless, judicial enforcement of IP should relate to overall judicial law enforcement abilities and infrastructure; and, as TRIPS emphasizes in Art. 41:5, there is no obligation to establish special IP courts (Ollier, 2008).[54]

Next to the judiciary, there are increasing tendencies to involve public authorities such as the prosecution office or the policy in ex-officio enforcement of IP rights: the draft EU directive on criminal enforcement measures extends the coverage of Art. 61 of TRIPS from the specific cases of trademark counterfeiting and copyright piracy[55] to all infringements of any type of IP (as long as they are committed intentionally and on a commercial scale).[56] A recent US legislative proposal allows the Justice Department to file a lawsuit against any person committing a copyright violation – thereby potentially targeting millions of individuals who use peer to peer file-sharing networks (McCullagh, 2008).[57] In Germany, state prosecutors are overwhelmed by applications for criminal proceedings against unknown acts of file-sharing so that the applicant rightholder can utilize state resources to obtain relevant data and user identity.[58] These examples provide anecdotal evidence towards a trend for externalizing the risks and resources to enforce IP rights away from the originally responsible right-holders towards state authorities. At the WTO, the US challenge of China's interpretation of Art. 61 TRIPS will not only clarify the policy space WTO Members have when implementing terms like commercial scale; it will more generally determine the scope of TRIPS obligations when broad and open terms in TRIPS provisions are at stake.[59]

Amongst the last subgroup, customs authorities are equally given an ever-increasing role to play in IP enforcement. Current tendencies to broaden the scope of border measures well beyond TRIPS[60] prescribe custom authorities a function that they cannot fulfil effectively. Border controls by customs should be limited to prima facie detectable infringing goods – which generally excludes the determination of patent and utility model infringements where infringement cannot be assessed without specific legal and technical expertise.[61] The attempts to extend the duties of customs authorities beyond the TRIPS baseline of acting against counterfeit trademarks and copyright piracy may well serve as a new form of non-tariff trade barrier, especially for industries that produce value-added products or follow-on innovations related to patented inventions (Mathew, 2008 and Narendranath, 2008). If generic drugs are targeted, public policy concerns such as access to medicines are equally affected. Another aspect is that – in the same manner as for public law enforcement bodies – customs offices are more and more required to take ex-officio action.[62] Such ex-officio actions, however, not only shift the initiative and costs for taking action to the state but also entail significant risks of damaging claims by affected importers whenever the goods suspended in the end are not IP infringing (Correa, forthcoming 2009, p. 40). In sum, one should recall that the primary role of customs is to prevent illegal trade while not threatening legal trade[63] and therefore must balance the need for IP enforcement with trade objectives.

Intermediaries

Finally, a fourth group can be identified that as such play a role that is rather minor in comparison to those of the three main groupings. However, as they do not fall within any of the three groups, I list them here separately as intermediaries who are involved in the transfer or dissemination of IP-protected material. The main interface with IP enforcement lies with Internet Service Providers (ISPs) such as access or host providers, or search engines that usually perform a purely technical function in the transfer or dissemination process and are not directly involved in a specific use of the IP-protected material. Outside the digital online environment, intermediaries such as postal services have recently been targeted to assume a greater role and responsibility in IP infringement (Li, 2008c).[64]

ISPs function as purely technical transmitters or disseminators of IP-protected content while their primary role is often to enable communication and access to information. The latter key functions, which are crucial for access to knowledge, should not be affected by indirect liability for IP infringements of their users, or by increasing responsibility to act against alleged infringers. Under the so-called 'notice and take-down' procedure established by the Digital Millennium Copyright Act (DMCA), ISPs in the United States must act immediately on a complaint that certain user content infringes IP rights and remove that content from the Internet if they want to avoid liability for contributory infringement.[65] In the United Kingdom and in France, ISPs had to enter into agreements with right-holders and the government dealing with their extended role in the prevention of IP infringements in order to themselves avoid liability. Further legislative measures are also under consideration: ISPs are required to send warning letters to their customers; possibly filter their traffic for IP-infringing content, and may end up having to cut off Internet connections of users if they are alleged to have used infringing material three times (Boiron and Tulquois, 2008, pp. 16–17; Sweney, 2008). This 'brave new world' for Internet users has serious implications for access to essential communication means like the Internet and thereby strongly affects the availability of information. It further impacts on user privacy and data protection principles.[66] Overall, the initiatives in the United Kingdom and France fit well into the trend of shifting away responsibilities in enforcing the right-holders' market exclusivity towards third parties.

A DEVELOPING COUNTRY AGENDA ON IP ENFORCEMENT

The preceding analysis has shown that based on the diversity of interests involved, issues of IP enforcement also include several offensive interests for developing countries. I, however, first address the rather obvious and well-known defensive interests in brief. They can be summarized in the need for developing countries to retain sufficient policy space to tailor the IP enforcement system to their domestic IP environment and to suit the interests of their stakeholders. This policy space is currently threatened by various international, regional or bilateral initiatives that focus exclusively on strengthening the position of right-holders. While some aspects of such a move may be an interesting option to consider for some (technically more advanced) developing countries, they certainly do not work in favour of the majority, let alone all developing countries. Apart from the specific flaws of these initiatives, there simply is no 'one size fits all' approach in IP protection in general, as well as in IP enforcement in particular (Grosse Ruse-Khan, 2008a, pp. 175–6).[67] More specific problems of the recent initiatives (which in turn translate into defensive interests for developing countries) include the need to avoid more pressure on scarce state resources in the enforcement of exclusive entitlements of right-holders. Various aspects of recent initiatives, for example the increased role of customs authorities in border measures or of the police and the prosecution office in criminal measures, entail a greater state responsibility in enforcing IP rights. Coupled with an increasing tendency for ex-officio actions, this shift from the original responsibility of the right-holders tends to circumvent the safeguards in Art. 41:5 of TRIPS and binds law enforcement resources that may be much more urgently needed in other areas of law enforcement.

Another defensive interest relates to the availability of permanent injunctive relief or provisional measures in the form of interim injunctions. Due to the further impact on free competition and potentially on other public policies whenever highly demanded goods (such as essential medicines) are concerned, developing country judiciaries should take a very cautious approach in granting such measures. Defendants in developing countries are most likely to be in greater need for protection against broad prohibitions due to their limited resources and experience in utilizing legal means for appeal or redress. Finally, developing countries should resist attempts to place a significant part of the IP enforcement responsibility on ISPs or other forms of intermediaries involved in the transfer and dissemination of IP-protected material. The above-described implications for access to communication networks and end user privacy are equally relevant for developed countries, but in (some) developing countries civil society and user organizations may be less able to place these concerns on the public agenda.

Turning to the offensive interests developing countries might have under the wider understanding of IP enforcement developed above, one should stress from the outset that any detailed assessment depends on the individual circumstances of the developing country at stake. Its technological, economic and cultural level of development, the public interests pursued and potentially affected by IP protection, the national actors involved in the IP system as well as the law enforcement mechanisms, all play a role in this regard. However, given that developing countries generally need to improve their technological and innovative capability, historical evidence and economic theory suggests that they are generally better off with a lax IP system that allows for certain forms of imitation and technological learning (CIPR, 2002; Trebilcock and Howse, 2005, pp. 397–401).[68] Taking TRIPS as a given baseline for international obligations to protect IP, offensive interests of developing countries will rather lie in giving proper effect to the requirements for protection, the limitations in scope and time as well as the exceptions to exclusive rights allowed under TRIPS. These elements of the IP system usually function to balance the exclusivity conferred upon right-holders and counters the latter's anti-competitive and access-restricting effect. They therefore can be utilized to promote the dissemination of technology (as mandated by Art. 7 of TRIPS) and function as safeguards for public interests outside the IP system, such as public health and nutrition (as recognised by Art. 8:1 of TRIPS).

Examples of specific offensive interests are (1) ensuring that exceptions to copyright protection are given effect over contractual limitations and the use of digital locks (in the form of TPMs and DRMs); (2) upholding a strict application of the requirements for granting exclusive rights, for example, to ensure quality patents and offering effective pre- or post-grant review procedures; (3) implementing provisions that tackle the abuse of IP rights (for example, in licensing agreements) and foster the transfer of technology and (4) including public interest considerations and fundamental rights safeguards in procedural measures such as injunctive relief, damage awards and criminal investigations.[69] However, in relation to the protection available to right-holders also, developing countries can surely have specific offensive interests. Next to an effective and adequate enforcement of market exclusivity in industries where developing countries have developed a comparative advantage, ensuring protection for small-scale innovations via utility models (petty patents), for example, could be a way forward to reward local small-step innovations, adaptations and improvements of existing technology. The most important area here will nevertheless be the effective protection and enforcement of traditional knowledge and traditional cultural expressions in line with the needs and interests of the knowledge-holders. Apart from pursuing the matter in international negotiations, which should focus on preventing misappropriation in (developed) user countries, developing countries should enact effective protection mechanisms in their home countries (McDermott, 2008).[70]

To conclude, currently the IP enforcement debate not only suffers from a disproportionate bias towards the interests of right-holders; it further blurs a more appropriate holistic perception of the matter, which addresses the concerns of all relevant stakeholders. Not surprisingly, the interests of developing countries, which are likely to focus more on other stakeholders than the right-holders, are marginalized. While developing countries have recently made good progress in fighting a continuous increase in the measures available to right-holders, they should put more effort into identifying and pursuing their positive interests in the IP enforcement debate. This arguably starts by adopting a wider, more holistic view on IP enforcement.

NOTES

1. I wish to thank Ruth Claussen for her research assistance and the participants of the second South Centre International Symposium on IP enforcement for their input. All errors remain mine. Email: henning-gr-khan@mpg.de.
2. Such as the TRIPS Council of the WTO, various bodies of the WIPO, the World Customs Organization (WCO), the World Health Organization (WHO), the Universal Postal Union (UPU), the Organisation for Economic Co-operation and Development (OECD), the Group of Eight (G8) as well as INTERPOL and the International Chamber of Commerce (ICC).
3. See, for example, Arts. 151–164 of the EU-CARIFORUM Economic Partnership Agreement (EPA) negotiated between the European Union and the Group of Caribbean States; Art. 15:11 of the Central American Free Trade Agreement (CAFTA) between the United States and Central American Countries; and Arts. 119–121 of the Japan-Indonesia Economic Partnership Agreement.
4. In the EU, see Directive 2004/48/EC of the European Parliament and the Council of 29 April 2004 on the enforcement of intellectual property rights and the amended proposal for a directive on criminal measures aimed at ensuring the enforcement of intellectual property rights, COM(2006) 168 final of 26 April

2006. Further, the EC has recently adopted a 'Strategy for the Enforcement of Intellectual Property Rights in Third Countries' (accessible online at http://ec.europa.eu/trade/issues/sectoral/intell_property/strategy_tc.htm, accessed 23 September 2008). In the United States, several recent legislative proposals deal with IP enforcement at home (see S.3325, the Enforcement of Intellectual Property Act of 2008, introduced on 24 July 2008) and abroad (see the International Intellectual Property Protection and Enforcement Act of 2008 introduced in the Senate in September 2008). Also, several developing countries such as China (National Strategy on the Protection of Intellectual Property Rights of 5 June 2008) or the Philippines (Five Point Strategy to Improve IP Enforcement of 3 July, 2008) have adopted measures that either include or exclusively address IP enforcement.

5. See Arts. 41–61 TRIPS. For a discussion on the attempts to add new obligations on IP protection in various international forums see Chapter 4 below and Chapter 1 above.

6. Such as the judiciary and certain administrative authorities (for example, customs); see the next section below.

7. For example, private use, education and disabled persons' exceptions in the field of copyright – for a comprehensive list see Art. 5 of the Directive 2001/29/EC of the European Parliament and of the Council of 22 May 2001 on the harmonization of certain aspects of copyright and related rights in the information society (EU Copyright Directive). In patent law, typical exceptions relate to research or experimental use (see sec. 60 (5) (b) of the UK Patents Act 1977) and obtaining regulatory approval to market drugs ('Bolar' exceptions: see the US case *Roche Products Inc.* v. *Bolar Pharmaceutical Co.*, 733 F.2d 858 (Fed. Cir. 04/23/1984) and 35 U.S.C. sec. 271 (e) (1)). In the field of trademarks finally, TRIPS itself mentions descriptive use of protected signs as one possible exception (see Art. 17 TRIPS).

8. Examples of such mandatory exceptions which can override contractual limitations, are Art. 5 secs. 2, 3 (making of back-up copies; idea–expression dichotomy) and Art. 6 (decompilation) both in connection with Art. 9 sec.1 of the EU Directive 91/250/EEC on the legal protection of computer programs as well as Art. 5 sec. 1 (certain temporary acts of reproduction) of the EU Copyright Directive (see note 4 above) and further Art. 6 sec. 1, Arts. 8 and 15 of the EU Directive 96/9/EC on the legal protection of databases.

9. Art. 6 sec. 4 of the EU Copyright Directive (see note 4 above) adopts a rather controversial approach that contains an obligation for EU Member States to ensure that beneficiaries of certain exceptions to copyright must be enabled to exercise these exceptions even in cases where right-holders limit access or use by technological protection measures. This obligation is, however, subject to 'voluntary measures taken by right-holders' and does not apply to works made available over the Internet (where right-holders thus remain free to effectively invalidate exceptions and the underlying public policies by technological measures).

10. For example, the interests of commercial users in creating follow-on innovations and value-added products or the interests of the general public in access to essential drugs, affordable foodstuffs and environmentally sound technology.

11. Emphasis added.

12. See Gervais (2003), paras. 2.72–2.80; Correa (2007), pp. 91–103; ICTSD/UNCTAD (2005), Part One, Chapter 6; for an analysis on the role of Art. 7 for TRIPS interpretation see Grosse Ruse-Khan (2008a).

13. Several commentators, however, equally stress the role of exceptions and limitations in safeguarding follow-on innovations, value-added products and services and competitive markets, which in turn are necessary elements for innovation;

see Okediji (2006), who points out the relevance of exceptions in line with the principle of 'standing on the shoulders of giants'; see also Geiger (2007), p. 707 and Geiger (2008), pp. 459–67.

14. Limitations to exclusive rights – for example, in form of substantive requirements for granting protection (see Art. 27:1 TRIPS on patent protection or Art. 15:1 TRIPS on trademarks) or limits on the duration of IP rights (see Art. 12 TRIPS on copyright and Art. 33 TRIPS on patents) – ensure the availability of underlying ideas, discoveries and concepts in the public domain and later (after expiry of protection) force the protected technology or other subject matter to arrive there as well. Exceptions to exclusive rights and compulsory or statutory licensing generally aim to make otherwise IP-protected material available to certain privileged users and/or for certain public purposes; see Bently and Sherman (2004).

15. Similar to the general exception contained in Art. XX GATT and Art. XIV GATS (but subject to an overall TRIPS consistency test), Art. 8:1 TRIPS provides that 'Members may, in formulating or amending their laws and regulations, adopt measures necessary to protect public health and nutrition, and to promote the public interest in sectors of vital importance to their socio-economic and technological development, provided that such measures are consistent with the provisions of this Agreement'. The interpretative importance of both Arts. 7 and 8 in the process of implementing TRIPS and utilizing its flexibilities has been emphasized in para. 5 (a) of the Doha Declaration on TRIPS and Public Health. On the post-Doha role of Art. 8 TRIPS see Grosse Ruse-Khan (2008b).

16. See UNCTAD (2007), World Bank (2001). On the historical evidence for tailoring national IP policy and regulation to the domestic economic, technological and development needs of a country see further CIPR (2002), and especially the two related background papers Khan (2002) and Kumar (2002). For an economic and trade theory justification see Trebilcock and Howse (2005).

17. This aspect is emphasized in the preamble of TRIPS indicating that the agreement was adopted by WTO Members 'recognizing that intellectual property rights are private rights'.

18. Compare CIPR (2002), as note 16 above.

19. See the SECURE initiative of the WCO, the recent amended proposal for a directive on criminal enforcement (as note 4 above), and the discussions on a new Anti-Counterfeiting Trade Agreement (ACTA). Whether the functions and interests of those who are increasingly targeted to take on new roles in IP enforcement justify such approaches shall be discussed below; for an analysis on the international initiatives see also Chapters 1 and 7.

20. They may, however, have an indirect interest here as they receive remuneration primarily from those who rely on such enforcement options.

21. On the issue of copyright contract regulation see Hugenholtz and Guibault (2002).

22. On a detailed regulation of such copyright levies see secs. 54–54h of the German Copyright Act (*Urheberrechtsgesetz*).

23. This is one of the issues addressed in the recent Declaration 'On a Balanced Interpretation of the Three Step Test in Copyright Law', available online at   http://www.ip.mpg.de/ww/de/pub/aktuelles/declaration_three_steps.pdf, accessed 30 September 2008.

24. The special status results from protection under Bilateral Investment Treaties (BITs): as they commonly include IP as protected investment, one standard of protection offered under BITs can have implications for IP enforcement: the guarantee to offer 'full protection and security', which is commonly understood as the active duty of a state to keep the investor free from harm from third parties

could entail a state obligation (potentially enforceable in investor–state arbitration) to prevent IP infringements beyond IP-specific obligations under TRIPS.

25. See the subsection on state authorities below.
26. See also the further discussion in the next subsection below.
27. On the issue of protecting personal data and enforcing IP rights see the European Court of Justice (ECJ) judgement of 29 January 2008 in the case of *Productores de Música de España Promusicae* v. *Telefónica de España* (C275/06) considering that the European law 'does not require member states to lay down an obligation to disclose personal data in the context of civil proceedings'.
28. Art. 61 TRIPS only prescribes criminal law measures in cases of copyright piracy on a commercial scale and wilful trademark counterfeiting. In the United States and Europe, right-holder organizations such as IFPI, the RIAA, MPAA and others increasingly target end users with criminal investigation and high damage claims; see the Electronic Frontier Foundation's (EFF) website at http://www.eff.org/issues/file-sharing, accessed 29 September 2008, for an overview.
29. International obligations on TPMs and DRMs exist under Arts. 11, 12 of the WIPO (WCT) Copyright Treaty as well as Arts. 18, 19 of the WIPO Performers and Phonograms Treaty (WPPT), which do not address the issue of exceptions; in the EU, Art. 6:4 of the Copyright Directive offers some protection for exceptions. For a detailed study on the matter see Parliament of Australia (2006).
30. That is, those who directly or indirectly compete with the right-holders by offering products or services that serve as market substitute for the protected good or service.
31. For example, follow-on innovators or producers of value-added goods and services.
32. According to Art. 50 TRIPS, provisional measures must be available to (1) prevent an infringement of any intellectual property right from occurring, and in particular to prevent the entry into the channels of commerce in their jurisdiction of goods, including imported goods immediately after customs clearance; and (2) to preserve relevant evidence in regard to the alleged infringement.
33. See Chapter 6 for details. The further public policy implications are also briefly discussed below.
34. Art. 40 TRIPS.
35. A lax application of the patent granting requirements of novelty, inventive step and industrial application (see Art. 27:1 TRIPS) will lead to poor-quality patents for no or few innovative products or processes that in turn monopolize relevant markets without any return in innovation.
36. Limits on the scope of IP rights, such as the idea–expression dichotomy in Art. 9:2 (in combination with the prohibition to protect data itself in Art. 10:2 TRIPS) serve a central function not only in upholding the public domain in general but also in allowing competitors and second-comers to utilize the underlying ideas and concepts for developing their own products and services.
37. An example of a codification of such an interface can be found in the rules on interoperability and decompilation in Art. 6 of the EU Software Directive – see also the recent judgement of Court of First Instance (CFI) in *Microsoft* v. *Commission* (T-201/04).
38. Indian generic companies have complained that the approach to counterfeiting in the WCO SECURE initiative is overly broad and can be used to prevent trade in generic medicines; see Mathew (2008) and Narendranath (2008); see further the discussion on the role of customs authorities below.
39. Although not traditionally the case, the group of licensees, however, can sometimes also include consumers as defined above: due to the digital revolution and the advent of the Internet, consumers become contracting parties in so-called

shrink-wrap or click-wrap licences, for example regarding the use of software or other digital content.

40. Art. 142:2 states: 'The EC [European Community] Party and the Signatory CARIFORUM States shall take measures, as appropriate, to prevent or control licensing practices or conditions pertaining to intellectual property rights which may adversely affect the international transfer of technology and that constitute an abuse of intellectual property rights by right-holders or an abuse of obvious information asymmetries in the negotiation of licences'.

41. This understanding effectively extends the territorial reach of competition law beyond the domestic market to those abroad where technology transfer should take place and is threatened due to restrictive licensing.

42. See Arts. 7 and 8 TRIPS and their role in the enforcement debate discussed in the section above.

43. *Hoffmann-La Roche Ltd.* v. *CIPLA Limited*, Delhi High Court, 20 March 2008 (CS(OS) 89/2008 and I.A. 1272/2008) – for an extensive debate on this judgement see http://spicyipindia.blogspot.com/search/label/Roche%20vs%20Cipla (accessed 23 September 2008).

44. US Supreme Court decision in *eBay Inc.* v. *MercExchange, L.L.C.*, 547 U.S. 388 (2006); for an analysis of the 'post-*eBay*' treatment of injunctive relief and the further implications of the decision see Petersen (2008).

45. See Correa (forthcoming, 2009), pp. 30–31.

46. See Arts. 41:2 and 42 TRIPS.

47. See Arts. 7 and 8:1 TRIPS.

48. Art. 41:5 TRIPS is an expression of this principle that clarifies that IP enforcement does not require preferential treatment and is subject to an autonomous decision on the use of domestic law enforcement resources.

49. This is particularly so when one focuses on enforcing exclusive entitlements of (foreign) right-holders; compare Correa (forthcoming 2009), as note 45 above, p. 51.

50. Especially, patent offices have an important role to play in ensuring and upholding the granting requirements.

51. According to Art. 15:5 TRIPS, Members shall publish trademark registrations (thus allowing transparency) and must afford a reasonable opportunity for petitions to cancel the registration. In addition, Members *may* afford an opportunity for the registration of a trademark to be opposed. Art. 32 TRIPS further implies the flexibility to patent office proceedings leading to the revocation or forfeiture of a patent.

52. On the enforcement function of granting requirements and limitations in scope see the two subsections above.

53. Arts. 41:2, 3 TRIPS and especially Art. 42 TRIPS set out some of these general standards for fair and equitable court proceedings leaving sufficient flexibility for domestic implementation tailored to and regardful of the domestic (IP) enforcement environment.

54. Still, several developing countries are diverting resources to set up IP-specific branches in their judicial system as the recent Five Point Strategy to Improve IP Enforcement of the Philippines shows; see Ollier (2008).

55. Compare Art. 61 TRIPS and especially footnote 14 to Art. 51 TRIPS, which defines these thus: (a) 'counterfeit trademark goods' shall mean any goods, including packaging, bearing without authorization a trademark which is identical to the trademark validly registered in respect of such goods, or which cannot be distinguished in its essential aspects from such a trademark, and which thereby infringes the rights of the owner of the trademark in question under the law of the country of importation; (b) 'pirated copyright goods' shall mean any goods which are copies made without the consent of the right holder or person

duly authorized by the right holder in the country of production and which are made directly or indirectly from an article where the making of that copy would have constituted an infringement of a copyright or a related right under the law of the country of importation.

56. See Arts. 1–3 of the EU draft directive on criminal measures, as note 4 above. The directive, however, currently faces opposition from the EU Parliament precisely for its extended criminalization of IP infringements.

57. See the recent proposal for an Enforcement of Intellectual Property Act, as note 4 above and McCullagh (2008).

58. A senior German prosecutor who refused to investigate in light of this abusive behaviour of state resources for rather minor offences found himself subject to prosecution; see 'Illegale Internettauschbörsen – Ermittlungen gegen den Staatsanwalt', *Focus*, 26 May 2008.

59. As in the WTO *Canada – Patents* dispute (*Canada – Patent Protection of Pharmaceutical Products* (WT/DS114/R), Panel Report (17 March 2000), paras. 7.24–7.26), a key issue will be whether individual Member States have the right to utilize the policy space such open terms imply fully (for example, by giving effect to the TRIPS objectives in the interpretation, compare Art. 31 VCLT and para. 5 (a) of the Doha Declaration) and so determine the scope of international obligations flowing from TRIPS. For the available legal documents on the WTO Dispute DS/362 see http://www.wto.org/english/tratop_e/dispu_e/cases_e/ds362_e.htm, accessed 25 September 2008. The dispute is further discussed in Chapter 7 below.

60. Such as in the SECURE initiative in the WCO; for a detailed discussion see Chapter 4 below.

61. The actions brought by Monsanto against the importation of processed soy-food where the soy beans used for growing soy contained an (in Europe) patent protected gene indicate the potential trade-restrictive effect of giving customs the power to act in cases of alleged patent infringements. On the Monsanto case, see the discussion in Chapter 5 below.

62. See Art. 9 of the WCO model provisions on border enforcement as well as Standard No. 7 of the WCO SECURE initiative; for a detailed discussion, see in Chapter 4 below.

63. Compare Art. 41:1 TRIPS, which generally requires an application of IP enforcement measures in a manner as to avoid the creation of barriers to legitimate trade.

64. On the initiative in the Universal Postal Union (UPU) see Li (2008c).

65. See the notice and take-down procedure under sec. 512 (c) of the US Digital Millenium Copyright Act (DMCA), which requires ISPs 'upon notification of claimed infringement' to respond 'expeditiously to remove, or disable access to, the material that is claimed to be infringing or to be the subject of infringing activity'.

66. Compare the ECJ judgement *Promusicae* v. *Telefónica* (as note 27 above).

67. See Grosse Ruse-Khan (2008a), as note 12 above, pp. 175–6 and the further references provided in note 16.

68. On the historical evidence see CIPR (2002), as note 16 above, and especially the two related background papers Khan (2002) and Kumar (2002), both as note 16 above; for an economic and trade theory justification on this point see Trebilcock and Howse (2005), as note 16 above, pp. 397–401.

69. All of them are discussed in greater detail in the second section above.

70. The Indian state of Kerala recently enacted an IP strategy that explicitly focuses on the protection and preservation of traditional knowledge; see McDermott (2008).

4. WCO SECURE: legal and economic assessments of the TRIPS-plus-plus IP enforcement

Xuan Li

INTRODUCTION

For many developed countries, one of the important strategies to enhance and maximize their economic benefits is through formulation of international IP standards, which may impede the development of countries in the South. Following the footprint of the Agreement on Trade-Related Aspects of Intellectual Property Rights (TRIPS) of the World Trade Organization (WTO), one of the most profitable deals for developed countries in international norm-setting exercise, some developed countries are now pushing for TRIPS-plus standards on IP enforcement as a new strategic priority. However, developed countries have met well-founded resistance from the developing countries in IP negotiations within the framework of the WTO and the World Intellectual Property Organization (WIPO). Given the sticky situation in traditional negotiation forums to achieve their TRIPS-plus IP enforcement initiatives, developed countries have strategically shifted the battlefield to other international forums, notably the World Customs Organization (WCO), which is relatively unknown to the international community as a forum for setting IP regulations and has actually no mandate to negotiate intellectual property legislation. Under this forum-shopping strategy, the intention of the North is to break the situation through the back door, that is, revise customs regulations with expansion of the authorities of customs administrations, and re-delineate the boundary of customs and other stakeholders. If the Provisional Standards Employed by Customs for Uniform Rights Enforcement (SECURE) is allowed to be adopted in its current form, these new border measures will inevitably be incorporated in the free trade agreements (FTAs) and Bilateral Investment Treaties (BITs) between major developed countries and developing countries at some point in the future. On this basis, developed countries could gradually legalize international TRIPS-plus-plus[1] rules without resorting to amending the TRIPS Agreement itself. In this context, SECURE has been developed and promoted by developed countries at the WCO.

SECURE contains a set of international standards on border measures that exceed those established by TRIPS. For developing countries, primarily SECURE poses a four-fold threat/concern: (1) it appears to be outside the boundary of the WCO's mandate and responsibility; (2) it will undermine the delicate balance as enshrined in the TRIPS as far as the role of customs is concerned; (3) it is contaminated with quite a number of TRIPS-plus-plus elements; (4) it is obviously tilted towards the interests of right-holders to the potential detriment of other parties. The standards included in the SECURE represent a significant departure from the TRIPS Agreement. These TRIPS-plus-plus measures would increase the power and authority of national border and customs authorities to seize goods that are suspected of infringing intellectual property rights. If adopted, SECURE will seriously erode the policy flexibilities available under TRIPS, undermine the implementation of WIPO's development agenda by developing countries and pose new trade barriers on the international trading system.

Aiming at fast-tracking SECURE at the WCO Council in June 2008, three SECURE Working Group meetings were organized with a view to concluding all technical discussions at its third Working Group meeting held on 24–25 April 2008. However, due to the effective coordination among developing countries, developed countries unexpectedly failed to pressurize the adoption of the SECURE standards at the WCO and their attempt to promote a TRIP-plus-plus agenda suffered a major setback when the WCO Council held on 26–28 June 2008 did not adopt SECURE and decided to send the text back to the Working Group for further examination.

This chapter provides the background information on WCO SECURE and the negotiation process of SECURE in the next section. The following section analyses the legal implications of the SECURE text. The fourth section assesses the economic implications of SECURE and the final section concludes with policy recommendations for developing countries.

BACKGROUND: WCO SECURE NEGOTIATIONS AND COORDINATION

WCO SECURE Negotiations

The WCO is an international organization with its headquarters in Brussels and represents 171 customs administrations. The WCO has a mandate to provide technical assistance to customs administrations and serves as a forum where delegates representing a wide variety of members can tackle customs issues on an equal footing.[2] Thus, the mandate of WCO has been limited to providing technical assistance to implement existing norms, rather than norm-setting activities.

The WCO SECURE initiative has an unusual origin in a meeting of the G8 group of developed countries. The reference to the G8 Summit was explicitly made in the draft SECURE text of 24 April 2008. The WCO considers that the July 2005 declaration of the G8 Summit leaders urging collective and concerted international action to combat counterfeiting and piracy has empowered the WCO through a political boost to substantially increase their mandate to develop IP enforcement legislation. Thus, responding to the concerns of the G8 to enhance global resources to combat counterfeiting and piracy, the WCO launched its SECURE Programme.

The evolution of WCO SECURE was rather speedy, matching with the eagerness of the Secretariat to have SECURE adopted at the WCO Council in June 2008. A first draft of the SECURE provisions was made public at the 26th Session of the WCO Enforcement Committee held in February 2007. One month later, a Working Group on SECURE, under the supervision and guidance of the WCO Policy Commission was created by the WCO IP Working Group. Subsequently, the draft text of SECURE was sent to member countries for comments, which were to be submitted for consideration by the WCO Policy Commission and Council by June 2007. In accordance with the decision of the WCO Council in 2007, the Working Group held its first meeting in October 2007 and convened a Virtual Drafting Group meeting. The second Working Group meeting was held in February 2008 with a view to adopting the SECURE draft at the 2008 Council Session in June. On 24–25 April 2008, the third Working Group on SECURE was held at the WCO, which was targeted as the last round of technical discussions by the developed countries before its submission for approval by the Council.

The WCO Policy Commission and Council held their annual meetings on 23–25 June 2008 and on 26–28 June 2008 respectively. After intensive debates, the Policy Commission 'asked [the Council] to instruct the SECURE Working Group to continue its examination of the Provisional SECURE Standards document, reporting to the Policy Commission in December 2008'. With the recommendation of WCO Policy Commission, the WCO Council decided to send back the SECURE draft to the Working Group for continued discussion. The SECURE Working Group was to 'continue its examination of the Provisional SECURE Standards document, reporting to the Policy Commission in December 2008'.[3]

The WCO Council is the highest decision-making body of the WCO and the Policy Commission has the mandate to make recommendations for approval by the Council. The Policy Commission consists of 24 members: Chair of the WCO Council (Finland), six Vice-chairs of the Council who also act as representatives of the six customs regions, namely, Canada (region: South America, North America, Central America and the Caribbean), India (region: Far East, South and South East Asia, Australasia and the Pacific Islands), Ireland (region: Europe), Jordan (region: North of Africa, Near and Middle East), Mozambique (region: East and Southern Africa) and Senegal (region: West and Central Africa), and 17 elected member states, namely, France, Japan, Nigeria, Norway, Russian Federation, Rwanda, Saudi Arabia, Slovenia, United Kingdom, United States, Argentina, Italy, Korea (Republic of), Mexico, New Zealand, Singapore and Spain. Decisions of the Policy Commission can be adopted by a majority vote consisting of two-thirds of the members present. Though the membership of the Policy Commission is dominated by developed countries, the expected adoption of the SECURE standards as pushed by developed countries did not happen due to the effective coordination among developing countries.

Coordination Among Developing Countries

South–South cooperation played a critical role in preventing the adoption of the SECURE draft at the 2008 WCO Council. During the third SECURE Working Group meeting (Brussels, 23–24 April 2008), Brazil, Ecuador, China, among others, presented a number of proposals to modify the SECURE standards. With contribution from the South Centre, further coordination was undertaken during the period between the third SECURE Working Group and the WCO Policy Commission and Council sessions. The coordination involved activities of communication between/among the Brussels and Geneva missions, missions and capitals, as well as different governmental authorities in the capitals of developing countries. The effectiveness of the coordination was reflected during the Policy Commission discussions. There were attempts by the SECURE Working Group Chair and the European Commission to send back to the Working Group only the bracketed parts of the standards. These attempts were rejected by Argentina. Also, during the Policy Commission discussions, India stated that a TRIPS-plus instrument is not acceptable and that further discussion was needed on the whole text. As a consequence, the Policy Commission made the recommendation that the SECURE draft should be sent back to the Working Group. Figure 4.1 features the coordination process among developing countries.

LEGAL ANALYSIS OF THE SECURE WORKING DRAFT

The SECURE draft (as of 23 April 2008) comprised an Introduction and four sections, that is, Section I (IPR Legislative and Enforcement Regime Development), Section II (Cooperation with the Private Sector), Section III (Risk Analysis and Intelligence Sharing), and Section IV (Capacity Building for IPR Enforcement and International Cooperation). Among these, the contents of the Introduction and Section I are most critical for the 12 proposed standards.

Section I of the SECURE Working Draft, 'IPR Legislative and Enforcement Regime Development', is the key component of the Working Draft. It is comprised of 12 standards. The scope and level of enforcement of the 12 standards proposed by developed countries are much higher than that of any previous international agreement and agenda, notably the TRIPS Agreement, which is considered as the most significant milestone in the development of multilateral intellectual property regime in the 20th century, and the WIPO Development Agenda adopted in September 2007, which is a landmark in the history of the endeavours by members to integrate development into IP policies. It enshrines provisional enforcement rules

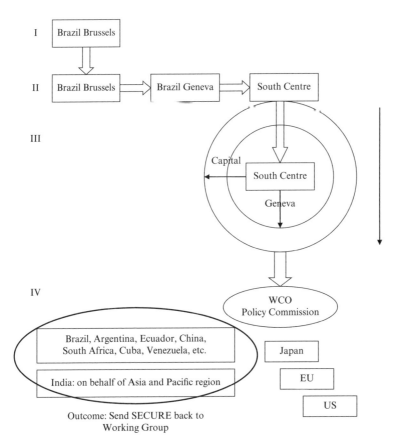

Figure 4.1   WCO coordination process (Feb. 2008–23 Jun. 2008)

and procedures for right-holders on one critical aspect of intellectual property rights enforcement: border measures.

Salient Features and Characteristics of SECURE

The SECURE Working Draft can be characterized as follows: (1) lack of clear and agreeable definition of IP infringement; (2) absence of appealing and review mechanisms; (3) unduly expanded scope; (4) absence of exemption and limitation provisions; (5) significantly enhanced rights of right-holders without proper balance between different stakeholders; (6) the power of customs authorities expanded without properly identified obligations; (7) enforcement costs are substantially shifted to states; (8) customs administrations generally lack the means to determine whether IP infringements exist – in particular, they have no capacity to address the complex legal and technical issues involved in patent infringement determination; (9) the enhanced power that right-holders would enjoy may lead to serious trade barriers, as the simple allegation of infringement of intellectual property rights may be enough to block legitimate competition; (10) trade in a wide range of products, including medicines, may be seriously distorted.

Legal Comparison Between SECURE Standards and WTO TRIPS Standards

Part III, Section 4 of the TRIPS Agreement, entitled 'Special Requirements Related to Border Measures' (Articles 51–60) established international obligations for WTO members to introduce border measures for the protection of IPRs. The section establishes the procedure and conditions under which a customs authority may, at the request of right-holders, suspend the release into circulation (seize at importation) any suspected counterfeit trademark or pirated copyright goods. The 12 standards under Section I of the SECURE Working Draft essentially correspond to Section 4 of Part III of the TRIPS Agreement.

Table 4.1 summarizes the differences between the SECURE draft and the TRIPS Agreement, and highlights the TRIPS-plus-plus elements of the former (Li, 2008b).

Compared with the TRIPS Agreement, the proposed SECURE standards are IP enforcement border measures that represent a significant departure from TRIPS provisions in terms of subjects, scope and measures of the protection, disposal methods and member states' obligations and rights.

First, the proposed SECURE standards expand the subjects and scope of enforcement of IPRs. Enforcement by customs administration under the TRIPS Agreement is compulsory only with respect to importation (Article 51). However, the scope of SECURE Standard 1 is much broader than the TRIPS Agreement, as Standard 1 extends the enforcement from importation to all types of transaction, including but not limited to export, transit, warehouses, transhipment, free zones, duty-free shops, and so on. Regarding the scope of protection,

Table 4.1 Comparisons of SECURE and TRIPS provisions

SECURE	Issue	TRIPS Agreement	Comments
Standard 1	Scope	Article 51	Extend the scope from 'import' to 'export, transit, warehouses, transhipment, free zones, duty-free shops', and so on
Standard 2	Definitions	Article 51	Extend the protection from trade-mark and copyright to all other types of intellectual property rights
Standard 3	Procedures	Article 51	Extend the procedure from 'suspension of the release of goods' to other types of procedures
Standard 4	Application and right of information	Articles 52, 57	Unclear what is the definition of 'costs to right-holders' and no justification why the costs to right-holders should be reduced. Remove the obligations of right-holders to provide adequate evidence to satisfy the competent authorities that there is prima facie an infringement to initiate the procedure
Standard 5	Central Office	Article 41	A single contact point governing applications should be designated by customs authorities, which imposed additional burden. Under Article 41 (5) of the TRIPS Agreements, however, WTO members are not obliged with respect to the distribution of limited resources as between enforcement of IPRs and the enforcement of law in general
Standard 6	De minimis import	Article 60	Establish a principle that the quantities of exempted goods should be as 'as low as possible'.
Standard 7	Ex officio	Article 58	Expand the right of customs authorities to take action upon own initiatives, but remove the obligations from remedial measures when they did not act in good faith

Table 4.1   (continued)

SECURE	Issue	TRIPS Agreement	Comments
Standard 8	Application	Articles 52, 58	Specify the right of right-holders to make request, but importer's minimum right of being notified promptly and properly is shrunk Reversed the burden to provide evidence from the right-holders to customs administration Under TRIPS, it is the obligation of the right-holders to provide evidence and satisfy the customs authority to make determination To satisfy, two evidences should be provided, (1) a prima facie infringement of an IPR under the laws of the country of importation; (2) a sufficiently detailed description of the goods to enable customs authorities to identify the goods in question.
Standard 9	Notification	Article 54	Under TRIPS, the importer and the applicant shall be promptly notified of the suspension of the release of goods Under SECURE, no safeguard is available for importers regarding the right of notification of suspension and detention
Standard 10	Remedies	Article 59	Under TRIPS, (1) it is the authority of judicial body rather than customs administration to dispose of or destroy the infringed goods; (b) it is upon the decision of the competent body to determine either destruction or disposal of infringing goods; (c) it established the procedure that any order to destroy or dispose of the goods is subject to a right of review by the importer or other defendant and without prejudice to the right-holders' rights of action

Table 4.1 (continued)

SECURE	Issue	TRIPS Agreement	Comments
			Under Standard 10, it (1) expands the authority of customs administration, (2) it regulates that all infringing goods should be destroyed
Standard 11	Disposal	Article 51	Under SECURE, (1) customs administration has authority to detail, move or seize IPR-infringing goods; (2) while specifying that the burdens of fee should not be unreasonable on right-holders, there is no security on other stakeholders
Standard 12	Criminal procedure	Article 61	Under TRIPS, members shall provide for criminal procedurals and penalties for . . . trademark counterfeiting and copyright piracy on a commercial scale
			Under SECURE, customs administration has legal authority to impose deterrent penalties against entities knowingly involved in the importation/exportation of goods under customs control that violate *any* IPR laws

it is proposed under SECURE Standard 2 that 'National legislation may extend the scope of Customs IPR legislation from trademark and copyright to other intellectual property rights'. However, the procedures for border measures under TRIPS are required to be made available to 'counterfeit trademark or pirated copyright goods' only (Article 51). As clearly defined in footnote 14 to Article 51, the definition of 'counterfeit trademark goods' only refers to *registered* marks, as 'counterfeit trademark goods' means:

> any goods, including packaging, bearing without authorization a trademark which is identical to the trademark validly registered in respect of such goods, or which cannot be distinguished in its essential aspects from such a trademark, and which thereby infringes the rights of the owner of

the trademark in question under the law of the country of importation. (Vrins and Schneider, 2006)

Second, the proposed SECURE standards tend to favour the right-holders, thus affecting the balance between the right-holders and importers under TRIPS. The balanced mechanisms under TRIPS have been bypassed under the SECURE standards, thus affecting the flexibilities contained in TRIPS. According to Article 52 of the TRIPS Agreement, it is the obligation of the right-holders to provide evidence and satisfy the customs authority to make the determination whether a product is a counterfeit. The aim of the TRIPS Agreement is to ensure that customs authorities would not impede legitimate trade and prevent right-holders from taking undue advantage of the border seizures and detentions to delay legitimate trade. To satisfy Article 52, two evidences should be provided: (1) a prima facie infringement of an IPR under the laws of the country of importation; (2) a sufficiently detailed description of the goods to enable customs authorities to identify the goods in question. However, when the SECURE Standard 4 and Standard 8 are read together, they point to an intention to shift the burden of proof from the right-holders to the customs administration by requesting customs administrations to provide samples of suspicious goods to right-holders, and for right-holders to determine the counterfeit nature of those samples.[4]

Third, the proposed SECURE standards may disrupt legitimate trade of non-infringing goods by re-delineating the responsibilities of determination of IP infringement among various authorities. Under the TRIPS, it is the authority of a judicial body, rather than the customs administrations, to dispose of or destroy the infringed goods. It falls upon the competent body to determine either destruction or disposal of infringing goods, as stated in Article 46 that is, 'the judicial authorities shall have the authority to order that goods that they have found to be infringing be, without compensation of any sort, disposed of outside the channels of commerce in such a manner . . . or, destroyed'. It also established the procedure that any order to destroy or dispose of the goods is subject to a right of review by the importer or other defendant and without prejudice to the right-holders' rights of action (Biadgleng and Muñoz, 2008a). However, under Standard 10, while expanding the authority of the customs administration, it regulates that all infringing goods should be destroyed. Therefore, the proposed border measures for the enforcement of IPRs embedded in the SECURE standards may significantly disrupt legitimate trade of non-infringing goods. Notably, SECURE provides no mechanism for appeal and review, which is destructive to the fairness of a system.

Comparison Between SECURE and WIPO Development Agenda

The adoption of 45 Recommendations of Development Agenda during the General Assembly of the World Intellectual Property Organization in 2007 was a historic achievement. It integrates the key concept of 'development' into functioning of the WIPO and serves as guiding principles to translate the concept of development into IP practices in both international and national contexts.

The adopted 45 recommendations for action are categorized into six clusters: Cluster A: Technical Assistance and Capacity Building; Cluster B: Norm-setting, Flexibilities, Public Policy and Public Domain; Cluster C: Technology Transfer, Information and Communication Technologies and Access to Knowledge; Cluster D: Assessment, Evaluation and Impact Studies; Cluster E: Institutional Matters including Mandate and Governance; and Cluster F: Other Issues.[5] In particular, Recommendation 45[6] (Cluster F) specifies that the WIPO's approach to enforcing IPRs should be undertaken 'in the context of broader societal interests', with a view that:

> the protection and enforcement of intellectual property rights should contribute to the promotion of technological innovation and to the transfer and dissemination of technology, to the mutual advantage of producers and users of technological knowledge and in a manner conducive to social and economic welfare, and to a balance of rights and obligations.

We should be aware of the fact that Recommendation 45 cross-references Article 7 of the TRIPS Agreement, which explicitly states that the protection and enforcement of intellectual property rights should be 'to the mutual advantage of producers and users of technical knowledge in a manner conducive to social and economic welfare'.

Compared with the recommendation of the WIPO Development Agenda, the proposed SECURE draft accords more benefits and less obligations to right-holders at the cost of other stakeholders, which is inconsistent with the call for more balanced IP protection mechanism for all stakeholders in Recommendation 45 of the WIPO Development Agenda.

Legal Effect of SECURE

Currently, the SECURE standards are proposed for implementation on a voluntary basis. However, developing countries should consider this issue in the broader context of the global strategy of developed countries in IP negotiations. The customary tactics of developed countries tend to be first breaking the weakest link by promoting new standards on a voluntary basis, and then making them compulsory through subsequent multilateral, bilateral or regional negotiations.

The proposed SECURE standards of the WCO, if adopted, will have far-reaching consequences. Although it was claimed to be non-compulsory with no legal effect, it has been a pattern for developed countries to promote new international regulations first on a voluntary basis before transforming them into compulsory regulations. Once SECURE is eventually adopted, it can be expected that developed countries will promote these standards in multilateral (WTO, WIPO), regional and bilateral negotiations. This was the case of the Framework of Standards to Secure and Facilitate Global Trade (SAFE) adopted by WCO in 2001, which was initially introduced on a voluntary basis and is currently being transformed into compulsory standards.

ECONOMIC IMPACT ASSESSMENT OF THE SECURE WORKING TEXT

Optimal IP Enforcement Regime

Establishing and strengthening the enforcement of IPRs is a costly exercise both in terms of budgetary outlays and the employment of skilled personnel. The enforcement cost should be borne by private parties as IPR is a private right in nature, and enforcement activities ought to be planned on a cost-effective basis from a socially optimal perspective aiming at achieving optimal IP enforcement (South Centre, 2008).

'Cost-effective approach' is a fundamental principle to determine an optimal level of IP regime and enforcement in a country. As IPRs create some static losses in the form of deadweight loss or consumer welfare losses, they must be regulated in a way to increase the dynamic gains achieved through grant of IPRs, that is, creation of new products and process through constant innovation. It is also evident that the static losses involve rent-seeking activities by right-holders, which leads to monopoly rents and transfer of welfare gains from consumers to producers (right-holders). The optimal IP enforcement strategy is one that balances the marginal cost of achieving compliance with the marginal benefit that derives from doing so. It should create appropriate incentives that maximize the discounted net present value of the difference between the social benefits and the social costs of information creation, including the costs of administering the system (Maskus, 2000). As IP is a private right, the cost of its protection should be borne by right-holders without costing the public resources of governments, as specified by TRIPS.

Economic Impact of SECURE

The economic impact of SECURE on developing countries will be two-fold: (1) within their territory, there will be increased obligations for the customs administration and increased cost of enforcement; (2) externally, the developing countries' enterprises are likely to face greater uncertainties due to new trade barriers.

On the former issue, the impact should be assessed based on a cost-effect analysis of implementing TRIPS-plus measures. As IP is a private right, the cost of its protection should be borne by right-holders without costing public resources. It is argued by many that border measures for intellectual property enforcement would give rise to increase of financial expenses and the needs for more human resource inputs. It may also lead to some internal restructuring and shifts of focus and priorities in a given customs office. At present, the fact is that many customs authorities in developing countries are facing the challenge of adapting to the changes in their roles while coping with the difficulties of limited availability of human, financial and material resources. In terms of capacity building, developing countries in general and LDCs in particular, need sufficient time and resources to prepare and update the dynamic contents of training for their competent functionaries including customs officials in accordance with relevant provisions of the TRIPS Agreement. It should be noted that developing countries have no legal obligation to extend border measures beyond the requirements of the TRIPS Agreement on a mandatory basis, but may choose to do so if they are able and willing to do that. They should undertake a careful analysis and thorough consideration before making the decision whether or not to extend the scope of customs involvement on IPR enforcement beyond the TRIPS provisions. In this exercise, it is suggested that particular attention should be given to such factors as availability of various resources needed, actual level of customs capacities, institutional constraints, potential disruption to normal trade and possible abuse by IP right-holders, and so forth.

Against the backdrop of its traditional role of revenue collection mainly in the form of import duties, today customs is required to perform more and more duties, including acting as an IPR enforcement agency. It is reasonable to say that this new function entails costs and these costs could be even huge vis-à-vis the various constraints in developing countries. Thus, developing countries are faced with uncertainty about the full implications of rising pressure on customs administrations to enhance IPR enforcement. Thus, customs and border authorities in developing countries are entitled to technical assistance and capacity building in the form of, among others, continuous and intensive training, and transitional periods through which to gain first-hand experience in implementing the system for border control of counterfeit and pirated goods as provided in the TRIPS Agreement. In this process, special attention should be paid to guard against any possible abuses by either IP right-holders or customs officials and other parties. It is of critical importance that the measures of implementation concerned should not constitute new barriers to trade. Under SECURE, due to unclear delineation of the cost concept, the direct and indirect costs of IP enforcement are being charged to the government and the public.

On the second issue, if SECURE is adopted, customs and IP holders would be accorded higher than appropriate powers in international trade. In the case of customs, with the new powers acquired under SECURE, developed countries would be able to put in place new border barriers to restrict imports from developing countries. Moreover, with more powers accorded to IP holders, the exports from developing countries would be easily treated as 'suspected' infringements and be blocked or even destroyed by the customs. Since there is no dispute resolution mechanism and channel for appeal put in place, the exports from developing countries are more likely to be treated unfairly.

In sum, the proposed SECURE standards will lead to higher enforcement costs within developing countries; and externally, it would incur new types of trade barriers for developing countries. Once adopted for implementation, SECURE will be detrimental to the economic growth of developing countries. It is important to maintain adequate policy space for the present and the future as part of short-run and long-run development objectives. It is necessary for developing countries to at least maintain the acquired rights and be on guard against any change in the international trade order that may be detrimental to their interests.

CONCLUSION

The SECURE standards of extreme TRIPS-plus nature has been sent back to the Working Group without adoption in the last WCO Council session. However, attempts by developed countries to promote the TRIPS-plus-plus agenda on international IP enforcement regulations are still underway.

If adopted, SECURE would seriously erode the legitimate flexibilities enshrined in the TRIPS Agreement, undermine the adopted recommendations of the WIPO Development Agenda, and pose grave constraints on the policy space of developing countries. For instance, Standard 1 of the proposed SECURE standards intends to extend the scope of protection from 'import' under Article 51 of the TRIPS Agreement to all other transactions including, but not limited to, 'export, transit, warehouses, transhipment, free zones and duty-free shops'. Compared with the WIPO Development Agenda, the proposed SECURE standards favour the IP right-holders, thus affecting the balance between the right-holders and other stakeholders, for example, importers, manufacturers, consumers, and so on.

Having noticed that the SECURE standards in their present form would generate significantly negative legal and economic impact for developing countries, continued active participation and effective coordination of developing countries in the upcoming discussions of the SECURE Working Group is imperative.

Substantively, the SECURE standards document is entirely open for discussion and nothing is agreed upon so far. A number of standards have already been scaled down to TRIPS level and more proposals from developing countries are expected. Procedurally, there are concerns with the conduct of the work by the current Chair of the Working Group. The terms of reference must be discussed and defined before moving into the discussion of the standards.

Strengthened coordination is much needed among developing countries. The major challenge to the effectiveness of developing country coordination is to bridge the divide that more often than not separates trade from customs within government structures. Developing countries should ensure that the role of the WCO on developing international standards on border measures remains limited and focuses on training of customs officials without going beyond its mandates. It is important to ensure that legislation intro-duced related to border measures for IPR enforcement in developing countries is balanced. Developing countries should take proactive measures and coordinate their efforts to put on hold or postpone the adoption of SECURE at the forthcoming WCO Council annual meeting.

NOTES

1. 'TRIPS-plus' generally refers to commitments that go beyond those already included or consolidated in the TRIPS Agreement. The expression 'TRIPS-plus-plus' is used to highlight the extent of the significant departure of SECURE from the existing TRIPS provisions regarding border measures.
2. http://www.wcoomd.org/home.htm.
3. Report of SECURE Working Group, WCO, 2008.
4. Standard 4 proposes that 'with respect to requests from rights holders for Customs intervention, Customs Administrations should develop standardized application forms requesting information consisting of basic, standard data at a cost not exceeding the costs of the processing of the application. . . . The initial period should be extended by simple notification, including evidence of the con-tinuing right and prima facie evidence of infringement'. Standard 8 proposes that 'Customs Administrations should adopt procedures enabling them to provide to rights holders free of charge samples of suspicious goods to determine the coun-terfeit nature of those samples'.
5. 'The 45 Adopted Recommendations under the WIPO Development Agenda', WIPO, www.wipo.int/ip-development/en/agenda/recommendations.html.
6. Recommendation 45: 'To approach intellectual property enforcement in the context of broader societal interests and especially development-oriented con-cerns, with a view that "the protection and enforcement of intellectual property rights should contribute to the promotion of technological innovation and to the transfer and dissemination of technology, to the mutual advantage of producers and users of technological knowledge and in a manner conducive to social and economic welfare, and to a balance of rights and obligations", in accordance with Article 7 of the TRIPS Agreement'. www.wipo.int/ip-development/en/agenda/recommendations.html#f.

PART II

CASES AND DEVELOPMENTS ON
IP ENFORCEMENT

5. Enforcing border measures: importation of GMO soybean meal from Argentina

Carlos M. Correa[1]

Requests for the detainment of Argentine soymeal shipments at the ports of Denmark, the Netherlands, Spain and the United Kingdom, a multi-million dollar claim over royalties and suits filed against European importers are some of the visible facts in an unusual dispute between the US multinational Monsanto on the one hand, and farmers and the Argentine government on the other. Curiously enough, the legal battle takes place in Europe rather than where the exported soybean was grown and processed. This chapter explains the reasons for as well as the possible consequences of this trans-national litigation. It illustrates the possible impact on legitimate trade of broad border measures, particularly when applied to alleged patent infringements.

THE SEED OF DISCORD

Soy-related products (particularly for feed) are Argentina's main export product to the European market, surpassing meat. Argentine soybeans and their derivates contain genes that were inserted arti-ficially into the seeds in order to confer the plants resistance to glyphosate, a widely used herbicide. These are, hence, by-products of a genetically-modified (GM) soybean.

Nowadays, GM soybeans account for over 90 per cent of the total soybean harvest in Argentina. Their rapid and broad dissemination is one of the factors explaining the soybean expansion in Argentina's agricultural production: the share of soybean in total crops doubled (standing at nearly 50 per cent) between the 1996/97 and 2004/05 harvests. In that period, the number of soybean planted hectares rose from 10 000 to over 14 million. Argentina is selling, in Europe alone, nearly 2 billion dollars worth of soybean-derived products per year (Delich and López, 2008).

This rapid expansion was the outcome of the insertion of a glyphosate-resistant transgene into the genome of a range of soybean varieties resulting from the excellent level of plant breeding existing in Argentina, as well as from the broad diffusion of no-tillage practices. This combination allowed for improvements in terms of production output as well as reductions in production costs. Another legal and commercial factor was also decisive for the expansion of soybean plantation: the glyphosate-resistant transgene (known in commerce as 'Round-Up Ready' or 'RR'), developed by Monsanto, has been and currently is within the public domain in Argentina, that is, it has been available for free use by seed companies. They can, hence, develop their own soybean varieties incorporating resistant gene, without requiring permission from or the payment of compensation in favour of Monsanto.

PATENTS AND TERRITORY

The RR gene was not patented by Monsanto in Argentina, although it was patented in other countries, such as the United States and European countries. Maybe as a result of a miscalculation about the commercial impact that RR soybean might have in Argentina, or for other reasons (either practical or strategic), Monsanto let due dates expire for obtaining a patent in Argentina.

The patent system has three major characteristics:

- It is of *voluntary* use, that is, inventors may choose to apply or not for a patent.
- It is *territorial* in nature,[2] which implies that a patent is only legally enforceable in the country where it has been applied for and obtained (therefore, a US patent is not valid in Argentina and vice versa).
- It is a system of *rewards and punishments*: if a patent is applied for before the invention loses its novelty (that is, it becomes publicly disclosed) and other conditions of patentability are fulfilled, the patent-holder may be granted a monopoly for its

exploitation over a period of 20 years (from the filing date). But if it fails to be applied for in due time, the holder can no longer claim any right: once disclosed (except when this has taken place by fraud against the inventor or in an authorized exhibition)[3] the invention falls into the public domain in all those countries where patent protection has been neither sought nor obtained.

The patent system has operated in this way since its inception in European countries five centuries ago, and indeed, the case in which an innovative company (least of all an individual inventor) applies for a patent in all countries around the world is very rare or nonexistent. On average, the number of countries where no patents are applied for (thus allowing the invention to be used by any person) is higher than the number of countries where expenses – which are significant – are incurred for acquiring and enforcing patent rights. One noticeable exception is the pharmaceutical industry, which normally obtains patents almost worldwide in order to secure a monopoly on the sale of new or variants and derivatives of existing medicines.

In an era of globalization it might be surprising to notice that the patent system is less global than what many people think or wish.[4] The lack of patent protection in a certain country cannot be compensated for – as now Monsanto intends – by the abusive exercise of patent rights conferred in another territory. The European or US patents the company may have can only be applied to acts that would constitute patent infringement under those jurisdictions. Unlike copyright, which is protected without the need to register or comply with any formalities, the protection of patents requires (to the advantage of patent attorneys) the processing and grant of patents in each country where they are to be enforced.

The lack of a global patent system is evidenced by another major fact: countries, even those that are members of the World Trade Organization and are therefore subject to the TRIPS Agreement[5] have a considerable margin to determine what is an invention and what is not. Thus, many countries consider that a gene cannot be patented because it is already a product of nature and cannot be 'invented', even when isolated and claimed as such. On this point[6] the legislation of developed countries differs from that of many developing countries (such as Argentina and Brazil) where the ownership of genetic resources through patents generates resistance and less permissive regulations that are nevertheless perfectly compatible with WTO rules.

BENEFITS WITHOUT PATENT PROTECTION

Returning to the Monsanto case, as mentioned above, the company deliberately left the RR gene in the public domain in Argentina, as it failed to file an application for patent protection in due time. Obviously, the free availability of this gene would prompt its dissemination through incorporation in a large number of soybean varieties developed and commercialized by local seed companies, with an important advantage for Monsanto: it has also commercialized (exclusively until the patent expired)[7] the glyphosate, the herbicide to which the soybean plant becomes resistant to. In this way, Monsanto managed to profit from sales of GMO seeds and from growing volumes of glyphosate sales.

Moreover, although Monsanto had no legal grounds to claim payment for the use of the RR gene, Argentine seed companies entered into private licence agreements involving payment of royalties for such use. A sign of the apparent harmony that prevailed is the fact that the National Seeds Institute registered nearly 200 plant varieties including the RR gene, of which only 30 were developed by Monsanto. But there is an even more revealing fact: Argentine law allows any third party to oppose the registration of plant varieties. Monsanto *never* made use of this right against the registration of a variety incorporating the RR gene: that is, it knowingly consented the use of the RR gene in the numerous soybean varieties that were registered. The availability of a diversity of soybean varieties was ultimately one of the key factors explaining the success of the RR gene in Argentina.

However, the dissemination of the RR soybean in Argentina not only served Monsanto's interests when it came to sell seeds and glyphosate in the domestic market but was the starting point for the dissemination of its products all over the Southern Cone. Argentina was the port of entry that Monsanto chose for the region, probably attracted by its openness to foreign investments and, above all, by its willingness to accept transgenic varieties, which were rejected in other parts of the world. For instance, the formal approval of the cultivation of GMO soybean was delayed for several years in

Brazil owing to legal actions. However, it was widely cultivated (particularly in the south of the country) with seeds imported from Argentina. As a result, the government's approval[8] just legalized what was already a fact.

TEN YEARS OF INACTION

The RR soybean was developed in 1991. The use in trade of a commercial variety containing the RR gene started in 1996. Argentina together with the United States and Canada was among the first countries to authorize its introduction, in spite of the global outcry against the cultivation of transgenic plants by several non-governmental organizations and the concerns about their impact on the environment.

For almost ten years, the Argentine situation seemed to satisfy the economic aspirations of Monsanto:

- RR soybean dominated almost the total production of one of the world's leading soybean producers and was disseminated in neighbouring countries.
- Monsanto participated in the market with the sale of both seeds and glyphosate.
- Argentine seed companies paid Monsanto royalties (even in the absence of patents).

Nevertheless, after having accepted and taken advantage of such a situation during that long period, Monsanto changed its commercial policy and requested that farmers pay compensation for the use of the RR gene. It demanded payment of up to 15 dollars per ton, an exorbitant amount that, in the event of being paid, would cause thousands of producers to go bankrupt.

The Argentine government – already skilled in major disputes (such as those resulting from the renegotiation of the external debt and IMF conditionalities) – rejected, in all its right, Monsanto's aspiration. By way of reprisal, the company threatened with filing requests – and finally did so – to hold up Argentine soymeal shipments at European ports, on the grounds that it contained the RR gene (something nobody argued about) and that such imports infringed its European patents on the gene.

The multinational company did not conceal its intentions: it filed actions against European importers of Argentine soymeal in order to obtain the payment of an additional fee for the RR technology from Argentine farmers. Monsanto speculated that, given the imminent threat of facing legal actions against each shipment of Argentine soymeal, European exporters would resort to other suppliers or eventually accept paying Monsanto a royalty, the cost of which would end up being transferred to Argentine producers and exporters. Monsanto expected that the Argentine government would choose to avoid these risks and implement a mechanism to allow Monsanto to collect a special compensation from farmers for the use of the (unpatented) RR gene.

While Monsanto was organizing this operation to put pressure on the Argentine government, the latter was paradoxically filing a complaint before the World Trade Organization (WTO) regarding the restrictions to trade in transgenic products imposed by a European 'moratorium' on the approval of new GMOs (Sindico, 2005; Devereaux et al., 2006). The resolution of the WTO panel, which rules in favour of the claimants,[9] will benefit – among others – Monsanto, which will be able to expand its business transactions in the European continent once the moratorium is lifted.

NO PATENT INFRINGEMENT

Monsanto's arguments behind the offensive launched against the Argentine government and farmers are vague: 'Monsanto acknowledges Argentina's contribution with regards to the expansion of biotechnology . . . but we cannot refrain from demanding payment because that is how it works all over the world'. From such a global and dogmatic perspective, it does not matter what the legal provisions and circumstances of each country are.

Just as in other countries and pursuant to the UPOV[10] Convention (1978 Act), farmers in Argentina may retain and use – as part of their own exploitation – seeds obtained from the cultivation of protected varieties. On the other hand, as also happens in other countries (including the United States), 'white bag' seeds that are grown without the authorization of breeders end up cutting down sales of the legitimate seed. This is a problem of enforcement that affects all seed producers, not just Monsanto, which cannot be solved by filing suit in a foreign jurisdiction, but rather by investing in improved mechanisms for the supervision and control of the production and trading of seeds. Intellectual property rights, as stated in the Preamble of the TRIPS Agreement, are private rights. Hence, the costs of their enforcement should be borne by the right-holders, not the states.

However, the option taken by Monsanto was to invoke the patents it holds until 2011 in European countries to prevent imports of Argentine soymeal. These patents protect DNA sequences encoding certain enzymes (class II EPSPS) with kinetic and immunological activities as well as the recombinant DNA molecules comprising them; methods to produce genetically modified plants by using the respective DNA sequence, cells and plants thus obtained; and finally, methods to selectively control weeds in a field cultivated with crops containing the respective DNA sequence.

Can someone who imports soymeal or even soybeans not intended for cultivation be committing a patent infringement? The process of manufacturing soymeal applies temperatures and physical compression that destroy the possibility of any particular DNA to perform its function in the meal, which is not any more a biological material. That process typically includes the following steps:

1. Harvested soybeans are collected from a variety of farmers, combined, cleaned and air-dried at about 180°F (about 82°C) to about 9.5–10 per cent moisture.
2. The beans are then placed in tempering bins for 24–72 hours.
3. The beans are cracked on rollers to remove the hulls (typically they are cracked in quarters and eighths of whole bean sizes.
4. The hulls are separated by aspiration using a flow of air.
5. The cracked beans are heated at 160°F (about 71°C) for about 20–30 minutes.
6. The resulting material is flaked between rollers to prepare pieces 0.012″ to 0.16″ thick.
7. The flakes are then often put through an expander to form 'collets' – this process involves putting the flakes under mechanical and steam pressure, which when released results in the formation of a porous, food-like substance, which remains on the extractor for a greater period of time.
8. The collets are subjected to a solvent extraction process (commercial hexane or isohexane) to remove the soy oil.

9.   The defatted soybean flakes and/or collets are then processed
     in the desolventizor toaster where direct and indirect steam is
     used to drive off the solvent. This stage lasts about 30 minutes
     and the material will reach temperatures of 212°F (100°C) for
     20 minutes.
10. The resulting meal is then dried and cooled.
11. The meal is then ground into particles of either 2 mm or 4 mm,
     or pelleted for transport.[11]

In the case of soymeal, even if DNA sequences – fit to perform
immunization against glyphosate – remained intact after processing,
they could certainly not be used for further cultivation. Therefore,
it is impossible to infringe those patents by importing soymeal,
since the patented gene is not performing there its claimed function.
The same can be applied to other by-products, such as soybean
oil. Likewise, the importation of soybeans, so long as they are not
used as seeds (but for food or further processing), does not infringe
said patents since there is no use in European territory of the gene-
resistance properties. The same reasoning is applicable to the RR
gene eventually remaining in soymeal. It is not only deprived of any
function but it is an undesirable element.

The implications of the case brought by Monsanto may be illustrated by this hypothetical situation: let us suppose that tomato plants
were treated with a pesticide in country A, they said pesticide not
being patented there. Tomatoes are subsequently exported to country
B where there is a patent on the pesticide. Naturally, if those tomatoes
were analysed, molecules belonging to that pesticide would be found.
Could the patent-holder block their import for that reason? It would
obviously be an absurdity. A positive answer would grant unlimited
power to patent-holders in terms of imposing trade restrictions, not
just on their own products but on everything that derives from or
comprises such products in some way, no matter how residual.

The European Law as contained in the Directive on the Legal
Protection of Biotechnological Inventions (Directive 98/44/EC of 6
July 1998) leaves Monsanto's audacious legal case before European
courts with little chance of success. Its Article 9 stipulates that the
protection conferred by a patent on a product containing or consisting of genetic information shall extend to all material in which
'the genetic information is contained and performs its function'.
Although the European Court of Justice has still not interpreted this

directive, it is quite clear that a patent cannot be invoked against acts involving products in which a protected gene is not performing 'its function' – in our case, to give resistance to glyphosate herbicide. This can only take place at sowing time with cells that are viable for such purpose, which is clearly not the case with the Argentine exported products.

Monsanto was able to interfere with the importation of Argentine soymeal based on requests for the detainment of shipments pursuant to the Council Regulation (EC) No. 1383/2003 of 22 July 2003 concerning customs action against goods suspected of infringing certain intellectual property rights and the measures to be taken against goods found to have infringed such rights.

Article 4.1 of this regulation epitomizes the dangers of broad border measures. It provides that:

> Where the customs authorities, in the course of action in one of the situations referred to in Article 1(1) and before an application has been lodged by a right-holder or granted, have sufficient grounds for suspecting that goods infringe an intellectual property right, they may suspend the release of the goods or detain them for a period of three working days from the moment of receipt of the notification by the right-holder and by the declarant or holder of the goods, if the latter are known, in order to enable the right-holder to submit an application for action in accordance with Article 5.

This provision gives the custom authorities powers beyond what is required by Article 51 of the TRIPS Agreement. Whereas trademark counterfeiting and copyright piracy may be easily established by customs authorities through visual inspection, it is extremely difficult or impossible for them to determine without appropriate testing or other evidence, and without technical and legal expertise, whether an infringement of a product or process patent, even if literal,[12] has taken place. For instance, custom authorities have no possibility of establishing without proper research or experimentation whether an imported pharmaceutical active ingredient infringes a patent covering a particular process for manufacturing it, or whether a patent covering a gene construct used in plants is violated by the importation of grains or a derivative product from such plants.

Pursuant to the strategy described above, in 2005 Monsanto requested and obtained the seizure of Argentina's soybean imported into Denmark, the Netherlands, Spain and United Kingdom. The application of the Council Regulation (EC) No. 1383/2003 implied, first, that the importers were bound to pay detention fees, which range from 20000 to 30000 euros per day. The cost of each detention for importers was between 200000 and 300000 euros.[13]

Second, importers were bound to provide a guarantee to eventually compensate Monsanto in case patent infringement was finally found. The guarantee requested by Monsanto was 100 euros per ton of soymeal. Following negotiations with Monsanto and the European importers, the amount of the guarantee was reduced to 15 euros per ton. On average, for a seizure of 40000 tons, the importer had to constitute a guarantee of 600000 euros. As a result, each seizure's cost for the importer was 850000 euros, an amount that remains blocked until the legal procedures are concluded (after many years). In exchange no bond or guarantee was requested from Monsanto.

The requests of Monsanto were treated by the customs administration on the sole basis of the arguments and documents presented by Monsanto who alleged that there was an infringement to its patent rights.

The importers who became engaged in legal procedures that may take years to conclude will operate under the uncertainty of pending litigation and the eventual condemnation to pay damages if an infringement were found. Moreover, they will bear the financial cost of the guarantees they had to constitute to be permitted to dispatch the imported soymeal.

THE FIRST COURT DECISIONS

Although no final decision has been reached in the legal procedures initiated by Monsanto, it is interesting to consider the rulings so far taken by the first instance courts in the United Kingdom, Spain and the Netherlands.

In the United Kingdom, the UK High Court of Justice, Chancery Division, Patents Court, issued its decision on 10 October 2007 in *Monsanto Technology LLC* v. *Cargill International and SA Cargill PLC*. The ruling made a thorough technical analysis of the patent claims and of the arguments submitted by the parties.

Monsanto claimed infringement of EP (UK) 0 546 090 entitled 'glyphosate tolerant 5-enolpyruvylshikimate-3-phosphate synthases' (referred to as EPSPSs).

The court noted that the defendants ('Cargill') purchased in Argentina soybeans grown from seeds carrying the gene for one of the EPSPSs disclosed in Monsanto's UK patent, and 'from it they or others manufactured meal which they import into the United Kingdom'. Monsanto requested detention of the cargo MV *Podhale* carrying out 5000 tons of soya meal. The court noted that the use of 'Round-Up Ready' seed 'had transformed the soya bean industry in Argentina, and represented a very substantial benefit to Argentinean growers and processors' and that it was told that '99% of soya bean meal exported from Argentina came from Round-Up Ready plants carrying the CP4R gene'. Cargill denied infringement of the UK patent and challenged its validity 'on the grounds of anticipation, obviousness and insufficiency', although Cargill accepted that 'the discovery of the CP4 enzyme was an invention'.

Cargill argued, inter alia, that at the priority date, the mode of operation of glyphosate, better known under the brand 'Round-Up', was well known. It submitted scientific papers that would have anticipated the invention. However, the arguments substantiating the challenge against the patent validity were examined but dismissed by the court, which found that the patent had been validly granted.

Regarding the alleged infringement, the court recalled that the acts related to the cargo of soybean meal on board MV *Podhale*. It reasoned as follows:

> To be justiciable here for present purposes the infringement must occur within the jurisdiction. There is no real doubt that the meal, or a very substantial part of it, is produced from Round-Up Ready soybeans in Argentina. The first question is whether importation of such meal is capable of infringing any of the method claims. The second question is raised by an allegation by Monsanto that the meal contains at least genomic fragments containing the whole of the Round-Up Ready gene. If this is so, are any of the claims relating to genetic material infringed?

In considering the possible infringement of the method claims, the court examined the protection conferred under Section 60(1)(c) of the UK Patent Act.[14] It relied on *Pioneer* v. *Warner* [1997] RPC 759. The judge considered that:

> The obverse situation was one in which the intermediate product had lost its identity and had become something else. The products of many, if not most, intermediate processes in chemical cases will suffer that fate. I take

it that *prima facie* the phrase 'directly obtained by means of the process' [Section 60(1)(c)] means 'the immediate product of the process', or, where the patented process is an intermediate stage in the manufacture of some ultimate product, that product, but only if the product of the intermediate process still retains its identity. In most cases, the assessment will be a matter of fact and degree but not always – *Pioneer* v. *Warner* was a strike-out case.

The court observed that the claimed method for producing genetically transformed plants starting with the insertion into the genome of a plant cell a double-stranded recombinant DNA molecule having the prescribed characteristics:

> is hardly an everyday operation: it will have been carried out only on the parent of every strain of Round-Up Ready soybeans. . . . The transformation of this plant was many generations ago. Since then, soybeans have been grown by seedsmen or retained by farmers for planting; the plants have been grown and the new beans harvested; and after some generations the harvested beans have been processed into the meal in the *Podhale* cargo. I accept that all the Round-Up Ready soybean plants in Argentina are lineal descendants of this original plant, and I can see how it can be said that this huge mountain of soybean meal (5000 tons on the *Podhale* alone) can be described as the ultimate product of the original transformation of the parent plant. But I cannot see that it can be properly described as the direct product of that transformation, a phrase I would reserve for the original transformed plant.

Another argument by Monsanto was that the meal:

> comes from beans produced by a plant which contained the Round-Up Ready sequence. It was the sequence that made the invention patentable, and the sequence has survived. Even though the meal comes from beans which are not the beans from the plant which underwent the original transformation, that is enough.

The court dismissed this argument noting that:

> this has nothing to do with the product of the process at all. It might be extravagant to say that the generation of plants producing the beans from which the *Podhale* meal was manufactured did not have an atom in common with the original transformed plant, but it must be close to the truth. I think that Monsanto's argument confuses the informational content of what passed between the generations (the Round-Up Ready genomic sequence) with the product, which is just soybean meal with no special intrinsic characteristics from one of the generations of plants. Put

another way, it is difficult to see how anything has survived into the meal if the sequence has not. It cannot be told apart from non-Round-Up Ready meal unless it contains traces of the gene, in which case other claims are relevant. What has not survived is the original transformed plant. I should add that I think it is dangerous to talk of reproductive material having in some way passed between the generations. While no doubt some reproductive material does pass between the first and second generations, the same material does not pass further. Copies pass thereafter.

Although Cargill argued that no single- or double-stranded DNA could survive the process of manufacturing meal but will be degraded – and, hence, the material will not infringe – the court found, on the basis of the results of Monsanto experiments, that 'there was present in the *Podhale* meal some genomic DNA which included the RR EPSPS gene, and that some or all of that DNA was double-stranded'. However, the court stressed that the DNA present in the meal:

is entirely irrelevant to the meal as an animal feedstuff, is present in small, variable, quantities and may not be present at all if processing conditions are changed. It is not in any serious sense genetic material. It is just the remains of the material which was in the soybeans from which the meal was extracted. This, it seems to me, is irrelevant.

Based on these and other considerations, the court concluded that no claim of the patent was infringed by the importation of soybean meal on board MV *Podhale*. It also allowed Monsanto to amend some of the patent claims. The ruling, however, did not address the legitimacy of the border measure requested by Monsanto to detain imports.

In the case of Spain, the decision by the Juzgado Mercantil No. 6, 27 of Madrid in *Monsanto Technology LLC* v. *Sesostris SAE*, in July 2007, addressed the alleged infringement of patent ES 2089232 covering a molecule of DNA that comprises DNA codifying EPSP resistant to glyphosate. The court set the framework for the decision by stating that a patent confers an 'authentic legal monopoly' but not 'unlimited rights' and by differentiating patents on products, processes and uses. It considered applicable Article 50.4 of the Spanish Patent Law, which incorporated Article 9 of the EU Directive on the Legal Protection of Biotechnological Inventions.

In interpreting the protection conferred to biotechnological inventions, the court concluded that the purpose of Article 9 of the directive was not to expand the protection of biotechnological inventions, and that patent law needs to be restrictively interpreted as patents constitute an exception to the principle of free enterprise.

In the view of the court, the protected invention in this case was not a DNA sequence but the *function it performs* and, hence, considered that the conditions of Article 50.4 needed to be met for an infringement to be established. As in the UK case, there was no question about the presence of the patented RR gene in the plants used to produce the soymeal. The court noted, however, the characteristics of the process utilized for producing the meal (including temperatures of up to 115°C). Although the evidence submitted did not allow establishing whether the protein detected in the imported meal was functional, practically the totality of the genetic material was degraded and did not supply any value-added to the soymeal, as glyphosate resistance was only a valuable feature while the plant develops. The court, hence, concluded that the meal obtained with transgenic seed was substantially equivalent to that obtained from conventional varieties.

Monsanto, finally, failed to demonstrate in the Spanish case that the genetic information had been incorporated into the meal and that it performed its function in the imported soymeal.

Based on the above considerations, Monsanto's action was dismissed. The court also did not consider the legitimacy of the border measure requested by Monsanto.

In the case of the Netherlands, an interim judgment has been issued by the District Court in The Hague, Civil Law Sector, on 28 September 2008, whereby the Dutch court requested the Court of Justice of the European Communities to reach a decision with regard to the following questions (paragraph 2.6.5):

1. Should Article 9 of Directive 98/44/EC of the European Parliament and the Council of 6 July 1998 on the protection of biotechnological inventions (OJ EC L 1998, No. 213 pp. 0013–0021) be interpreted such that the protection offered by this article can also be invoked in a situation as in the present proceedings in which the product (the DNA) constitutes part of a material (soya meal) imported in the European Union and is not performing its function at the moment of the alleged infringement, but did however perform the same (in the soy plant) or could possibly, after this has been isolated from the material and introduced to the cell of an organism, again perform its function?

2. Assuming the presence of the DNA sequence described in claim 6 of the patent with number EP 0 546 090 in the soya meal imported into the Community by Cefetra and ACTI and assuming that the DNA is, in the sense of Article 9 of Directive 98/44/EC of the European Parliament and the Council of 6 July 1998 on the protection of biotechnological inventions (OJ EC L 1998, No. 213 pp. 0013–0021), processed in soya meal and that it is not performing its function in the same; does the protection of a patent for biological material, as prescribed by the Directive, and in particular in Article 9, prevent the national patent legislation[15] from (in addition) conferring absolute protection on the product (the DNA) as such, regardless of the fact whether the DNA performs its function, and should the protection of Article 9 of the Directive thus be considered to be exhaustive in the situation intended by this article in which the product consists of genetic information or contains such information, which product has been processed in material and in which material the genetic information is incorporated?

3. Does it make a difference to the answer to the previous question that the patent with number EP 0 546 090 is filed and granted (on 19 June 1996) before Directive 98/44/EC of the European Parliament and the Council of 6 July 1998 on the protection of biotechnological inventions (OJ EC L 1998, No. 213 pp. 0013–0021) had been established and that this kind of absolute product protection was provided according to the national patent law before this Directive had been established?

4. Could you involve the TRIPS Convention in the answer to the preceding questions, in particular Articles 27 and 30 thereof?

This request will give the European Court of Justice the opportunity to provide an interpretation, for the first time, of key provisions of the Directive 98/44/EC of the European Parliament and the Council of 6 July 1998 on the protection of biotechnological inventions. Clearly, the interpretation to be provided about Article 9 of the directive will have a decisive impact on the way claims in biotechnological patents are to be read. If the court confirmed the interpretation already made by the European Commission, as noted above, trade, innovation and competition in secondary markets may be preserved. Critical for the application of the directive would be, in particular, the way in which the European Court of Justice addresses the query about the subsistence of 'absolute protection' despite the provision of Article 9 of the directive. An expansive interpretation may not only be rejected by many European countries given the sensitivity of this sensitive area, but could lead to deleterious implications for the internal market.

As in the other two cases mentioned above, the Dutch court did not address issues relating to the border measure that had been obtained in the Netherlands, as it was not a matter subject to review. These cases, therefore, do not help to clarify the extent of the power that customs authorities may exercise.

CONCLUSIONS

Monsanto's action against European soymeal importers represents a handbook case of 'strategic litigation'. Parties filing these cases often have little chances of success or no real interest in obtaining a final judgment; the legal action is used to put pressure on and create uncertainty for targeted parties so as to impose on them certain commercial terms and conditions. Large companies such as Monsanto allocate substantial resources to engage in strategic litigation.

In the case analysed here, the dispute goes beyond the private interests of the parties involved. It affects the Argentine economy, which at the time the dispute had begun, was getting out of the biggest crisis ever in the history of the country. European importers being sued by Monsanto are strictly circumstantial victims. The company aims at twisting the arm of the Argentine government and imposing a 'tailor-made' solution, bypassing Argentine and international law. In fact, much more than the interpretation of patent law is at stake in this case. It is an important test for the way in which disputes between multinational companies and the states where they operate are to be settled.

The broad powers conferred to customs authorities under Regulation (EC)1383/2003 of 22 July 2003 illustrate the risk of TRIPS-plus border measures, particularly as they may be used to detain goods allegedly infringing product or process patents. It also alerts us about the deleterious impact that the internationalization of such TRIPS-plus standards, as recently proposed at the World Customs Organization (Li, 2008b), may have on global trade.

NOTES

1. This chapter is partially based on a paper originally published under the title 'La disputa sobre soja transgénica. Monsanto vs. Argentina' in *Le Monde Diplomatique/El Dipló*, April 2006, and in *Resurgence*, No. 203–204, 2007.
2. In accordance with Article 4*bis* of the Paris Convention for the Protection of Industrial Property, '(1) Patents applied for in the various countries of the Union

by nationals of countries of the Union shall be independent of patents obtained for the same invention in other countries, whether members of the Union or not. (2) The foregoing provision is to be understood in an unrestricted sense, particularly in the sense that patents applied for during the period of priority are independent, both as regards the grounds for nullity and forfeiture, and as regards their normal duration'. The principle of territoriality of patents has not been affected by the adoption of the Agreement on Trade-Related Aspects of Intellectual Property (TRIPS Agreement). Paragraph 6 of the WTO Decision of 30 August 2003 confirmed the application of this principle ('It is understood that this will not prejudice the territorial nature of the patent rights in question').

3. Some countries, for example, United States, Mexico, Argentina, allow for a 'grace period' whereby an invention may be disclosed up to a year before the filing without losing novelty.

4. The World Intellectual Property Organization (WIPO) launched in 2001 a 'Patent Agenda' aiming at harmonizing patent law at the global level, but it has faced resistance by developing countries and generated strong disagreement among developed countries themselves, who are proposing such harmonization. The negotiation of a new 'Substantive Patent Law Treaty' has been frozen.

5. Argentina implemented the obligations established by the TRIPS Agreement in 1995, through enactment of Law No. 24.481.

6. Likewise, in Europe and many other countries, no patents are granted for plant varieties as such, in contrast to the policy followed, for instance, in the United States and Japan.

7. Monsanto held a patent on glyphosate in Argentina and many other countries (Robin, 2008).

8. See Provisional Measure 223/04 (enacted into Law No. 11.092/2005).

9. See the WTO panel reports WT/DS291/R, WT/DS292/R and WT/DS293/R.

10. UPOV is the Union for the Protection of New Varieties of Plants.

11. See *Monsanto Technology LLC* v. *Cargill International and SA Cargill PLC*, discussed below.

12. In most countries infringement can also occur 'by equivalence', when it is found that certain patent claims have not been literally violated but the alternative product or process is equivalent, structurally and functionally, to the patented invention. The 'theory of equivalence' applied in various jurisdictions differs considerably as there is no international standard on the matter. See, for example Franzosi (1996).

13. In Spain, for instance, more than 70 000 tons of soymeal were detained.

14. Section 60(1): 'Subject to the provisions of this section, a person infringes a patent for an invention if, but only if, while the patent is in force, he does any of the following things in the United Kingdom in relation to the invention without the consent of the proprietor of the patent, that is to say . . . (c) where the invention is a process, he disposes of, offers to dispose of, uses or imports any product obtained directly by means of that process or keeps any such product whether for disposal or otherwise'.

15. Article 53 of the Dutch patent law reads as follows: 'A patent grants the patent holder . . . the exclusive right: a. to manufacture, use, market or further sell, lease, deliver or otherwise trade the patented product or to offer, import or store the same for any of those purposes'.

6. Flexible application of injunctive relief in intellectual property enforcement (with reference to lessons from the emerging US jurisprudence)

Joshua D. Sarnoff[1]

INTRODUCTION

Although the existence of a right normally implies the existence of a remedy for its violation, substantial judicial discretion may exist in determining what particular remedy to apply. Such discretion provides flexibility to accomplish policy goals, and thus may be considered one of many important 'policy levers' that may be applied to accomplish legislative purposes and enhance social welfare, without creating excessive specificity or differentiation in the legislation itself.[2] Retail differentiation of remedies by judges in particular cases may be less risky for innovation policies, less costly to administer, more sensitive to contextual information or more politically feasible than wholesale differentiation of rights and remedies at the legislative level.[3] Such legislative specificity, moreover, would encourage rent-seeking. Few (except perhaps lawyers) would want intellectual property legislation to look like the tax code or environmental regulations.

In both common law and civil law jurisdictions, some form of equity jurisprudence invariably exists as an alternative to or correction to a more rigid, codified, and universal system of enforcing legal rules, whether or not this alternative system of justice is applied by separate municipal courts.[4] Nevertheless, separate courts of equity have a long pedigree, tracing back at least to Roman law.[5] The basic nature of equity jurisprudence is for courts to have 'jurisdiction in

cases of rights, recognized and protected by the municipal jurisprudence, where a plain, adequate, [or] complete remedy cannot
be had in the courts of common law'.[6] Equitable jurisdiction and
remedies thus are sometimes concurrent with, exclusive of or aux-
iliary to the remedies available at law, and provide the flexibility to
render complete justice among the parties.[7] Equity jurisprudence is
distinguished by its flexible application to factual context and by the
policy discretion vested in the judiciary to achieve substantive justice
and more complete relief.[8] Foremost among the remedies authorized
by equity is the prospective injunction, which is directed to a party so
as to prevent a wrong, when courts at law can only redress the wrong
after it occurs.[9] Injunctions can compel or prohibit different kinds of
conduct, including the payment of compensation.

This chapter examines the developing law in the United States
applicable to judicial decisions to grant or to deny various forms of
equitable injunctive relief as a tool for intellectual property rights
enforcement. It proceeds first by addressing recent trends in US
intellectual property jurisprudence, describing lower court trends
(particularly over the last two decades) to restrict judicial discretion cases to deny prospective injunctive relief that orders infringers to cease their infringing activities. It then analyzes a recent US
Supreme Court decision, *eBay, Inc.* v. *MercExchange, L.L.C.*,[10]
which has restored greater flexibility and discretion to trial court
judges in this regard. It then places such flexibility in an international
context, explaining why the Agreement on Trade-Related Aspects
of Intellectual Property Rights (TRIPS)[11] does not meaningfully
limit domestic legislative and judicial decisions to grant or to deny
prospective injunctive relief. Finally, it reviews some of the developing US jurisprudence since the *eBay* decision, to identify important
considerations for legislators and judges in other countries. These
considerations include: the amount of compensation considered to
be fair and adequate for different types of intellectual property right-
holders; the costs of judicial supervision of injunctive remedies and
concerns that such remedies may excessively empower right-holders;
the potential for injunctive remedies to deter legitimate challenges to
the validity of asserted rights; and the public interests that warrant
authorizing prospective infringement.

Specifically, developing countries may wish to make different
choices from those of the United States, and potentially codify
different policies by legislation, in regard to whether or when:

- to tailor remedies to domestic economic conditions, addressing concerns such as the need to promote domestic innovation
  and foreign direct investment;
- preliminary injunctions should be refused, to better assure that
  any intellectual property rights being asserted will have their
  validity fully tested when examination and rights-granting
  practices are insufficiently rigorous; and
- to identify a broader range of public interests – particularly
  competition and public access concerns – that will justify
  denying injunctions that would require infringers to cease
  infringing activity, including determining whether to award
  compensation for such continuing infringement.

RECENT LIMITS ON JUDICIAL DISCRETION TO DENY INJUNCTIONS TO STOP INFRINGING ACTIVITY

For many decades, judges in the United States have with ever-
increasing rigidity applied one specific and extremely powerful
equitable remedy for cases of patent infringement – injunctive relief
in the inflexible form of an order to cease any continued infringing
activity. Before the creation of the US Court of Appeals for the
Federal Circuit (Federal Circuit) – which has nearly exclusive jurisdiction over patent appeals – federal Circuit Courts of Appeals frequently granted injunctive relief once a patent was found (or found
likely) to be valid and infringed.[12] At least by 1988, the Federal
Circuit had stated that a permanent injunction 'should issue once
infringement has been established unless there is a sufficient reason
for denying it'.[13] This presumption in favor of injunctive relief had
expanded by 2005 to limit the reasons for denying injunctions to the
point that the Federal Circuit could state a 'general rule that courts
will issue permanent injunctions against patent infringement absent
exceptional circumstances'.[14]

In regard to preliminary injunctions, which are an 'extraordinary
remedy',[15] the Federal Circuit had developed a strong presumption
of irreparable harm upon a sufficient showing that a patent was
valid and was infringed. This presumption applied without regard
to differences among patent-holders who licensed their inventions
and those who made and sold their inventions in the market.[16]

Consequently, preliminary injunctions were routinely issued to cease patent-infringing activities, which might result in a settlement or other termination of the litigation before a decision on the merits.

Similar presumptions in favor of prospective injunctive relief to stop infringing conduct have also been applied for a longer time in trademark and copyright cases within all of the federal circuits. In trademark cases, the difficulties of quantifying harm to market share, goodwill or reputation and the public interest in avoiding consumer confusion typically resulted in granting permanent injunctions, and courts provided a presumption of irreparable harm for preliminary injunctions when there was a sufficient showing of likely success on the merits.[17] Similarly, in copyright cases, courts have traditionally granted permanent injunctions once copyright infringement was proven, and have presumed irreparable harm upon a sufficient showing of a likelihood of success. Such injunctions and presumptions reflected concerns over the forced sharing of the creative works of authors, although courts also sometimes refused to order infringement to stop when to do so would impose harms that were disproportionate to the infringement or based on the public's interest in free expression or in access to the infringing work.[18]

Because intellectual property infringement normally does not require culpable intent, infringers often may have made substantial but reasonable investments in creativity, manufacturing, marketing and other activities. By 1986, however, the Federal Circuit had stated that the potential to put the infringer out of business was not a sufficient reason to deny a prospective injunction requiring the infringer to cease infringing activity. As the Federal Circuit put it, '[o]ne who elects to build a business on a product found to infringe cannot be heard to complain if an injunction against continuing infringement destroys the business so elected'.[19] This was true even though patent injunctions are authorized by law only 'in accordance with the principles of equity'.[20] Equitable principles traditionally required consideration of (among other factors) the balance of hardships to the parties, but the Federal Circuit's rigid approach precluded the flexible and contextual weighing of the equities.[21] Particularly when the infringement related only to a component of a larger product, the potential for injunctive relief and the presumption of irreparable harm from proof of likely infringement consequently has posed a significant 'holdup problem' that may have resulted in recent decades in extortionate settlements and unreasonable licensing demands and fees (imposing on society what are commonly referred to as 'holdup costs').[22]

In earlier times, decisions about whether to grant such injunctive relief were left to the sound discretion of trial courts, which applied equitable principles in their traditional, flexible and context-specific manner. For example before the 20th century, patent injunctions were refused where: they would cause disproportionate harm to defendants relative to the benefits to plaintiffs or would prevent the use of an essential process or device;[23] they would be harmful to the convenience as well as the safety of the public;[24] the defendant acted in a good faith belief in the inapplicability of or in ignorance of the patent when making substantial business investments;[25] or the patent-holder had an established fee for licensing the invention (and the defendant was solvent).[26]

At the beginning of the 20th century, the Supreme Court in *Continental Paper Bag Co.* v. *Eastern Paper Bag Co.* had stated that exclusion is 'the very essence of the right conferred by the patent', and 'that the right can only retain its attribute of exclusiveness by a prevention of its violation'.[27] The Court thus held that equity jurisdiction exists to grant injunctive relief even when the patent-holder did not itself use or license the patented invention.[28] Given this language, some have argued that appellate courts have been justified in routinely granting injunctive relief, finding a presumption of irreparable harm and inadequacy of damages for infringements of valid patents.[29] Nevertheless, the Court in *Continental Paper Bag* had reiterated general equitable principles in reaching its conclusion, specifically the concern that damages at law might not remedy continuing harms, and expressly refused to decide whether 'the situation of the parties in view of the public interest' might justify withholding an injunction.[30] Further, the view expressed in *Continental Paper Bag* – and a later Supreme Court case affirming *Continental Paper Bag*'s holding in the context of a refusal to grant a patent[31] – addresses only whether the patent-holder must work or license the patented invention in order to assert the patent right, and not what the remedy should be for any specific violation of that right. In the 1952 Act, the Congress reaffirmed the right to relief and simultaneously retained judicial discretion over the remedy.[32]

As with the patent experience, during the 20th century courts also became less willing to refuse copyright injunctions than in an earlier era. In earlier times, no presumption of such relief existed, no 'overheated rhetoric about copyright being a sanctified form of property' was employed, courts 'revealed a balanced, and in some cases skeptical attitude toward the need for such relief', and copyright-holders were required as a condition for injunctions to reimburse innocent infringers who lacked notice before making investments that would be destroyed.[33]

THE *eBAY* DECISION AND RESTORED JUDICIAL FLEXIBILITY TO DENY INJUNCTIONS

In 2006, in *eBay, Inc.* v. *MercExchange, L.L.C.*,[34] the US Supreme Court explicitly rejected the Federal Circuit's 'general rule' that after finding infringement of a valid patent a permanent injunction to cease infringing activity should issue. The Supreme Court made clear that the right to exclude does not necessarily imply the powerful exclusionary remedy of such an injunction:

> According to the Court of Appeals, this statutory right to exclude alone justifies its general rule in favor of permanent injunctive relief. . . . But *the creation of a right is distinct from the provision of remedies for violations of that right.* Indeed, the Patent Act itself indicates that patents shall have the attributes of personal property '[s]ubject to the provisions of this title'. . . including, presumably, the provision that injunctive relief 'may' issue only 'in accordance with the principles of equity'. . . .[35]

The importance of the highlighted statement cannot be overstated. It denies any necessary legal entitlement to an injunction, and reflects a fundamentally different understanding than that expressed by the Federal Circuit regarding the nature of exclusive patent rights and of equitable limitations on enforcing that right. The Federal Circuit had repeatedly stated its view that an exclusionary right implies the need for an exclusionary remedy, because a patent grants 'the right to invoke the state's power in order to exclude others from utilizing the patentee's discovery without his consent', and without this power, 'the right to exclude granted by the patent would be diminished, and the express purpose of the Constitution and Congress, to promote the progress of the useful arts, would be seriously undermined'.[36] Although the Federal Circuit's language reflects a view of the importance of exclusivity granted by the patent right similar to that expressed by the Supreme Court in *Continental Paper Bag*, the Court in *eBay* had requested briefing on whether to reconsider its prior precedents and referenced *Continental Paper Bag* only to reject any categorical rule precluding injunctive relief.[37] Further, the Supreme Court implicitly reiterated that the burden is on the patent-holder to prove each of the traditional equitable factors, when noting that even non-working entities 'may be able to satisfy the traditional four-factor test'.[38] Thus, the Supreme Court in *eBay* signaled a significant change to how intellectual property is viewed in the United States.

The Supreme Court's reaffirmation of the right-remedy distinction in *eBay* also implicitly overruled a line of Federal Circuit cases dating back at least to 1987 regarding preliminary injunctive relief. The Federal Circuit had held in that context that irreparable harm should be 'presumed when a clear showing has been made of patent validity and infringement', because the patent's term will continue to run during any litigation and because the '*nature of the patent grant* . . . weighs against holding that monetary damages will always suffice to make the patentee whole, for *the principle value of a patent is its statutory right to exclude*'.[39] As the Supreme Court noted in *eBay*, however, the exclusive right does not as a matter of law mandate an exclusionary remedy; this is true whether or not a diminution in the value of that right to the patent-holder might result. It is only the flexible judicial decision to afford substantive justice in equity (considering the effects on a patent's value of any infringement of the exclusive right) that supplies the basis for an injunctive remedy.

Nevertheless, as discussed below, some courts have refused to abandon this presumption of irreparable harm, seeking instead to limit the effects of *eBay* to the permanent injunction context. Such courts either have refused to resolve the question of whether a presumption of irreparable harm exists or have held that the Supreme Court at most overruled only a presumption that injunctive relief must be granted following proof on the merits of patent validity and infringement. That the Supreme Court overruled such a presumption in regard to permanent injunctions is crystal clear. The Court had analogized its decision in patent cases to that in earlier copyright cases, where it had refused to 'replace traditional equitable considerations with a rule than an injunction automatically follows a determination that a copyright has been infringed'.[40]

The Supreme Court also reiterated that injunctive relief in regard to patent infringement is subject to the traditional four-factor test established by courts in equity, which places the burden on the plaintiff to prove:

(1) that it has suffered an irreparable injury; (2) that remedies available at law, such as monetary damages, are inadequate to compensate for that injury; (3) that, considering the balance of hardships between the plaintiff and defendant, a remedy in equity is warranted; and (4) that the public interest would not be disserved by a permanent injunction.[41]

In remanding the case for proper evaluation under the traditional test, the Court rejected both: (a) the 'broad classifications' of the District Court that the patent-holder's willingness to license and failure to practice the patent necessarily precludes injunctive relief; and (b) the Federal Circuit's 'categorical grant' of relief except in 'the "unusual" case, under "exceptional circumstances" and "in rare instances . . . to protect the public interest"'.[42] Thus, the Supreme Court made clear that these equitable principles should be applied in their traditional, context-specific manner. The Court also made it clear that the 'public interest' factor should encompass and should properly weigh all relevant public interests, and was not constrained to the small list of exceptions previously recognized by the Federal Circuit. The Federal Circuit had limited those exceptions to when the '"patentee's failure to practice the invention frustrates an important public need for the invention", such as the need to use an invention to protect public health'.[43]

Since the 2006 *eBay* decision, a body of case law has been developing regarding the conditions under which preliminary and permanent injunctions should and should not issue in patent, trademark, copyright and other intellectual property law cases. In an increasing number of cases, which inform the discussion below, preliminary or permanent injunctive relief is being denied (although permanent injunctions continue to be routinely granted in cases of direct competition).[44] Following judgments of validity and infringement, prospective compensation is sometimes being awarded in the form of an equitable 'ongoing royalty' injunction,[45] which some argue (wrongly, as explained below) is a compulsory license[46] even though the authorization to continue infringing conduct is in the form of a court order limited to the parties to the dispute.[47] An ongoing royalty injunction is a prospective monetary award based on a previously determined royalty amount, and which may require continuing judicial supervision of the parties' prospective conduct to determine the amount of payment over time.[48] Because the amount of the royalty for continuing infringement is judicially imposed rather than voluntarily negotiated, the right-holder may view the injunction as providing inadequate compensation.

These decisions to deny injunctions to stop infringement reflect the roots of injunctive relief in equity, demonstrating its flexibility and its sensitivity to the factual context and the positions of the parties in achieving substantive justice. Moreover, the developing case law reflects renewed recognition of the fact that equitable remedies were not to be supplied where damage remedies at common law were adequate to compensate the plaintiff.[49] Significantly, because the *eBay* decision has restored their flexibility to deny injunctive relief, trial court judges may be encouraged to uphold the validity of intellectual property rights and to find liability more often in difficult cases, where they would otherwise have been reluctant to impose the high costs of injunctive relief on defendants or on society. The *eBay* decision may thereby bring 'into alignment the issues of liability and remedy'.[50]

The body of case law that is being developed in the United States through the discretionary judgments of trial judges may be instructive to other developed and to developing countries in assessing whether, when and how to grant prospective injunctive relief. This is true even if legislators and judges in those countries choose to exercise their policy discretion differently from judges in the United States. To the extent that social conditions or policy preferences differ from those in the United States, legislators or judges in other countries may choose to specify different conditions under which injunctive relief should be granted. Similarly, legislators may choose to codify different factors for judges to consider, different weights to be accorded or different degrees of delegated policy discretion.

DOMESTIC POLICY FLEXIBILITY FOR INJUNCTIVE RELIEF UNDER THE TRIPS AGREEMENT

US legislation regarding intellectual property rights has always authorized the flexibility reflected in the recent injunctive relief case law. The US Congress has supplied an express, discretionary authorization for federal courts to grant injunctive relief in patent and copyright cases since 1819, although federal courts granted injunctive remedies even earlier in diversity jurisdiction cases.[51] Specifically, the 1819 Act provided that federal courts 'should have authority to grant injunctions, *according to the course and principles of courts of equity*'.[52] As currently phrased in the US Patent Act, federal courts '*may* grant injunctions in accordance with the principles of equity to prevent the violation of any right secured by the patent, *on such terms as the court deems reasonable*'.[53] Similar discretionary language and references to equity exist in regard to providing injunctive authority to redress violations of other intellectual property rights.[54]

The discretionary authority vested in trial courts by the US Congress is further reinforced by deferential appellate review standards for grants and denials of preliminary and permanent patent injunctions. Such judgments are subject to reversal or modification only for an 'abuse of discretion', that is, 'a clear error of judgment in weighing the relevant factors, or based a decision upon a clearly erroneous factual finding or an erroneous legal standard'.[55] Similar discretionary deferential review standards apply in regard to other intellectual property rights.[56]

Such domestic policy flexibility in determining whether, when and how to award injunctive relief for infringements of intellectual property rights was expressly authorized by the TRIPS Agreement. Article 44.1 of TRIPS requires only that 'judicial authorities *shall have the authority to order a party* to desist from an infringement, inter alia to prevent the entry into the channels of commerce . . . immediately after customs clearance of such goods'.[57] Article 44.1 also recognizes that Members are not required to provide such injunctive relief authority in regard to protected subject matter (typically products that infringe patents, copyrights or trademarks) against parties that lack 'reasonable grounds to know' of infringement.[58] Similarly, Article 45.1 of TRIPS requires that the judicial authorities 'shall have the authority to order' payment of damages 'adequate to compensate for the injury the right-holder has suffered' from infringers with 'reasonable grounds to know' of the infringement.[59] And Article 50.1 requires that the judicial authorities 'shall have the authority to order prompt and effective provisional measures . . . to prevent an infringement . . . from occurring', preserving domestic discretion in regard to whether, when and how to grant preliminary injunctive relief.[60]

Article 44.2 of TRIPS provides additional policy flexibility. Members are not required to provide injunctive relief authority but rather may limit judicial remedies to the 'payment of remuneration' in accordance with Article 31(h)[61] – which requires payment of 'adequate remuneration'[62] – in the special circumstances of governmental use or compulsory licensing, so long as they comply with other TRIPS provisions applicable to governmental use or compulsory licensing.[63] Article 44.2 specifically refers to the ability to limit remedies 'against such use',[64] which necessarily refers only to these special circumstances. Finally, Article 44.2 provides that where injunctive relief would be inconsistent with national law, Members may provide for a declaratory judgment and 'adequate compensation'.[65] For this reason, resort to Article 13, Article 30 or any other limited authorizations[66] to adopt domestic exceptions to exclusive rights are wholly unnecessary to justify even categorical legislative exclusions of injunctive relief.

Because Article 44.2 provides additional flexibility rather than imposes additional restrictions on the required injunctive relief authority under Article 44.1, Article 44.2 *has no application whatsoever* to judicial decisions to provide ongoing royalty injunctions (or other conditional injunctions that authorize continuing infringement) in particular cases. Such injunctions are simply a particular equitable remedy exercised as part of the broader injunctive relief authority required by Article 44.1. The reference to compulsory licensing in Article 44.2, moreover, is the object (rather than the consequence) of the additional authorization for Members to dispense with injunctive relief authority in specified circumstances. Nor would Article 44.2 apply to damage awards that include a market entry fee or other prospective compensation, thereby authorizing prospective infringing conduct without the grant of an injunction; rather, the only limitation for such a damage award is that it be 'adequate to compensate for the injury the right-holder has suffered' under Article 45.[67] (The adequacy of such compensation, and whether it is to be determined from an objective perspective or from the subjective perspective of the right-holder, is discussed further below.)

It is critically important not to confuse such ongoing royalty injunctions, damage awards authorizing continued infringing conduct or refusals of courts to grant preliminary injunctive relief with compulsory licenses granted by the government.[68] (For this reason, the Paris Convention's authorization for and limits on the grants of compulsory licenses also are inapplicable to judicial remedy decisions.[69]) Such remedial decisions authorizing continuing infringement have long been a part of the judicial arsenal of equitable and legal remedies.[70] Given such long-standing practices, it seems highly unlikely that the negotiating parties would (without any discussion) have subjected the continued use of such remedies to the highly controversial administrative procedures and substantive restrictions employed for compulsory licenses in Article 31.[71] Articles 44, 45 and 50 all use the standard, discretionary language employed for the powers that Members must supply to their judicial branches – 'shall have authority to' – and do not require any specific actions by the judiciary in particular cases.

Further, the negotiating history of the TRIPS Agreement reflects significant concerns to preserve differences among national legal systems in regard to enforcement authorities. These concerns resulted not only in a provision assuring that Members were not required to enforce intellectual property laws differently from other laws, but more importantly resulted in the limitation of Article 44.1 on the requirement for Members to supply injunctive relief authority in cases of innocent infringement.[72] It is only in this context of *limiting* Members' judicial obligations that any reference is made to compulsory licenses, and it seems highly unlikely that the drafting parties would have imposed *additional* obligations for judges to comply with Article 31 when doing so. Any argument of nullification or impairment of benefits from judicial decisions not to order parties to cease infringement in particular cases would similarly be very difficult to sustain, particularly absent 'a systematic refusal (which would be difficult to demonstrate)'.[73]

In summary, TRIPS Members retain substantial discretion to determine their legislative policies and to delegate policy discretion to their judges to decide whether, when and how to grant preliminary and permanent injunctive relief, as well as to award damages that authorize continued infringing activity. Thus, we should expect significant differences of national treatment in this regard. Finally, although beyond the scope of the present analysis, additional flexibility and complexity may attend decisions regarding inter-jurisdictional enforcement of intellectual property rights, where one jurisdiction must decide whether to enforce remedial judgments issued in a differing jurisdiction.[74] The TRIPS Agreement does not harmonize or impose any requirements on such decisions (although a non-violation complaint is a theoretical possibility).

THE DEVELOPING EQUITABLE JURISPRUDENCE OF INJUNCTIVE REMEDIES AFTER *eBAY*

An exhaustive survey of recent decisions regarding injunctive relief and of each factor of the four-factor test in each of the different fields of intellectual property law is beyond the scope of the present discussion, and in any event would soon become outdated. Rather, this section seeks to identify some critical issues by reference to the developing equitable jurisprudence, focusing principally (but not exclusively) on the patent cases. These issues are to some extent interrelated, and raise important choices for policy-makers on fundamental questions regarding the nature of intellectual property rights and their functions in society. The issues are: (1) the adequacy of damage remedies and irreparable harm in regard to right-holders who make and sell products or services (practicing entities), as well as for those who only license their rights (non-practicing entities); (2) judicial supervision and holdup-cost concerns in regard to determining compensation and prospective remedies; (3) the potential for injunctive relief to deter socially beneficial challenges to the validity of intellectual property rights; and (4) the balancing of various public interests in permitting or prohibiting continuing infringement. In particular, judges in the United States (and by extension judges and legislators in other countries) must make policy choices regarding: (1) the types of harms that should be compensable and whether to protect intellectual property owners' subjective valuations of the worth of their rights; (2) the degree of remedial precision required for fairness (that is, whether rough judgments should be considered adequate compensation), whether courts should be actively involved in supervising the parties' obligations and whether in doing so courts can avoid sending signals that may exacerbate holdup costs; (3) the degree to which decisions to grant injunctions, and the timing of preliminary injunction decisions, may deter potentially successful, socially beneficial validity challenges; and (4) the kinds and weights of public interests to recognize and in particular whether and when to exert judicial control over market prices and anticompetitive behaviors. Again, different jurisdictions may and do adopt very different policies.

Assessing Adequacy of Damages and the Potential for Irreparable Harm

A historic premise of US patent law is to award damages so as to put the patent-holder in the economic position that it would have been in had the infringement not occurred.[75] But it is not always possible or sensible to base a damage award on actual economic harm (for example, if the patent-holder only licensed its patent, there may be no prior license with the infringer on which to determine the extent of the economic harm) and thus determining adequate compensation may sometimes require approximation of economic harm or valuation of the harm to the legal right itself. Patent law provides practicing patent-holders with the ability to recover not only for lost sales, but also for the erosion of prices affecting the profits made on sales that are nevertheless completed by the patent-holder.[76] Thus, it is principally the practical problem of determining lost sales and price erosion[77] – and other effects on market share or future activities resulting from infringing competition (such as lost goodwill, lost licensing and cross-licensing opportunities)[78] – that might render a prospective damage award inadequate. To the extent that a retrospective damage award includes a right-holder requested prospective, paid-up license or market-entry fee, then there is no inadequacy to the award, no potential for irreparable harm and no basis for prospective injunctive relief.[79]

The adequacy of a prospective damage award and the corresponding potential for irreparable harm also reflects policy judgments regarding the kinds of harms that should or should not be compensable. Damages should be considered inadequate to remedy more remote consequences (for example, loss of cross-licensing abilities) only when those harms are legally or equitably cognizable and rise above a level where their exclusion from the damage remedy renders it not 'adequate to compensate for the infringement'.[80] As with proximate causation in tort cases, not all but-for harms are legally compensable, but rather only those 'fairly attributable to the defendant'.[81] The issue of what damages are legally cognizable, proximate and sufficient to warrant recovery most commonly arises in regard to whether lost profits should include the value of either: (1) unpatented components sold with the patented invention (under the 'entire market value' rule, where the value of the patented invention is the source of demand for the entire product); or (2) product sales not directly incorporating the patented invention but competing with the infringing product (so-called 'diverted' or 'convoyed' sales).[82] Further, in order to assert that damages are inadequate, the plaintiff itself must be the party suffering the relevant harms (for example, non-practicing entities cannot assert the inadequacy of damages on behalf of their exclusive licensees).[83] These rules are controversial precisely because they incorporate basic notions of fairness, which differ not only domestically but internationally.

In contrast to practicing entities who may recover lost profits from infringing competitors, non-practicing entities (both those that have licensing programs and those that do not) are entitled to damages that 'in no event [are] less than a reasonable royalty for the use made of the invention'.[84] The question thus arises as to whether such entities are entitled to any damages beyond a reasonable royalty, including royalties that by definition are in excess of what is objectively reasonable. For non-practicing entities that have established licensing programs, the answer is typically no.[85] Damage awards in such cases can be based on straightforward prospective royalty calculations that will be considered fully adequate to compensate for any harm to the patent-holder. This is true even though the patent-holder *could have* chosen to hold out for a higher voluntary licensing fee (ex ante or in settlement) in regard to the particular infringer.

Where there is not an established program of licensing, courts have recognized that non-practicing entities may suffer irreparable harm to goodwill, reputation, potential licensing prospects or other opportunities that are difficult to measure.[86] Nevertheless, the majority of courts since *eBay* have denied permanent injunctions to stop infringing activities for non-practicing patent-holders, given that the infringers do not directly compete with them, and thus reasonable royalty damages are considered to be fair and adequate compensation for such entities even if some remote harms to their interests result.[87] Similarly, although courts 'are understandably reluctant to "set" prices or rates or interfere with the freedom of copyright owners to establish their own fees', they nevertheless evaluate the adequacy of damages and market harm by carefully scrutinizing proposed licensing fees 'in the context of prevailing rates in the industry and the licensing history and fees of copyright owners and users'.[88] Judges thus routinely engage in market regulation, as discussed further below.

So long as a court can fairly determine a prospective 'reasonable royalty' – which they are required to do for retrospective damage award calculations based on past history and objective market norms, using a complicated multi-factor test[89] – an injunction to cease infringement necessarily must protect either *more than objectively reasonable* compensation for the value of the invention or the *subjective* value to the patent-holder of refusing to license the invention at all. Refusal to license an invention may be a right conveyed to the patent-holder, subject over time to any working requirements, compulsory licensing or government use imposed by national law.[90] But jurisdictions are not required to provide equitable remedies to protect against harms to objectively excessive valuations or to the subjective value of suppressing exclusive rights, particularly when those valuations are balanced against harms to infringers or to public interests of which equitable injunctive relief also requires consideration. TRIPS Article 44 clearly does not require that result. TRIPS Article 45 similarly requires judges only to have authority to order the recovery of damages 'adequate to compensate for the injury the right-holder has suffered',[91] leaving to national law decisions about whether to treat the injury as a legal or economic one, what injuries are cognizable and what compensation is adequate. Any concerns that the judicial refusal to prohibit infringement compels the patent-holder to license its invention against its will, moreover, are likely to be much less strong in the patent context than similar concerns in copyright and trademark contexts, where creative expression and public confusion are at issue. This is particularly true in countries other than the United States that have a strong tradition of protecting moral rights.[92]

Thus, for non-practicing entities, whether damages are adequate and whether irreparable harm will occur absent an injunction to cease infringing activity thus will depend principally on fundamental policy choice regarding the fairness of rejecting compensation for right-holders who refuse to license unless they receive a subjectively desired and voluntarily accepted level of compensation. Such decisions reflect a larger policy debate, commonly referred to as the choice between property rules (leaving valuations to private, market-based determinations) and liability rules (authorizing governmental determinations of prices).[93] Again, countries have substantial policy discretion to make different choices in different contexts, in general as well as in regard to intellectual property rights. But even the rhetoric may matter here, as it may determine whether to view patents, copyrights and trademarks as private property rights subject to constitutional protections or as governmental privileges subject to governmental adjustment and regulation.[94]

Precision in Determining Remedies, Supervision of Relief and Concerns Over Holdout Behaviors

Some patent cases after *eBay* continue to state that irreparable harm *necessarily* follows from the fact of infringement by direct competition and the consequent diminution of value of the exclusive right.[95] Other cases reject the existence of a presumption of irreparable harm from proof of validity and infringement.[96] In these cases, the courts have focused on the potential for price erosion and consequent effects on sales, market share, licensing opportunities and goodwill to demonstrate irreparable harm.[97] The trademark cases have long recognized the difficulty of assessing the effects of infringing conduct on market behaviors resulting from reductions in goodwill and reputation, and courts in cases decided since *eBay* continue to make the same point.[98] Similarly, copyright cases since *eBay* continue to recognize irreparable harm either from the mere fact of continued infringement[99] or from specific facts that typically exist in regard to copyright infringement, such as the reduced incentives and value for further works of the same author or of potentially competing works.[100]

The cases have not provided any meaningful analysis of a threshold for determining inadequacy of damages in regard to these hard-to-measure effects or of the degree of diminished value to the exclusive right that is sufficient to render a damage remedy inadequate and the harm irreparable. 'Normal business losses' associated with direct competition are not necessarily incalculable, and economists and accountants regularly calculate such damages.[101] Thus, a key question arises as to the degree of 'reasonable precision' required in determining whether a damage award would be adequate to compensate the right-holder, the absence of which requires resort to equitable remedies.[102] Stated differently, the question is whether the somewhat rougher justice of legal damage award remedies is considered sufficient to assure fair treatment.[103]

The increased precision involved in providing equitable remedies to assure fairer treatment than that available at law, however, comes at the cost of greater judicial involvement and greater expenditure of governmental resources. Prospective injunctions require monitoring. Injunctions ordering prospective compensation may require more monitoring (to address potential changes in market conditions relating to the relevant technologies[104]) than injunctions that simply prohibit continuing infringement (although they may trigger contempt proceedings or subsequent requests for modification or dissolution).

However, the very premise of equitable injunctive relief is to *minimize* the burdens on courts and the unfairness to property owners of repetitive judicial damage actions at law.[105] Injunctions that prohibit continued infringement thus may induce the parties to enter settlement agreements or consent decrees that authorize the conduct, thereby restoring to the parties themselves the obligation to monitor compliance and to assess changes in market conditions. But even then, such settlements or consent decrees may simply defer conflicts into the future, requiring judicial resources to resolve continuing disputes in contempt proceedings or to address future infringements that are not authorized by the earlier voluntary resolution or addressed by the earlier injunction.

The question of whether to grant injunctive relief thus may ultimately depend less on what is best for the particular parties to the dispute than on decisions about the best uses of scarce judicial resources. Such decisions are likely to be better made on a retail basis by judges in particular cases than on a wholesale basis by legislative directives. Determining whether to grant and the form of prospective injunctive relief requires careful consideration and calibration to the conditions.

Intellectual property injunctions, moreover, are not necessarily harder to supervise than other types of injunctions. In many contexts, courts must supervise compliance in ways that pose much greater judicial burden, for example when addressing such controversial and recalcitrant issues as school desegregation and prison conditions.[106] Courts thus have not hesitated to impose or uphold ongoing royalty injunctions when they have thought it appropriate, even when they have recognized that it would be preferable to have the parties voluntarily reach agreement over the financial terms.[107] Accordingly, there may be substantial wisdom in preserving the traditional flexibility of equitable remedial discretion in determining the need for and the form of injunctive remedies.

Nevertheless, the mere potential for judicial involvement to prohibit continued infringement raises concerns about potential direct costs and sequential innovation effects on infringers and on the public (to whom competitors pass on the costs and harms). Infringers may have to pay higher settlements or higher licensing fees than they would otherwise voluntarily negotiate in the absence of the threat of injunctive relief. These holdup-cost concerns are particularly great in regard to patents held by non-practicing entities, including universities.[108] Non-practicing entities may not need to cross-license their intellectual property rights, and are unlikely to be defendants (or, if state entities, may not have to pay damages due to sovereign immunity[109]). Thus, universities and other non-practicing entities may exercise significantly less restraint in seeking to maximize litigation and licensing revenues. The lack of restraint, coupled with the potential for injunctive relief, may threaten payments far exceeding any objectively reasonable royalty. Similar holdup-cost concerns also apply to patents for inventions that are only components of larger products, as the attendant costs to the infringer of an injunction are correspondingly greater,[110] and to patents of dubious validity or uncertain scope, given the questionable value of the patent and the attendant difficulties of avoiding its application.[111]

The decisions that courts make in granting or denying injunctions, and in deciding on their form, send important signals to right-holders and potential infringers that either may encourage holdup-cost behaviors or that may inadequately deter infringement. The existence of strong expectations in regard to such injunctions may predetermine these behaviors. In contrast, the greater uncertainty resulting from increased judicial flexibility and sensitivity to factual context may limit the transmission of signals that would encourage either set of behaviors. Again, the flexibility provided by equity jurisprudence and discretionary review standards may be the best solution to avoid sending the wrong signals.

These holdout and signaling concerns, moreover, apply to decisions to grant adequate compensation in damage awards, given the potential to recover under the 'entire market value rule' lost profits that are based on the larger products sold by the patent-holder that incorporate the patented invention, or 'reasonable royalties' based on the larger products that are sold by the infringer.[112] A vigorous debate thus is currently raging in regard to whether to amend US patent law to further limit royalty damages to the apportioned value of the inventive contribution of the patent to the infringing product.[113] So long as the entire market value rule authorizes recoveries that may extend beyond the objective contribution of the patented invention to the value of the products at issue, greater judicial flexibility to determine adequate compensation may be justified not only as providing fairer compensation but also to avoid having judges send the wrong signals.

These concerns about judicial supervision of remedies and holdup-costs may be of particular concern to developing countries, which may lack extensive judicial infrastructure and the ability for the public to readily pay for the more expensive goods and services that more extensive intellectual property remedies may create. Further, developing countries may be more concerned with promoting local industries and innovation, and more extensive remedies may preferentially advantage foreign right-holders and inventors:

> [S]tronger global [intellectual property rights] could reduce the scope for [developing country] firms to acquire new, and even mature, technologies at reasonable costs. The natural competitive disadvantages of follower countries may become reinforced by a proliferation of legal monopolies and related entry barriers that result from global minimum intellectual property (IP) standards.[114]

Conversely, depending on their particular situation, the provision of more extensive remedies may have the potential to attract additional foreign direct investment.[115] Thus, careful consideration is required for developing countries to best calibrate their remedial discretion to their economic and social needs, and their choices are unlikely to reflect those of developed countries.

Concerns About Deterring Legitimate Challenges to Validity

Because injunctions that stop infringing activity may result in substantial lost investments for innocent infringers and may increase the litigating power of patent-holders to obtain greater than objectively reasonable compensation, they may excessively deter socially valuable infringing conduct. Of perhaps greater concern, such injunctions may deter legally permissible conduct that does not infringe any valid intellectual property right. The potential to grant permanent injunctive relief potentially discourages challenges to intellectual property rights that are not valid (or to overbroad assertions of valid rights). Strong public policy interests exist in assuring vigorous challenges to invalid intellectual property rights, so as to free the public from the burdens that such rights impose.

At least since 1969, the US Supreme Court has affirmatively encouraged litigation challenges to the validity of granted patents, prohibiting contractual licensing provisions that would foreclose or deter such challenges by parties with the greatest incentives to litigate.[116] Nevertheless, it is widely recognized that inadequate incentives exist for bringing validity challenges or for maintaining validity defenses, in light of the costs and risks of litigation compared with license fees or settlements that may be demanded by the patent-holder.[117] Collective action problems also exist in regard to such challenges, resulting in part from the legal rule that patent-holders cannot assert validity in future litigation once their patent has been declared invalid.[118]

Concerns about deterring potentially successful challenges to the validity of granted intellectual property rights are particularly strong in regard to grants of preliminary injunctive relief. (It is possible that determining the likelihood of success on the merits when seeking preliminary relief may differ from the standards of proof at trial. For many years, the Federal Circuit has required the party opposing preliminary relief to show only a 'substantial question' concerning the validity, enforceability or infringement of a patent that the patent-holder cannot show to 'lack substantial merit'.[119] More recently, the Federal Circuit has called this differential standard into question, stating that the standard for likelihood of success should track the burdens of proof at trial.[120]) Such relief may induce parties to settle prematurely rather than to litigate validity issues to their conclusion. Although such settlements may be subject to antitrust scrutiny for collusive behavior, such as recent reverse-payments settlements in pharmaceutical patent litigation, such scrutiny in the United States is highly deferential.[121]

Judges thus may need to consider more carefully the effects that preliminary injunction decisions may have on prematurely terminating what would otherwise be successful validity challenges. To do so, however, may conflict with other important public policies, such as encouraging settlements of complex disputes to avoid expending judicial resources.[122] Further, it may require not only careful balancing of the relative hardships to the parties (as already required by equitable principles), but also careful assessment of whether these hardships will lead to premature settlements. More routinely denying the extraordinary relief of preliminary injunctions to encourage validity challenges also will diminish somewhat (albeit temporarily) the value of granted intellectual property rights ultimately held valid, and thus will diminish somewhat the incentives provided for investment, invention, disclosure or distribution.[123] All of these concerns may be taken into account under traditional equitable balancing principles of relative hardship to the parties and the public interest.

Although the cases since *eBay* have not directly addressed this issue, they have implicitly done so when evaluating the relationship (if any) that exists between proof of success on the merits and other preliminary injunction factors, particularly irreparable harm. Some cases have called into question the presumption of irreparable harm for proof of likely patent infringement,[124] as well as for proof of likely trademark infringement or false advertising.[125] Others have limited the presumption of irreparable harm to cases where a clear showing of likely success on the merits has been made, and have refused to find irreparable harm based on the possibility of lost revenues and price erosion, lost market share, lost research opportunities, inability to service debts and lost employees where the defendants were solvent.[126] As one court noted, it 'would convert the "extraordinary" relief of a preliminary injunction into a standard remedy'.[127] Nevertheless, other cases (including those decided by the Federal Circuit) have consciously avoided resolving whether a presumption of irreparable harm should result from a strong showing of validity and infringement.[128] In the copyright context, some cases continue to hold that a presumption of irreparable harm should exist upon a prima facie showing of copyright infringement,[129] and other cases question the presumption but find irreparable harm on the facts without significant analysis of the presumption question.[130]

Of more explicit relevance, some courts have adopted a presumption that absent a showing of likely success on the merits, the public interest factor weighs strongly in favor of denying a preliminary injunction.[131] Clearly this presumption is more favorable to the policy of not discouraging validity challenges. But it could also be more nuanced, distinguishing more clearly between likelihood of success in regard to validity and in regard to infringement. Courts also could be more conscious about the timing of their preliminary injunction rulings, deciding explicitly whether to defer decisions on preliminary injunctive relief that might cause litigation to terminate before evidence of invalidity can be fully developed and evaluated.

Competing Conceptions of the Public Interest and of Judicial Control Over Market Prices and Behaviors

Courts since *eBay* differ significantly in their views regarding whether public interests other than those relating to health and safety (and sometimes even those so relating) are sufficient to warrant denying injunctive relief. Recall that the Supreme Court in *eBay* expressly rejected the Federal Circuit's constricted view (as unusual, exceptional or rare) of the public interest grounds for denying injunctions. Nevertheless, some courts have repeated the earlier view that exceptions to injunctive relief on public interest grounds are 'rare and limited',[132] and that the diminution in value of the exclusive right by permitting continued infringement (and consequent diminution in ex ante incentives provided by the right) will necessarily outweigh any other public interest concerns. Thus, one court granted a permanent injunction by according (without reference to the particular facts of the case) superior weight to the public interest of encouraging investments in research and development over the public interest in obtaining lower prices and increased access to products.[133] Another court did the same, explaining that without an injunction, the exclusive right '"would have only a fraction of the value it was intended to have, and would no longer be as great an incentive to engage in the toils of scientific and technological research"'.[134] Yet another court suggested categorically that any diminution in the value of a patent would favor the patent-holder when balanced against any harm incurred by an infringer, and that the public interest in 'protecting patent rights, which encourage the development of useful inventions' categorically outweighs the public interest in 'low cost generic alternatives to branded drugs' resulting from earlier market entry.[135]

Other courts have focused on the particular language of the four-factor equitable balancing test articulated in *eBay* (that 'the public interest would not be disserved') to place the burden on the defendant opposing injunctive relief to show that the public interest would be disserved by granting an injunction, even though *eBay* makes clear that the plaintiff bears the burden of proof.[136] In the context of preliminary relief, moreover, one court suggested that the public interest factor should be governed by the likelihood of success factor, because of the public interest to enforce patents or copyrights.[137] Significantly, many of these cases rely on pre-*eBay* Federal Circuit dicta suggesting that continuing an infringement can never be found to be a paramount public interest. For example, "'selling a lower-priced product does not justify infringing a patent'' , , . or "excuse infringement of a valid pharmaceutical patent'".[138] Similar categorical language can be found in some copyright cases. For example, since "'Congress has elected to grant certain exclusive rights to the owner of a copyright in a protected work, it is virtually axiomatic that the public interest can only be served by upholding copyright protections and, correspondingly, preventing the misappropriation of the skills, creative energies and resources which are invested in the protected work'".[139]

But even without such categorical language, in many copyright cases the policy balance of production incentives is generally determined (without reference to the particular facts) to outweigh access concerns. For example, '[t]he public interest in receiving copyrighted content for free is outweighed by the need to incentivize the creation of original works'.[140] Conversely, some courts have made the opposite error of categorically ignoring the public interest in the greater incentives provided by the increased value of patents when injunctions to cease infringement are granted. For example, in a case that refused to enjoin a product incorporating the patented invention as a small component, the court focused on the somewhat speculative negative effects that would result from an injunction and stated that it was 'unaware of any negative effects that might befall the public in the absence of an injunction'.[141]

These categorical views of the public interests and their relative weights are untenable in the light of *eBay,* which required elaboration and careful consideration of the competing harms. As one court put it when denying an injunction:

> although it is true that the protection of patent rights generally fosters innovation, that, in itself, is insufficient to justify permanent injunctive relief. As the Supreme Court has cautioned us, we must consider the facts of each patent case on its own merits, and not grant permanent injunctive relief based on broad principles, and generalities, of patent law.[142]

However, it is difficult to determine how the courts are actually weighing the competing interests, as they may identify the competing interests and state their balancing outcome without detailing their reasoning.[143]

Thus, more nuanced attention by judges to the factual context and the different public interests, and more explicit development and articulation of the competing policy judgments is clearly warranted. In particular, determining the public interest in regard to injunctive relief requires explicit balancing of the short-term interest in reduced prices, increased access and cumulative innovation that denying injunctions may provide against the long-term interest in promoting investment, creativity, disclosure and distribution that enforcing the exclusive right may provide.[144] Yet, such policy-based judgments are often intentionally eschewed by judges as best left to legislators,[145] even though the legislature in the case of injunctions has delegated the policy-making decisions to the courts in equity. Thus, other countries may wish to more clearly identify the relative weight to be accorded to the competing policy considerations by legislation, and certainly need not follow the precedents of the United States in categorically privileging production and distribution incentives over competition and access considerations.

The concerns typically expressed in opposing compulsory licensing regimes regarding the fairness and social efficiency of involuntary compensation are highly relevant to the choice to grant injunctions to stop infringement (and to impose ongoing royalty compensation). These concerns include: (1) depriving right-holders of liberty and compelling actions they would otherwise refuse; (2) failing to include valuable terms that would be included in voluntary licenses or to adjust for changes to market conditions and the value of the rights over time;[146] (3) converting courts into regulatory bodies that set prices, licensing terms and other industry requirements;[147] (4) interfering with markets in ways that are not economically efficient and that reduce dynamic product competition;[148] and (5) diminishing incentives for investment, invention, disclosure and dissemination.[149] Similar concerns have been expressed in the academic literature in regard to judicial refusal to enjoin continuing infringement, including: (1) unfairly depriving inventors of the worth of their contributions (including when it is incorporated into complex products); (2) increased resort to trade secrecy (and consequent reductions in public disclosure); (3) reduction of capital investments and of consequent market competition (particularly for individuals and small enterprises); and (4) discouragement of the transition from university-based research to commercial products.[150] But the competing values of access and of assuring only objectively reasonable compensation and market behaviors by right-holders have not been thoroughly explored. These issues are ripe for additional scholarly analysis. As part of such analysis and of the developing jurisprudence on preliminary and permanent injunctions, and notwithstanding the traditional hostility in the United States to the issue,[151] it may be appropriate to look to earlier precedents granting compulsory licenses (typically by the judiciary to remedy patent misuse and antitrust violations, but also by the Federal Trade Commission).[152] The compulsory licensing precedents may be particularly relevant to determinations of whether, when and on what conditions to grant ongoing royalty awards. Similarly, courts could look for guidance for ongoing royalties to the developing body of decisions of the Copyright Royalty Board in establishing royalty rates for statutory copyright licenses.[153]

Perhaps more importantly, the concerns expressed against compulsory licensing reflect a philosophic view that intellectual property rights, as exclusive market rights, should convey power to be free not only from competition but also from price regulation[154] and from antitrust (competition law) scrutiny and misuse doctrines when selling products within the scope of the granted rights.[155] As noted above, courts tend to believe that the public's long-term interest in promoting innovation necessarily trumps its short-term interest in obtaining low-cost access to protected goods, and thus price regulation and competition concerns should not be applied to limit market returns for intellectual property rights within their scope of application and during their term. Similarly, a recent Federal Circuit decision has held that the grant of a patent conveys broad immunity from state price regulation of patented products, at least for pharmaceuticals and other medical inventions subject to patent term extensions, because of the careful balance of incentives established by the national legislature to permit such patent-holders to charge what the market will bear so as to create incentives for investment, invention, regulatory approval and ultimate marketing.[156] There are reasons to believe that these cases are wrongly decided and overbroad,[157] given that federal price and product regulation may co-exist with intellectual property rights[158] and given the long-standing recognition that patents grant only a right to exclude and not any affirmative rights (including 'rights to a return on investments in creating patented inventions') or any authorization for market conduct or other immunity from market regulation for patented products.[159] As the Supreme Court held many years ago, '[t]he franchise which the patent grants *consists altogether in the right to exclude* every one from making, using, or vending the thing patented without the permission of the patentee. *This is all that he obtains by the patent*'.[160]

Here, in particular, differences of philosophical approach exist between the US experience and that of other developed and developing countries. Other jurisdictions view intellectual property rights grants and their relation to market regulation differently, adopting disparate approaches to price regulation of goods and services embodying exclusive rights[161] and to determining whether and when intellectual property rights convey antitrust immunity.[162] The TRIPS Agreement does not address price regulation of patented products, except potentially as a non-violation complaint,[163] and at most imposes minimal restrictions on domestic competition policies that regulate intellectual property rights.[164] Accordingly, other countries may choose to permit greater judicial policy-making discretion to regulate market conduct than is thought to exist in the United States. Alternatively, they may further specify by legislation when the violation of an exclusive intellectual property right either should not entail an injunctive remedy or should entail only a remedy that regulates price and private market conduct through prospective conditions (that may include ongoing royalty payments).

CONCLUSION

Although the developing US experience with injunctive relief after *eBay* is highly instructive, other developed and developing countries may choose different approaches in light of the TRIPS Agreement's flexibilities, and thus may and do make different choices regarding each of the many issues involved. Further, countries may point to the increasing flexibility in the developing equitable jurisprudence in the United States to respond to recent pressures being applied in the context of trade negotiations to restrict such flexibility and policy discretion in regard to injunctive relief.

In the context of efforts to negotiate an Anti-Counterfeiting Trade Agreement (ACTA), a proposal is circulating that would require countries to adopt border 'measures to ensure that goods are not released into channels of commerce . . . in cases where goods have been determined by the competent authorities to be infringing IPR'.[165] Such measures would therefore significantly restrict the equitable discretion to determine to refuse to grant permanent injunctions or to grant injunctions on specific terms that would authorize continued infringement. Similarly, trade pressures are being exerted when injunctive relief is not ordered in particular cases, even though such decisions may properly reflect the facts of specific cases, judicial discretion and domestic policy choices. For example, in the context of a report identifying perceived unfair trade practices, the United States recently stated that:

> Argentina amended its patent law in December 2003, as required by a May 2002 agreement between Argentina and the United States. The intention of the amendment was to provide protections for process patents and to ensure that preliminary injunctions were available in intellectual property court proceedings. However, the injunctive relief process has thus far been too slow to be an effective deterrent to patent [infringement].[166]

Whether or not the failure to grant preliminary injunctions adequately deters infringement in the view of any specific country, all countries retain substantial discretion to determine their policies for assessing the adequacy of damages and deciding whether to grant injunctive relief, and to apply those policies flexibly in specific cases. Such retained discretion and flexible application are particularly important for developing countries, given recognition of 'differential and more favourable treatment' under Articles 7 and 8 of the TRIPS Agreement[167] and of the universal premise that the increased flexibility of equity jurisprudence improves the quality of substantive justice.

NOTES

1. The author thanks Michael Carroll, Peter Jaszi and David Ryan for helpful insights and Ida Wahlquist-Ortiz for research assistance.
2. See Carroll (2007): 422–6. See generally Burk and Lemley (2003): 1575.
3. See Carroll (2006): 848.
4. See, e.g., Story (1870): § 3, at 3–4; id., §§ 7–9, at 6–10; id., §§ 25–35, at 19–26.
5. See id., §§ 4–6, at 4–6; id., §§ 36–7, at 26–7.
6. Id., § 33, at 24.

7. See id.
8. See, e.g., id., § 28, at 20–21 ('one of the most striking and distinctive features of courts of equity is, that they can adapt their decrees to all the varieties of circumstances, which may arise, and adjust them to all the peculiar rights of all the parties in interest'); *Hecht Co.* v. *Bowles*, 321 US 321, 329 (1944).
9. Story (1870), *Commentaries on Equity*, supra, 1: § 30, at 21–2.
10. 547 US 388 (2006).
11. Agreement on Trade-Related Aspects of Intellectual Property Rights (TRIPS), 15 Apr. 1994, 33 I.L.M. 81.
12. See, e.g., *Chisum on Patents*, 7–20 (2008): § 20.04[1][e] (Matthew Bender & Co. online edition).
13. *W.L. Gore & Assocs., Inc.* v. *Garlock, Inc.*, 842 F.2d 1275, 1281 (Fed. Cir. 1988).
14. *MercExchange, L.L.C.* v. *eBay, Inc.*, 401 F.3d 1323, 1339 (Fed. Cir. 2005), rev'd in part, 547 US 388 (2006).
15. *Roper Corp.* v. *Litton Sys., Inc.*, 757 F.2d 1266, 1273 (Fed. Cir. 1985).
16. See, e.g., id. at 1271–3.
17. See, e.g., *Opticians Ass'n of Am.* v. *Indep. Opticians of Am.*, 920 F.2d 187, 196 (3d Cir. 1990); *Talley-Ho, Inc.* v. *Coast Cmty. Coll. Dist.*, 889 F.2d 1018, 1029 (11th Cir. 1989); *Int'l Kennel Club, Inc.* v. *Mighty Star, Inc.*, 846 F.2d 1079, 1092 (7th Cir. 1988); *Omega Importing Corp.* v. *Petri-Kine Camera Co.*, 451 F.2d 1190, 1195 (2nd Cir. 1971). See generally *Gilson on Trademarks*, 3–14 (2008): § 14.02[3] [b][ii] (Matthew Bender & Co. 2008 online edition).
18. See, e.g., *Taylor Corp.* v. *Four Seasons Greetings, L.L.C.*, 403 F.3d 958, 967 (8th Cir. 2005); *Silverstein* v. *Penguin Putnam, Inc.*, 368 F.3d 77, 84–5 (2nd Cir. 2004); *Johnson Controls, Inc.* v. *Phoenix Control Sys., Inc.*, 886 F.2d 1173, 1174 (9th Cir. 1989); *Abend* v. *MCA, Inc.*, 863 F.2d 1465, 1478–80 (9th Cir. 1988); *Pac. & S. Co.* v. *Duncan*, 744 F.2d 1490, 1499 (11th Cir. 1984). See generally *Nimmer on Copyright*, 4–14 (2008): § 14.06[A]&[B] (Matthew Bender & Co. 2008 online edition).
19. *Windsurfing Int'l, Inc.* v. *AMF, Inc.*, 782 F.2d 995, 1003 n.12 (1986).
20. 35 USC § 283.
21. See *eBay, Inc.* v. *MercExchange, L.L.C.*, 547 US 388, 391 (2006).
22. See Lemley and Carl Shapiro (2007): 1992–3.
23. See Robinson (1890) (vol. 3): § 1200, at 619 and n.3.
24. See id. § 1200, at 620 and n.4.
25. See id. § 1197, at 611 and n.1.
26. See id. § 1088, at 400 and n.2.
27. *Continental Paper Bag Co.* v. *Eastern Paper Bag Co.*, 210 US 405, 429–30 (1908).
28. See id.
29. See, e.g., Ryan (2008), at 3–18 (unpublished draft 28 July 2008).
30. Id. at 430.
31. See *Specialized Equipment Co.* v. *Coe*, 324 US 370, 375–80 (1945).
32. See 35 §§ 271(d)(4), 283. Cf. Ryan, supra, at 88.
33. *Patry on Copyright* (2008) (vol. 6): § 22.3 (Thomson Reuters/West, online edition). See id. § 22.4 (citing Copyright Act of 1909, § 21).
34. 547 US 388 (2006).
35. Id. at 392 (emphasis added) (quoting 35 USC § 283).
36. *Smith Int'l, Inc.* v. *Hughes Tool Co.*, 718 F.2d 1573, 1577–78 (Fed. Cir. 1983). See Schoenhard (2008), at 196.
37. See *eBay*, 547 US at 393.
38. Id.

39. *H.H. Robertson Co.* v. *United Steel Deck, Inc.*, 820 F.2d 384, 390 (1987) (emphasis added) (citing *Smith Int'l, Inc.*, 715 F.2d at 1581, and *Connell* v. *Sears Roebuck & Co.*, 722 F.2d 1542, 1548 (Fed. Cir. 1983)). See *Chisum on Patents*, supra, 7–20, § 20.04[1][e][i].
40. Id. at 392–3 (citing *New York Times Co.* v. *Tasini*, 533 US 483, 505 (2001)), *Campbell* v. *Acuff-Rose Music, Inc.*, 510 US 569, 578 n.10 (1994), and *Dun* v. *Lumbermen's Credit Ass'n*, 209 US 20, 23–4 (1908)).
41. *eBay*, 548 US at 391.
42. Id. at 393–4 (citations omitted).
43. *MercExchange, L.L.C.*, 401 F.3d at 1338 (quoting *Rite-Hite Corp.* v. *Kelley Co.*, 56 F.3d 1538, 1547 (Fed. Cir. 1995) (*en banc*)). See, e.g., *Hybritech, Inc.* v. *Abbott Labs*, 4 USP.Q. 2d 1001, 1015 (C.D. Cal., 1987) (excepting infringing medical test kits for cancer and hepatitis from permanent injunction, to avoid requiring switching to unavailable or less effective technologies).
44. See, e.g., Ellis et al. (2008): 442–3.
45. *Paice L.L.C* v. *Toyota Motor Corp.*, 504 F.3d 1293, 1313 and n.13 (Fed. Cir. 2007).
46. See id. at 1316–17 (Rader, J., concurring).
47. See id. at 1314–16.
48. See id. at 1313 n.13.
49. See *Root* v. *Lake Shore & M.S. Ry. Co.*, 105 US 189, 206–16 (1881); Robinson (1890), *Law of Patents*, supra, 3: § 1084, at 394–5; id., § 1086, at 396–7.
50. Dannay (2008): 459.
51. See Robinson (1890), *Law of Patents*, supra, 3: §§ 1082–3, at 891–3.
52. Patent Act of 1819, ch. 19, 3 Stat. 481–2 (15 Feb. 1819) (emphasis added).
53. 35 USC § 283 (emphasis added).
54. See, e.g., 17 USC § 502(a) ('may . . . grant temporary and final injunctions on such terms as it may deem reasonable' for copyright infringement); 15 USC § 1116(a) ('shall have power to grant injunctions, according to the principles of equity and upon such terms as the court may deem reasonable' for registered and unregistered trademark infringement and unfair trade practices). See also 15 USC § 1116(a), § 1125(c) (trademark dilution).
55. *Tate Access Floors, Inc.* v. *Interface Architectural Resources, Inc.*, 297 F.3d 1357, 1364 (Fed. Cir. 2002) (preliminary injunctions). See *Int'l Rectifier Corp.* v. *Samsung Elecs. Co.*, 361 F.3d 1355, 1359 (Fed. Cir. 2004) (same for permanent injunctions).
56. See, e.g., *Perfect 10, Inc.* v. *Amazon.com, Inc.*, 487 F.3d 701, 713 (9th Cir. 2007) (copyright preliminary injunctions); *Boston Duck Tours, L.P.* v. *Super Duck Tours, L.L.C.*, 531 F.3d 1, 11 (1st Cir. 2008) (trademark preliminary injunctions); *Christopher Phelps & Assocs., L.L.C.* v. *Galloway*, 492 F.3d 532, 543–7 (4th Cir. 2007) (copyright permanent injunctions); *Angel Flight of Georgia, Inc.* v. *Angel Flight America, Inc.*, 522 F.3d 1200, 1208 (11th Cir. 2008) (trademark permanent injunctions).
57. TRIPS, supra, Art. 44.1 (first emphasis added).
58. Id.
59. Id. Art. 45.1.
60. Id. Art. 50.1.
61. Id. Art. 44.2.
62. Id. Art. 31(h).
63. Id. Art. 44.2.
64. Id.
65. Id.
66. See, e.g., id. Arts. 13, 30.

67.   Id. Art 45.1. See id. Art. 31(a)–(l).
68.   See, e.g., Wegner (2008), 1 (referring to an 'ongoing royalty license' as a compulsory license); id. at 2–18 (suggesting that such remedies are subject to TRIPS Art. 31 and may violate treaty requirements). Cf. *Innogenetics, N.V.* v. *Abbott Labs.*, 512 F.3d 1363, 1381 (Fed. Cir. 2008) (referring to a judgment imposing a 'running royalty' damage award as a compulsory license); *Finisar Corp.* v. *The DirecTV Group, Inc.*, 2006 WL 2037617 (E.D. Tex. 7 July 2006) (final judgment denying injunctive relief, granting a 'compulsory license' and ordering payment of an 'ongoing royalty'), vacated, 523 F.3d 1323 (Fed. Cir. 2008).
69.   Paris Convention for the Protection of Industrial Property, 20 Mar. 1883, revised 14 July 1967, 21 UST 1583, 828 U.N.T.S. 305, Art. 5.A(2) and (4) ('Paris Convention').
70.   See, e.g., *Shatterproof Glass Corp.* v. *Libbey-Owens Ford Co.*, 758 F.2d 613, 628 (Fed. Cir. 1985); *Foster* v. *Am. Mach. & Foundry Co.*, 492 F.2d 1317, 1324 (2nd Cir. 1974); *Royal-McBee Corp.* v. *Smith Corona Marchant, Inc.*, 295 F2d 1, 6 (2nd Cir. 1961).
71.   See, e.g., Gad (2008): 355–63 (discussing WTO dispute settlement understanding panels and appellate body approaches regarding general principles of interpretation and deference to national law under the TRIPS Agreement).
72.   See Gervais (2003): 289, 296, 299 (discussing TRIPS Arts. 41.5, 44.1, 44.2 and 45.1).
73.   Id. at 293 (discussing the 'shall have the authority' language in Art. 43.1).
74.   See, e.g., American Law Institute, *Intellectual Property: Principles Governing Jurisdiction, Choice of Law, and Judgments in Transnational Disputes: Proposed Final Draft* (American Law Inst. 30 March 2007): § 412, at 294–9 (injunctions); id. at § 413, 299–300 (validity, infringement and ownership). See generally Dreyfuss (forthcoming 2009)
75.   See, e.g., *Aro Mfg. Co.* v. *Convertible Top Replacement Co.*, 377 US 476, 507 (1964); *Yale Lock Mfg. Co.* v. *Sargent*, 117 US 536, 552 (1886).
76.   See, e.g., 35 USC § 284; *Crystal Semiconductor Corp.* v. *Tritech Microelectronics Int'l, Inc.*, 246 F.3d 1336, 1357 (Fed. Cir. 2001).
77.   See, e.g., *Canon, Inc.* v. *GCC Int'l Ltd.*, 263 Fed. Appx. 57, 62 (Fed. Cir. 2008); *Sanofi-Synthelabo* v. *Apotex, Inc.*, 470 F.3d 1368, 1381–3 (Fed. Cir. 2006).
78.   See, e.g., *Sanofi-Synthelabo*, 470 F.3d at 1383; Carroll (2007), supra, at 433.
79.   See, e.g., *Innogenetics, N.V.* v. *Abbott Labs.*, 512 F.3d 1363, 1379–81 (Fed. Cir. 2008); *Rite-Hite Corp.*, 56 F.3d at 1574 and n.21 (Nies, J., dissenting).
80.   35 USC § 284.
81.   *Anza* v. *Ideal Steel Supply Corp.*, 547 US 451, 466 (2006).
82.   Compare, e.g., *Rite-Hite Corp.*, 56 F.3d at 1546–51, with id., 56 F.3d at 1556–74 (Nies, J., dissenting).
83.   See *Voda* v. *Cordis Corp.*, 2008 WL 3822801, at *15 (Fed. Cir. 18 Aug. 2008).
84.   35 USC § 284.
85.   Cf. Carroll (2007), supra, at 434–5 (distinguishing 'productive licensing' patent-holders from other non-practicing entities that either do not license or do not have established rates, based on the uncertain effects on licensing market behaviors).
86.   See, e.g., *Commonwealth Scientific and Indust. Res. Org. (CSIRO)* v. *Buffalo Tech. Inc.*, 492 F. Supp. 2d 600, 604–06 (E.D. Tex. 2007).
87.   See, e.g., Prakash-Canjels and Hamilton (2008); Keller (2008): 434.
88.   Dannay, supra, at 458.
89.   See *Georgia-Pacific Corp.* v. *US Plywood Corp.*, 318 F. Supp. 1116 (S.D.N.Y. 1970).

90. See, e.g., Paris Convention, supra, Art. 5.A; TRIPS, supra, Art. 31; 42 USC § 28 USC § 1498(a).

91. TRIPS, supra, Art. 45.1.

92. See, e.g., Santilli (1997): 89; DaSilva (1980): 1.

93. See generally Sterk (2008): 1285.

94. See, e.g., Isaacs (2007): 23–5, 40–41; Drahos (1996): 32–3.

95. See, e.g., *Visto Corp.* v. *Seven Networks, Inc.*, 2006 US Dist. Lexis 91453, at *12 (E.D. Tex. Dec. 19, 2006); *Muniauction, Inc.* v. *Thomson Corp.*, 502 F. Supp. 2d 477, 482 (W.D. Pa. 2007). See also, e.g., *Perdue Pharma L.P.* v. *Boehringer Ingelheim GmbH*, 237 F.3d 1359, 1363 (Fed. Cir. 2001) (rebuttable presumption of irreparable harm from likelihood of success in preliminary relief context). See generally Stiefel (2008): 62 (BNA).

96. See, e.g., *MercExchange, L.L.C.* v. *eBay, Inc.*, 500 F. Supp. 2d 556, 568 (E.D. Va. 2007); *z4 Technologies, Inc.* v. *Microsoft Corp.*, 434 F. Supp. 2d 437, 440 (E.D. Tex. 2006).

97. See, e.g., *Sanofi-Synthelabo*, 470 F.3d at 1382; *Abbott Labs.* v. *Sandoz, Inc.*, 500 F. Supp. 2d 807, 843 (N.D. Ill. 2007).

98. See, e.g., *JA Apparel Corp.* v. *Abboud*, 2008 WL 2329533, at *22 (S.D.N.Y. 5 June 2008).

99. See, e.g., *Propet USA, Inc.* v. *Shugart*, 2007 WL 4376204, at *2 (W.D. Wash. 13 Dec. 2007).

100. See, e.g., *Warner Bros. Ent. Inc.* v. *RDR Books*, 575 F. Supp. 2d 513, 519 (S.D.N.Y. 2008) at *63–*65.

101. Ellis et al. (2008) supra, at 446.

102. *Power-One, Inc.* v. *Artesyn Techs., Inc.*, 2008 US Dist. Lexis 30338, at *5 (E.D. Tex. 11 Apr. 2008).

103. See, e.g., *Visto Corp.*, 2006 US Dist. Lexis 91453, at *13; *Brooktrout, Inc.* v. *Eicon Networks Corp.*, 2007 US Dist. Lexis 43107, at *4–*5 (E.D. Tex. 14 Jun. 2007); Carroll (2007), supra at 422 and n.47.

104. See, e.g., *CSIRO*, 492 F. Supp. 2d at 606; *The Mortg. Mkt. Guide, L.L.C.* v. *Freedman Report, L.L.C.*, 2008 US Dist. Lexis 56871, at *131–*2 (D.N.J. 28 July 2008).

105. See, e.g., *Continental Paper Bag Co.*, 210 US at 430; Brief for *General Elec. Co., 3M Co., the Proctor & Gamble Co., E.I. DuPont De Nemours and Co., and Johnson & Johnson as Amici Curaie Suggesting Affirmance, eBay, Inc.* v. *MercExchange L.L.C.*, 547 US 388 (2006), at 14 (citing Story (1870) *Commentaries*, vol. 2 at 236, and *Archer* v. *Greenville Sand & Gravel Co.*, 233 US 60, 63–6 (1911)).

106. See, e.g., *Swann* v. *Charlotte-Mecklenburg Bd. of Ed.*, 402 US 1, 22–32 (1971).

107. See, e.g., *Paice*, 504 F.3d 1314–15; id. at 1316–17 (Rader, J., concurring).

108. See, e.g., Lemley (2008): 611–19. See generally Lemley and Shapiro (2007), supra.

109. See, e.g., *Biomedical Pat. Mgmt. Corp.* v. *State of Cal.*, 505 F.3d 1328 (Fed. Cir. 2007).

110. See *eBay*, 547 USat 396–7 (Kennedy, J., concurring); *z4 Technologies, Inc.*, 434 F. Supp. 2d at 440–41.

111. See Carroll (2007), supra, at 436–9.

112. See, e.g., *Rite-Hite Corp.*, 56 F.3d at 1549 (citing *State Indus. Inc.* v. *Mor-Flo Indus., Inc.*, 883 F.2d 1573, 1577 (Fed. Cir. 1989), *Velo-Bind, Inc.* v. *Minnesota Mining & Mfg. Co.*, 647 F.2d 965 (9th Cir. 1981), and various cases applying the entire market value rule to lost profit and reasonable royalty damage awards).

113. See, e.g, S.1145, 110th Cong., 2nd Sess. § 4 (2008) (as reported by Committee

on Judiciary); *Georgia-Pacific*, 317 F. Supp. at 1120 (factor 13, discussing the 'portion of the realized profit that should be credited to the invention as distinguished from non-patented elements'). See generally Bensen and White (2008).

114. Maskus and Reichman (2005).
115. See generally Maskus (1998): 109.
116. See *Lear* v. *Adkins*, 395 US 653, 670–72 (1969). Cf. *Medimmune, Inc.* v. *Genetech, Inc.*, 127 S. Ct. 764, 769–77 (2007) (holding that licensees need not breach their agreements in order to have standing to file declaratory actions challenging patent validity). See generally Sarnoff (2008): 1044–50.
117. See, e.g., Farrell and Merges (2004): 948–60; Sag and Rohde (2007): 22–3.
118. See *Blonder-Tongue Labs., Inc.* v. *Univ. of Ill. Found.*, 402 US 313, 317–49 (1971).
119. *Genentech, Inc.* v. *Novo Nordisk A/S*, 108 F.3d 1361, 1364 (Fed. Cir. 1997). But see *Abbott Labs* v. *Sandoz, Inc.*, 2008 WL 4636167, at *22–*28 (Fed. Cir. 21 Oct. 2008) (raising a substantial question may be insufficient to negative likelihood of success on the merits under the applicable burden of proof).
120. See *Abbott Labs* v. *Sandoz, Inc.*, 544 F.3d 1341, 1344–5, 1363–71 (Fed. Cir. 2008) (citing, inter alia, *Gonzales* v. *O Centro Espirita Beneficiente Uniao do Vegetal*, 546 US 417, 429 (2006)).
121. See, e.g., *In re Ciprofloxacin Hydrochloride Antitrust Litig.*, 2008 WL 4570669, at *6–*10 (Fed. Cir. 15 Oct. 2008); *In re Tamoxifen Citrate Antitrust Litig.*, 466 F.3d 187, 205 (2nd Cir. 2006). See generally Holman (2007): 490.
122. See, e.g., *Gambale* v. *Deutsche Bank AG*, 377 F.3d 133, 143 (2nd Cir. 2004); Holman (2007), supra, at 549–50.
123. See Sarnoff (2008), supra, at 1000.
124. See, e.g., *Tiber Labs. L.L.C.* v. *Hawthorn Pharms. Inc.*, 527 F. Supp. 2d 1373, 1380 (N.D. Ga. 2007); *z4 Technologies, Inc.*, 434 F. Supp. 2d at 440. See generally Stiefel (2008), supra, at 62.
125. See, e.g., *N. Am. Med. Corp.* v. *Axiom Worldwide, Inc.*, 522 F.3d 1211, 1226–9 (11th Cir. 2008).
126. See, e.g., *Altana Pharm. AG* v. *Teva Pharms. USA, Inc.*, 532 F. Supp. 2d 666, 681–4 (D.N.J. 2007) (citing *Nutrition 21* v. *United States*, 930 F.2d 867, 871 (Fed. Cir. 1991)).
127. Id. at 683 (D.N.J. 2007) (quoting *Eli Lilly & Co.* v. *Am. Cyanamid Co.*, 82 F.3d 1568, 1578 (Fed. Cir. 1996), and *Illinois Tool Works, Inc.* v. *Grip-Pak, Inc.*, 906 F.2d 679, 683 (Fed. Cir. 1990)).
128. See, e.g., *Everett Labs., Inc.* v. *Breckenridge Pharm., Inc.*, 2008 WL 4053447, at *8–*9 (D.N.J. 26 Aug. 2008) (citing, inter alia, *Amado* v. *Microsoft Corp.*, 573 F. Supp. 2d 855, 865–66 (D.N.J. 2008).
129. See, e.g., *Lennon* v. *Premise Media Corp.*, 556 F. Supp. 2d 310, 319 and n.1 (S.D.N.Y. 2 June 2008).
130. See, e.g., *Warner Bros. Ent.*, 575 F. Supp. 2d at 552–3.
131. See, e.g., *Abbott Labs* v. *Andrx Pharms., Inc.*, 452 F.3d 1331, 1384 (Fed. Cir. 2006).
132. *CSIRO*, 492 F. Supp. 2d at 607.
133. See, e.g., id.
134. *Telequip Corp.* v. *The Change Exchange*, 2006 WL 2385425, at *2 (N.D.N.Y. 15 Aug. 2006) (quoting *Honeywell Int'l, Inc.* v. *Universal Avionics Sys. Corp.*, 397 F. Supp. 2d 537, 547 (D. Del. 2005)).
135. *Everett*, 573 F. Supp. 2d at 870.
136. See, e.g., *Brooktrout, Inc.*, supra, 2007 US Dist. Lexis 43107, at *5; *O2 Micro Int'l Ltd.* v. *Beyond Innovation Tech. Co.*, 2007 US Dist. Lexis 25948, at *9 (E.D. Tex. 21 Mar. 2007). Cf. *eBay*, 547 US at 391.

137. See, e.g., *Sun Optics, Inc.* v. *FGX Int'l, Inc.*, 2007 US Dist. Lexis 56351, at *3 (2 Aug. 2007); *National League of Junior Cotillions* v. *Porter*, 2007 US Dist. Lexis 58117, at *34 (W.D. N.C. 9 Aug. 2007).

138. Everett Labs., 573 F. Supp. 2d at 870–71 (quoting *Pfizer, Inc.* v. *Teva Pharms, USA, Inc.*, 429 F.3d 1364, 1382 (Fed. Cir. 2005)).

139. *Advance Magazine Pubs.* v. *Leach*, 466 F. Supp. 2d 628, 638 (D. Md. 2006) (quoting *Apple Computer, Inc.* v. *Franklin Computer Corp.*, 714 F.2d 1240, 1254–5 (3rd Cir. 1983)). See also *UMG Recordings, Inc.* v. *Blake*, 2007 US Dist. Lexis 46414, at *8 (E.D.N.C. 26 June 2007).

140. *Metro-Goldwyn-Meyer Studios, Inc.* v. *Grokster, Ltd.*, 518 F. Supp. 2d 1197, 1222 (C.D. Cal. 2007). See also *Disney Enters. Inc.* v. *Delane*, 446 F. Supp. 2d 402, 408 (D. Md. 2006).

141. *z4 Technologies, Inc.*, 434 F. Supp. 2d at 444.

142. *Respironics, Inc.* v. *Invacare, Corp.*, 2008 US Dist. Lexis 1174, at *17 (W.D. Pa. 8 Jan. 2008).

143. See, e.g., *Sanofi-Synthelabo* v. *Apotex, Inc.*, 492 F. Supp. 2d 353, 397 (S.D.N.Y 2007).

144. See, e.g., Carroll (2007), supra, at 440–41.

145. Cf. *Festo Corp.* v. *Shoketsu Kinzoku Kogyo Kabushiki Co.*, 535 US 722, 732 (2002) (referring policy objections to the doctrine of equivalents to Congress); *Novartis Pharms Corp.* v. *Teva Pharms USA, Inc.*, 2007 US Dist. Lexis 65792, at *43 (6 Sept. 2007) (recognizing valid public interest arguments of both parties but denying a preliminary injunction 'based on the other parts of the analysis').

146. See, e.g., *CSIRO*, 492 F. Supp. 2d at 606.

147. See, e.g., Nielsen and Samardzija (2007): 535.

148. See, e.g., Whitaker (1974): 165–8.

149. See id. at 161.

150. See, e.g., Beckerman-Rodau (2007): 194–202.

151. See, e.g., Dratler (1994): § 3.03[2].

152. See, e.g., Reichman and Hasenzahl (2003): 21–2.

153. See 17 USC § 114. See generally Robertson (2008): 543.

154. See, e.g., Epstein (2008): 227.

155. See, e.g., *Professional Real Estate Investors, Inc.* v. *Columbia Pictures Indus., Inc.*, 508 US 49, 56–60 (1993); *Monsanto* v. *McFarling*, 363 F.3d 1336, 1341 (Fed. Cir. 2004); *Virginia Panel Corp.* v. *Mac Panel Co.*, 133 F.3d 860, 868–74 (Fed. Cir. 1997); *Mallinkrodt, Inc.* v. *Medipart, Inc.*, 976 F.2d 700, 703–09 (Fed. Cir. 1992). Cf. *Ill. Tool Works Inc.* v. *Indep. Ink, Inc.*, 547 US 28, 42–3 (2006); *United States* v. *Masonite Corp.*, 316 US 265, 277 (1942). See generally Economides and Herbert (2008): 460–68.

156. See *Biotechnology Indus, Org.* v. *Dist. of Columbia*, 496 F.3d 1362, 1371–4 (Fed. Cir. 2007) (citing the Drug Price Competition and Patent Term Restoration Act of 1984 (the 'Hatch-Waxman Act'), Pub. L. No. 98–417, 98 Stat. 1585 (codified as amended at 35 USC §156)), pet. for reh'g denied, 505 F.3d 1344 (Fed. Cir. 2007).

157. The decision did not properly apply the standard for federal conflicts pre-emption of state laws. See Sarnoff (2007): 31–2.

158. See id. at 32–3.

159. Id. at 33. See id. at 34.

160. *Bloomer* v. *McQuewan*, 55 US 539, 549 (1852)) (second emphasis added).

161. See, e.g., Abraham (2002): 236 (discussing price regulation of pharmaceuticals in the UK); Vernon et al. (2006): 182 (noting that lower drug prices result from price regulation and lower incomes in countries such as Canada); Wechkin

(1995): 247–50 (discussing drug price regulation in New Zealand); Faunce (2007): 1–3 (discussing price reimbursement regulation in Australia).
162. See, e.g., Coco (2008): 10–24.
163. See, e.g., Abbott (2000): 172.
164. See, e.g., Apostolopoulos (2007): 267–8, 273.
165. 'Discussion Paper on a Possible Anti-Counterfeiting Trade Agreement' (leaked draft 2008): 3, available at http://ipjustice.org/wp/wp-content/uploads/ACTA-discussion-paper-1.pdf.
166. '2008 National Trade Estimate Report on Foreign Trade Barriers' (2008): 24, available at http://www.ustr.gov/assets/Document_Library/Reports_Publications/2008/2008_NTE_Report/asset_upload_file365_14652.pdf.
167. Reichman (2008b), supra at 80 (discussing TRIPS, supra, Arts. 7, 8).

7. Enforcement for development: why not an agenda for the developing world?

Hong Xue[1]

INTRODUCTION

Enforcement has become a new battlefield in international intellectual property law. While insistently consolidating enforcement in their legal system, which is most clearly exemplified by the United States' Digital Millennium Copyright Act (DMCA) and the European Union's Directive on the Enforcement of Intellectual Property Rights (Enforcement Directive), the developed countries are steadily pushing their enforcement agenda to the developing world. A score of developing countries have been sued at the Dispute Settlement Body (DSB) of the World Trade Organization (WTO) for not only the issue of protection but enforcement of intellectual property.[2] An Enforcement Agenda has been put on the table of the World Intellectual Property Organization.[3] Most prominently, a new treaty-making process to create a new global standard for intellectual property enforcement has just been launched 'secretly' by the developed world led by United States, the European Commission, Japan and Switzerland. The new treaty, the Anti-Counterfeiting Trade Agreement, which is well-known for its fancy acronym 'ACTA', is undeniably primarily targeting the developing world.[4]

Tightening and increasing the requirements on intellectual property enforcement in international intellectual property law has a tremendous negative impact on the developing countries, which are already striving to meet the substantive standards on intellectual property protection required by the TRIPS Agreement. Under the stick-and-carrot policy (trade sanctions, WTO DSB, technical assistance, and so on), the developing countries are being pressed hard to revamp their domestic enforcement system to meet the standards set out by the developed world. Through analyzing the case of the United States versus China at the WTO, this chapter attempts to show the caveats of imposing the enforcement agenda on the developing countries, and advocate that the developing countries should resist the unreasonable pressure and make their own pro-development agenda.

AN ANATOMY OF UNITED STATES VERSUS CHINA AT THE WTO

On 10 April 2007, the United States filed a complaint with the World Trade Organization (WTO), requesting consultations with China concerning certain measures pertaining to the protection and enforcement of intellectual property rights in China. Although the United States has been, since 1992, monitoring several rounds of bilateral negotiation to press China to upgrade its intellectual property protection (Xue, 2005), this is the first time that it resorts to the WTO dispute settlement system. On 25 September 2007, the WTO Dispute Settlement Body, at the second request of the United States,[5] established a panel to review the complaint against China's protection and enforcement of intellectual property rights.[6] On 18 July 2008, the panel communicated with the Chair of the DSB that the panel would not be able to complete its work within six months from the date of the panel's composition.[7] The panel had planned to issue the final report by November 2008, but under vigorous contest in the parties, the final report was not released until the end of January 2009. On 9 October 2008, an 'interim' draft report made by the panel was leaked to the media.[8] It said that the interim report was circulated to the United States and China as a part of the WTO dispute settlement process. Under the WTO rules, the parties to a dispute may file comments with a panel following an interim ruling, which the panel can take into account before issuing its final decision. Panels rarely make major changes between their interim and final rulings. The final ruling was rendered on 26 January 2009. Apart from a few procedural clarifications and minor corrections, the panel's findings and conclusions are substantively consistent with the interim report. At the time of writing this chapter, the formal report of the panel is still yet to be issued.

The United States' complaint filed on 10 April 2007 addresses four matters on China's intellectual property enforcement measures. On 21 August 2007, the United States filed the Request for the Establishment of a Panel to the WTO, stating that the consultations with China on 7–8 June 2007 provided some helpful clarifications but did not resolve the whole dispute. It seems that one of the 'helpful clarifications' is that the United States dropped one of the claims against Chinese criminal penalties.[9] So, there are only three matters in the United States' complaint, namely the thresholds for criminal procedures and penalties, disposal of goods confiscated by customs authorities that infringe intellectual property rights and denial of copyright and related rights protection and enforcement to works that have not been authorized for publication or distribution within China. This chapter will anatomize these claims to demonstrate how the enforcement agenda imposes the TRIPS-plus obligations and squeezes out the policy flexibilities.

Thresholds for Criminal Procedures and Penalties

The United States complained that China's lack of criminal procedures and penalties for commercial-scale counterfeiting and piracy as a result of the thresholds appears to be inconsistent with China's obligations under Articles 41.1 and 61 of the TRIPS Agreement.

Strengthening criminal penalties has always been one of the key agendas of the United States' trade negotiation with China. In accordance with Chinese Criminal Law, certain acts of trademark counterfeiting and copyright piracy may only be subject to criminal procedure and penalties 'if the circumstances are serious' or 'if the amount of illegal gains is relatively large', or 'if the circumstances are especially serious'. Numerical standards are set up for implementation in the judicial system. One of the most famous examples is the drop of the threshold for criminal prosecution from seizure of 1000 pirate optical discs to 500 copies.[10] Both the establishment and the modification of the numerical standards are clearly pushed by the United States Trade Representative (USTR).[11] Despite all these efforts, the USTR still filed the complaint to the WTO five days after China dropped the threshold to 500 copies.

According to the United States' complaint, Chinese criminality thresholds violate Article 61.1 of the TRIPS Agreement by failing to effectively combat any act of willful trademark counterfeiting or copyright piracy on a commercial scale. However, Article 61.1 of the TRIPS Agreement, in addition to willfulness, provides another criterion, that is, seriousness.[12] Only where willful trademark counterfeiting or copyright piracy reaches 'a commercial scale', should it be subject to criminal proceeding and penalties. The threshold for criminality provided in Chinese Criminal Law is exactly the criterion of seriousness. Since the TRIPS Agreement does not define what a commercial scale is, Chinese Criminal Law has the liberty to set out the calibrations commensurate to the domestic social economic situations.[13] Therefore, it is baseless for the United States to claim that the Chinese criminal thresholds, per se, are violating the TRIPS Agreement. China should be able to, like any other WTO Members, define what 'commercial scale' is in its domestic law. The author of this chapter has submitted on several international occasions that the WTO DSB should not be utilized to squeeze out the policy wiggle room permitted by the TRIPS Agreement. Unifying the implementation standards and intervening in a Member's legal details are equivalent to TRIPS-plus.[14]

According to the leaked interim draft report, the WTO panel actually echoes this view and sided with China on this issue, concluding that the United States had not provided sufficient evidence that smaller-scale piracy (below 500 optical discs) qualified as 'commercial-scale' piracy. The panel report marked the first time a WTO panel was asked to interpret the issue of 'commercial scale'.

The dispute over criminal threshold, if assessed in a broader legal context, has another legal significance. Criminal proceedings have never been the primary enforcement mechanism for intellectual property rights. Instead, most claimants make use of the civil process, partly because its technique and atmosphere are appropriate to the assertion of private property rights among businesspeople, and partly because the types of remedy – in particular injunctions and damages – are more useful than punishment in the name of the state (Cornish and Llewelyn, 2007, pp. 60–64). Most important of all, criminal proceedings impose a high burden of proof on the prosecution side, which inevitably prevents many infringing acts, on a commercial scale or not, from being subject to criminal penalties. The criminal proceeding, which is by nature a peripheral and supplemental element in the enforcement system, cannot succinctly reflect the overall effectiveness of intellectual property enforcement for the purpose of Article 41.1 of the TRIPS Agreement.

From another perspective, the thresholds in Chinese Criminal Law are generally applied to many types of crimes, not specifically for crimes against intellectual property rights. The threshold-setting is related to the whole prosecution policy and administrative system. In the Chinese legal system, there is a distinction between ordinary offences (comparable to 'misdemeanours') and crimes (comparable to 'felonies'). The former are largely handled through administrative procedures, instead of criminal proceedings. One of the considerations for such systematic design is that it would be extremely costly and inefficient to prosecute each and every ordinary offence through criminal proceeding in a country as big and populous as China. The thresholds help to filter a large percentage of cases into the more dynamic administrative procedures and make sure the criminal proceedings are only targeting the serious cases that are most detrimental to the public interests.

The TRIPS Agreement does not prevent a country, with a legal culture and structure suited to its own needs, from conforming to any other model of legal proceedings with comparable efficacy. The United States' claim against the Chinese criminal thresholds is, however, violating the principles of the TRIPS Agreement, Article 1.1 and Article 41.5, which allow the Members to determine the appropriate method of implementing the provisions of this agreement with their own legal system and practice and to make sure that the enforcement requirements do not create any obligation to put in place a judicial system for the enforcement of intellectual property rights distinct from that of the enforcement of law in general. The Chinese thresholds for criminal proceedings and penalties are generally applied in the enforcement of law, not specifically for the enforcement of intellectual property rights. If the criminal thresholds were only removed with respect to trademark counterfeiting and copyright piracy, it would make the whole criminal system unbalanced, which is not an appropriate method to implement the TRIPS Agreement within the Chinese legal system and practice and, more seriously, makes the intellectual property enforcement distinct from the enforcement of law in general, which could disturb the normal allocation of judicial resources.

The United States' claim is heavily relying on Article 61.1 of the TRIPS Agreement. It seems true that some of the willful trademark counterfeiting and copyright piracy cannot be subject to the criminal proceeding in China due to the thresholds set at in Chinese Criminal

Law. However, Article 61.1, a provision in the enforcement part of the agreement, should be interpreted coherently with the General Provisions and Basic Principles of the Agreement. The United States' claim actually raises one of the most fundamental issues in the implementation of the TRIPS Agreement: is there a hierarchy between the principles and general provisions and specific provisions? When there is a conflicting interpretation, should the principles and general provisions prevail? Since Article 61.1 is only a specific provision on enforcement, while Article 1.1 is a principle and Article 41.5 a general provision to the whole section on enforcement, it should not be cited out of context of the TRIPS Agreement or isolated into an absolute obligation on WTO Members.

Disposal of Goods Confiscated by Customs Authorities that Infringe Intellectual Property Rights

In the United States' complaint, China's customs measures for disposing of confiscated goods that infringe intellectual property rights appear to be inconsistent with China's obligations under Article 46 of the TRIPS Agreement, primarily because the relevant Chinese laws require the customs authorities to give priority to disposal options that allow such goods to enter the channels of commerce (for instance, through auctioning the goods after removing their infringing features). Only if the infringing features cannot be removed must the goods be destroyed.

According to the leaked interim draft report, the WTO panel found that China violates Article 46 of TRIPS by auctioning off counterfeit goods seized by the government after removing the infringing trademark. Article 46 of the TRIPS Agreement states that infringing goods should be 'disposed of outside the channels of commerce in such a manner as to avoid any harm caused to the right-holder' or destroyed. It specifies that this should be done 'without compensation' to the infringer in order to provide an 'effective deterrent.' Article 46 also states that the removal of a fake trademark 'shall not be sufficient, other than in exceptional cases', to justify releasing goods back into the market.

The panel's ruling, although not completely baseless, is not unarguable. Under the Chinese Customs Intellectual Property Rights Regulations and the Implementing Measures, the confiscated infringing goods can be:

- used for charitable purposes;
- sold to the right-owner with their consent;
- auctioned off after removing the infringing features; or
- destroyed.[15]

Therefore, the confiscated goods are disposed hierarchically. The first and the last option can effectively keep the goods out of the commercial channel. The second option, selling to the right-owner, is roughly consistent with Article 46 of the TRIPS Agreement. Only the third option, public auctioning off the goods, is controversial, but it is only in third place in the hierarchy. Disposal by auction is conditional and exceptional. Such disposal option is never prioritized, as against the claim of the United States. The option also emphasizes the removal of the infringing features from the goods before auctioning off any goods. Article 46 of the TRIPS Agreement does allow a disposal option distinct from destruction of the goods. The only issue is how to make sure the disposal does not cause any harm to the right-owner. The third option seemingly disposes of the goods in the channel of commerce. However, as far as the infringing features have been thoroughly and completely cleared, the goods are no longer infringing and cannot cause any harm to the right-owner any more. It is very unreasonable if such purely physical objects are banned from being appropriately utilized. Additionally, auction does not 'compensate' the infringer in any sense since all the income goes to the state.

Article 46 of the TRIPS Agreement does specify that simple removal of the trademark unlawfully affixed is not sufficient to permit the release of counterfeit trademark goods into the channels of commerce, but that requirement is only applied to 'counterfeit trademark goods'. The United States' complaint attempts to generalize such special stipulation to all the confiscated goods that are infringing to the other intellectual property rights, such as geographical indications.

Even with respect to counterfeit trademark goods, removal of infringing features from the goods as prescribed by the Chinese Customs Intellectual Property Rights Regulations is not equivalent to the 'simple removal of the trademark unlawfully affixed'. It may well involve repackaging, rearranging or reorganizing. In this regard, the wording in Article 59 of the TRIPS Agreement provides some clue.[16] Under Article 59, the authorities shall not allow the re-exportation of the counterfeit trademark goods 'in an unaltered state'. Once it is in an altered state with all the infringing features cleared, why should it not be allowed to be re-exported or sent back to the channels of commerce otherwise?

Denial of Copyright and Related Rights Protection and Enforcement to Works that Have Not Been Authorized for Publication or Distribution Within China

The United States claims that China appears to be acting inconsistently with its obligations under the TRIPS Agreement by denying the protection of its Copyright Law to creative works of authorship that have not been authorized for, or are otherwise prohibited from, publication or distribution within China.

With respect to this issue, the WTO panel found that China violates Articles 9.1 and 41.1 of TRIPS Agreement by denying copyright protection to works that do not meet the standards of Chinese censorship. In China, a work is not protected by copyright if it has been rejected by censors for distribution in China; however, a work still being reviewed by censors is protected. The WTO panel ruled that all copyrighted works must be protected.

It seems that China has a rather slim chance of championing against this claim. The primary target of the claim is Article 4 of the Chinese Copyright Law, under which works the publication or distribution of which is prohibited by law shall not be protected by this law. Under Article 9.1 of the TRIPS Agreement, which assimilates the automatic protection principle of the Berne Convention, the enjoyment and the exercise of copyright shall not be subject to any formality. Although the Chinese law states that copyright shall be protected on the date when a work is created,[17] the censorship system on publication and distribution is above copyright and any other legal protection.

Where the publication or distribution of a work is legally prohibited, any attempt of enforcement of the 'copyright' will be an immediate violation of the law.[18] On the other hand, any 'piracy' against such a work will be directly violating the law and public order as well. In such a circumstance, the sanctions by the public authorities will supersede any private remedy.[19]

If viewed in a broader context, the dispute may involve the *ordre public* exception under Article 17 of the Berne Convention or public morals exception under Article XX GATT.[20] But the author of this chapter has very little sympathy with these arguments. Neither exception implies that the power of censorship can restrict or replace the obligation to copyright protection. In other words, resorting to the censorship argument does not mean that censored works (or yet-to-be-authorized works) do not enjoy copyright protection.[21]

Nonetheless, Article 4 of the Chinese Copyright Law is one of links of the nationwide censorship system. If the United States had any hidden political agenda beyond the claim on copyright enforcement, it is filing a claim *ultra vires* and suspiciously abusing the WTO DSB proceeding.

The Case as a Tester

The case is still in proceedings. Many predict that both parties will compromise and eventually settle the dispute because of the tremendous trade interest between the two economic giants. Whatever the decision will be, the dispute concerning intellectual property enforcement between the largest developed country and the largest developing country has already illustrated some critical issues. It presents a vivid example of how a developed country intervenes, irrespective of any socioeconomic impact, into the details of law-making and enforcement of a developing country. The case is testing the cornerstone of modern international intellectual property law, that is, the principle of territoriality, testing whether calibrations of various doctrinal devices of national law are still viable as against the sweeping one-size-fits-all approach, testing whether the TRIPS Agreement still cherishes its objectives and principles that enshrine the higher level of value than enforcement, and testing whether implementation of the TRIPS Agreement should be in harmony with the international trend of access to knowledge that has been recognized by the Doha Declaration on TRIPS and Public Health and World Intellectual Property Organization (WIPO) Development Agenda.[22] The case is a gold tester and the whole world is watching.

CAVEATS OF THE ENFORCEMENT AGENDA

The developed countries' enforcement agenda does not confine itself to any particular international forum or any specific plan or scheme. It is a blanket of systematic programmes from existing strategic forum to emerging new forum, from bilateral agreements to multilateral regime, from the soft conversion through technical assistance to the hard push through trade sanctions.[23] Its detrimental effect has not been fully revealed to the developing world, but the caveats on law-making, enforcement measures and innovative development is becoming clear.

Intervening Law-making

The enforcement agenda does not merely intend to enforce the rules that have been set out but to create new, rigid and comprehensive norms. For instance, integrating the WIPO Internet Treaties into the enforcement agenda will make the developing countries liable to enforce the protection of technological measures and rights management information. Enforcement has become a new medium to impose an intellectual property maximalist approach and TRIPS-plus or even TRIPS-plus-plus obligations.

The developing countries that do not have a full-grown checks-and-balances political system and mature civil society, are particularly vulnerable to the pressure on the legislative demands. One fundamental principle of democracy is the balance between powers. If and when executive governments want to impose unacceptable threats to citizens' freedoms, legislative power should be able to stop this attempt and judiciary authorities can counterbalance it with fundamental rights. One of the striking examples is that the European Parliament voted decisively against the 'three strikes' act strongly proposed by the French government because termination of Internet access is in conflict with 'civil liberties and human rights and with the principles of proportionality, effectiveness and dissuasiveness', all core values of the European Union.[24] But in a country with only rubber-stamped legislature, the maximalist law can easily be adopted as far as the executive is bent to the pressure on enforcement. Civil society can play an important role in lobbying against the biased and partial legislative initiatives from the interest groups. For instance, a number of civil society organizations have begun to push back against ACTA by either arousing the public awareness or lobbying to the domestic legislators.[25] But in many developing countries, the bottom-up civil movement against maximalism is still at the very primitive stage and hardly has any substantive influence on law-making.

The WIPO's technical assistance scheme could have provided a useful guide to the developing countries. Unfortunately, the technical assistance fails to fulfill its mission. An officer of the WIPO Advisory Committee on Enforcement stated in an interview:

> we inform them (developing countries) that a specific provision is not in line with the international obligations that their country has agreed to, or we tell them that this is an issue which is not dealt with in international agreements. Even where there is no obligation and the country is free to choose, we may have to advise the government officials that according to our experience the solution which they have in mind is unlikely to work in practice.[26]

Such inside views show that the WIPO technical assistance actually adopts the maximalist approach. For fear of 'un-workability' warned of by the WIPO and the threat of lawsuit at the WTO DSB, the developing countries may well ignore or be unaware of their long-term interests and trade off intellectual property legislation for their immediate trade interests.

Burdening the Enforcement System

The developed countries have been pushing very hard to make the developing world strengthen their intellectual property enforcement measures, especially criminal and administrative measures. However, these measures can only be enforced at tremendous public expense. Increment and strength of public enforcement measures will inevitably impose an economic burden on the developing countries and divert the priorities of these countries, such as prosecution of violent crimes or relief of poverty. Some countries will have to set up special law enforcement systems and thus unnecessarily assume the TRIPS-plus obligation.

The widespread use of criminal proceedings and penalties is a big concern. Even within the developed countries, uniformity of criminal law encounters strong resistance. For instance, the EU Enforcement Directive has to leave the criminal penalties at the disposal of the Member States' jurisdiction.[27] Criminal punishments are related to human rights protection. Expansion of criminal punishment to uncommercial activities (non-profit facilitation), such as peer-to-peer file-sharing, is not only TRIPS-plus but endangering overall balance of the criminal system. Such serious public policy issues should not be decided one-sidedly and hastily.

Border control and other administrative measures are at the expense of public resources and should not be used by the intellectual property industry as their private police. In addition, custom measures have their inherent limits. Overreaching these measures can unreasonably impair the other parties' legitimate interests. Under Article 51 of the TRIPS Agreement, a Member shall apply the customs measures to 'the importation of counterfeit trademark or pirated copyright goods', but is not obliged to extend such measures to the 'other infringements of intellectual property' or 'exportation' of the goods.[28]

There is rationale behind such distinctions. For instance, a patent infringement is very hard to determine through superficial observation of the goods by the customs officers who might not have the relevant technological expertise;[29] and, targeting the exported goods would inevitably harm a manufacture-based economy that heavily relies on the overseas market.

Although it is not in the interests of the developing countries to go beyond what is required by the TRIPS Agreement, the enforcement agenda is clearly pushing to make all the optional measures mandatory and urging the developing countries to follow the more rigid and extensive customs enforcement adopted by the developed countries. For example, the European Council Regulation (EC) No. 1383/2003 on customs actions against goods suspected of infringing intellectual property rights covers not only counterfeit and pirated goods but also goods that infringe a patent and other intellectual property rights.[30] The regulation covers not only imports but also exports or re-exports.[31] Chinese Regulations on Customs Protection of Intellectual Property Rights slavishly follows EC No. 1383/2003,[32] which has seriously damaged the exportation of the Chinese OEM-reliant manufacture industry.[33] Ironically, the WIPO Advisory Committee on Enforcement believes that the other developing countries should follow the Chinese model.[34]

Legalizing Private Enforcement

ICT (information and communication technologies) and the Internet offer new opportunities for the developing world. But the enforcement agenda is threatening development countries' innovative development. Those legalized private enforcement measures are hampering IT (information-technology) companies, most of which

are small or medium-sized enterprises, from optimizing their technological innovations in the new economy.

Under tremendous pressure from the content industry, the Internet
service providers (ISPs) are being forced to become the private police
for copyright enforcement. Instead of adapting the old business
model to the new network-based communication environment, the
copyright industry is determined to make the ISPs responsible for
falling profits and losing customers. Unfortunately, no matter how
hard the ISPs try to prevent the people from swapping music on the
Internet, they are not likely to save the phonogram industry from
falling sales of CDs.[35] The highhanded content industry is backed
by the law. If ISPs do not help with the fight against music or any
other content piracy, then the government will bring in legislation
to make them cooperate. Since the notice-and-takedown measures
came to life from the Digital Millennium Copyright Act (DMCA), a
number of the developing countries have followed the step in fear of
the trade sanctions.[36]

Private enforcement is legalized in other aspects. Among others,
Digital Rights Management (DRM) is now sheltered and perhaps
sharpened by the law. Copyright-owners can always adopt technological measures to protect their rights as far as they have the
capacity and resources to do so,[37] but it is dubious why the law
should intervene and provide an additional layer of protection to the
technological protection measures. Although the anti-circumvention
law exemplified by the DMCA fuels tension between copyright and
the Internet, the developing world has been pushed hard to follow.[38]
Its negative impacts of locking up the useful contents and hindering
people's access to knowledge deserve careful assessment from the
prospective of the developing countries (Xue, 2007).

AN ENFORCEMENT AGENDA FOR DEVELOPMENT

The enforcement agenda is growing into a seamless web surrounding
the developing world and suffocating healthy and balanced social
economic development. It could even be a life-or-death fight. The
developing countries, despite their tremendous diversity, must set up
a united front, develop a series of practical strategies and proactively
initiate a pro-development enforcement agenda.

From Defensive to Proactive

The developed countries' enforcement agenda is, to a large extent, relying on the tactic of forum-shifting. Once the developing countries manage to adapt to an international forum and are able to resist the unreasonable initiatives, developed countries will shift to a new forum. International intellectual property management was shifted from the WIPO to the WTO TRIPS Agreement, which contains a lengthy chapter on enforcement. In the post-TRIPS era, enforcement requirements are being shifted to more rigid bilateral or regional trade agreements and a number of alternative or new international forums, such as the World Customs Organization, World Health Organization, Interpol, Universal Postal Union and ACTA.[39] Proliferation of forums is particularly useful to impart TRIPS-plus obligations. Developed countries are being pressed to assume additional enforcement obligations on the new forums.[40]

Proliferation of forums disadvantages the developing countries, which can hardly respond to the dynamics among the different forums in a timely and strategic way. Forum-shifting has been keeping the developing world defensive. The developing countries are busy catching up with the various new initiatives from the developed countries. Frequently, they are left with little time to digest the information, assess the impact and collaborate with peers. In a worse scenario, the multilateral treaty's scope and priorities are negotiated by the few countries invited to participate in the early discussions. The text of the treaty (such as ACTA) is then 'locked' and other countries who are later 'invited' to sign-on to the pact will not be able to renegotiate its terms.

A way out of the enforcement agenda capitalized on forum-shifting is to proactively take the control of the agenda-setting. Once the developing countries have an enforcement agenda of their own, they can walk out of the shadow of being chased, manipulated and intervened upon.

The WIPO Development Agenda marks the beginning of a new epoch for the developing countries. A pro-development enforcement agenda can be built in the ambit of the Development Agenda. The Development Agenda contains a provision requiring enforcement to be in line with international agreements, such as the TRIPS Agreement, which requires that enforcement and protection contribute to innovation, technology transfer and be conducive to social and economic welfare as well as to a balance of rights and obligations.[41] A group of developing countries reach consensus that all enforcement efforts should be channeled through WIPO as the central United Nations forum dealing with intellectual property issues.[42]

The pro-development agenda will inevitably encounter the strong resistance of the developed countries, which are more experienced and resourceful in the international context. So far, developed countries have been forcefully restricting discussion of enforcement to a WIPO Advisory Committee with no policy-making powers. On the other hand, there may be mounting difficulties given the non-hegemony nature of the developing world. Solidarity of the developing countries will be essential for the success of this strategy.

However, nothing shall intimidate the developing countries from taking proactive actions. There are scholars who suggest that developing countries develop their own set of data on intellectual property infringements and start recording enforcement abuse cases. The basic research would help to 'instill a sense of ownership in all'.[43] With respect to the new-shifted forums such as the World Customs Organization, the developing countries may initiate the pro-development enforcement measures against the abuse of rights and procedures. The next step could be developing the soft law, such as enforcement guidelines, for the developing world.[44] The guidelines can help the developing countries to understand the minimum enforcement obligations and requirements in international law and guide them to set up the enforcement system that is commensurate with their domestic environment and development stage. Although a treaty of the developing world may not be viable in the near future, the consensus to set a ceiling to prevent the indefinite expansion of intellectual property protection could be put onto the agenda.[45]

Issue Linking Against Maximalism

Enforcement is not always the weapon of the developed countries. The developing countries can consciously utilize it to serve positive ends. An effective method to counteract the forum-shifting is to link up those relevant but ignored issues to enforcement. Enforcement should not be isolated from the context of international intellectual property law.

One tactic of the developed countries that is demonstrated by the case of the United States versus China is isolating the enforcement provisions from the principles and objectives of the TRIPS Agreement. However, intellectual property protection and enforcement, which is inherently subject to the principles and objects, has never become an end in itself, but a means for promoting the public interest, innovation and access to knowledge. Linking up the principles and objectives to enforcement provisions can prevent the partial and biased interpretations of any specific enforcement obligation under the TRIPS Agreement.

Intellectual property law is like an ecosystem. The exclusive rights are merely small islands in the ocean of the public domain. It tends to protect the islands only, irrespective of the environment of the ocean. The limitation and exceptions to the rights should be enforced as well as the legal protection of the rights. The enforcement of limitations and exceptions can prevent the abuse of the rights that harm the consumers' interests or adversely affect the market competition.[46]

One of the proposals for amendment of the TRIPS Agreement is to provide for proportionate, efficient and deterrent remedies against mala fide use of intellectual property rights, in particular the making of unjustified threats.[47] The proposal is primarily based on the Article 8.2 and Article 40 of the TRIPS Agreement.[48] The proposal can actually be extrapolated to a wide scope, particularly against the abuse of the intellectual property enforcement procedures, including the WTO dispute settlement procedure. According to the second half of Article 41 of the TRIPS Agreement, these (enforcement) procedures shall be applied in a manner as to 'provide for safeguards against their abuse'. If developed countries not only deliberately manipulate and distort the enforcement requirements in the TRIPS Agreement for their own agenda but raise untruthful and suspicious claims to intimidate a developing country, it itself shall be subject to punishments.

There has been little scrutiny of developed country efforts to fulfill their obligations under Article 66.2 of the TRIPS Agreement to provide incentives for technology transfer to least-developed country members.[49] In reality, many of the activities that developed countries present in their reports on their actions to fulfill Article 66.2 are training and capacity-building activities, which do not necessarily lead to transfer of technology or fulfill Article 66.2 requirements. How to enforce the developed countries' obligations should be one of the priorities in the pro-development agenda.

Another issue that should be linked to enforcement is the costs. More aggressive and extensive enforcement requirements demand higher costs at the public expense. Any TRIPS-plus enforcement demand should be subject to careful cost–benefit assessment.

Diversify for Development

Developed countries have been pushing for unifying the protection standards and enforcement measures. Uniformity, however, is not consistent with the principles of international intellectual property law.

Territoriality and minimum standards of protection are the two cornerstones of international intellectual property law. To achieve the purpose of intellectual property protection,[50] each country should be allowed certain latitude to derogate from the international treaty obligations by means befitting its unique circumstances and societal constraints.

Enforcement is particularly a territorial issue. Under the Berne Convention, the extent of protection, as well as the means of redress afforded to the author to protect his or her rights, shall be governed exclusively by the laws of the country where protection is claimed.[51] The TRIPS Agreement, despite its detailed enforcement requirements, leaves sufficient room for the territorial differentiations. Article 1.1 and Article 41.5 of the TRIPS Agreement particularly provide such a possibility. Article 1.1 allows the Members to determine the appropriate method of implementing the provisions of this agreement with their own legal system and practice. Article 41.5, on the other hand, ensures that the enforcement requirements do not create any obligation on a Member to put in place a judicial system for the enforcement of intellectual property rights distinct from that for the enforcement of law in general.

Article 41.1 of the TRIPS Agreement has been frequently used by the developed countries to blame the developing countries for the so-called defective enforcement. Article 41.1, which is at the front of the TRIPS Agreement's enforcement part, is believed to set the tone for the whole part. Under the first half of Article 41.1, the Members shall ensure that enforcement procedures as specified in this part are available under their law so as to permit effective action against any acts of infringement of intellectual property rights covered by this agreement. Different from the developed countries' interpretations, what can be seen from this provision is, most importantly, the deference to the territorial enforcement, that is, enforcement procedure shall be subject to 'their' (Members') law. Therefore, what is 'effective action' should not be interpreted uniformly either. As far as they are equivalently effective, different procedures, measures or remedies should be allowed to be adopted in different developing countries.

Apart from territorial differences, enforcement measures should be diversified in terms of the different categories of intellectual property rights. Enforcement of patents is very different from the enforcement of copyright or trademarks. A blanket of enforcement could not only burden the enforcement system but damage the interest of an innocent third party. The TRIPS Agreement actually acknowledges and confirms the differentiations. For instance, Article 46 states, in considering civil remedies, the need for proportionality between the seriousness of the infringement and the remedies ordered as well as the interests of third parties shall be taken into account. The same provision also singles out the remedies against counterfeit trademark goods from the remedies available in general.[52] Under Article 51 of the TRIPS Agreement, customs measures are only required for 'the importation of counterfeit trademark or pirated copyright goods', not mandatory extension to the 'other infringements of intellectual property' or 'exportation' of the goods.[53]

If going even further, different subject matters in the same category of rights may be enforced differently. For example, enforcement of software patents may be different from enforcement of pharmaceutical patents. A diversified and cost-effective enforcement system will better serve the interests of developing countries.

CONCLUSION

Developing countries must leave the shadow of the old enforcement agenda manipulated by the developed countries and strive for their own pro-development agenda. Instead of unifying the standards, squeezing out flexibilities and stifling diversity, the norms and practices of enforcement should be diversified, flexible and commensurate to development. To achieve this goal, the developing countries must achieve solidarity, resist the developed countries' tactics of separating and severing them and effectively link the issues and forums to counteract the forum-shifting and maximalism. The WIPO Development

Agenda demonstrates the developing countries' capacity for agenda-setting. Solidarity will win them more bargaining power. The time has come for the developing world to act.

NOTES

1. E-mail: hongxueipr@gmail.com.
2. China, Argentina, Brazil and India have all been sued at the WTO for violation of the TRIPS Agreement one or more times. See WTO Dispute Settlement, at http://www.wto.org/english/tratop_e/dispu_e/dispu_status_e.htm.
3. See Intellectual Property Watch, 'Inside Views: The WIPO View On Enforcement, Idris And Development Agenda', 27 May 2007, at http://www.ip-watch.org/weblog/index.php?p=617.
4. See 'IP Justice White Paper on the Proposed Anti-Counterfeiting Trade Agreement (ACTA)', at http://ipjustice.org/wp/2008/03/25/ipj-white-paper-acta-2008/.
5. See WTO Case File WT/DS362/7. The countries that reserved their third party rights in the proceeding are Argentina, the European Communities, Japan, Mexico, Chinese Taipei, Australia, Brazil, Canada, India, Korea, Thailand and Turkey. On 3 December 2007, the United States requested the Director-General to compose the panel. On 13 December 2007, the Director-General did so. There is another independent complaint filed by the United States against China, WTO Case File WT/DS363, which is on China's Measures Affecting Trading Rights and Distribution Services for Certain Publications and Audiovisual Entertainment Products. Although indirectly related to the intellectual property enforcement case, DS363 is primarily a dispute on service trade.
6. The United States said that the bilateral discussions on matters related to the panel request had not resulted in a mutually agreed solution, which was the reason for the panel request. China declared it was regrettable that the United States asked for a panel a second time and added that it remained confident China's measures were consistent with WTO rules. China stated that the United States attempted to impose on developing countries extra obligations going beyond the TRIPS Agreement. China concluded it would defend its interests throughout the process. See http://www.wto.org/english/news_e/news07_e/dsb_25sep07_e.htm.
7. See WTO Case File WT/DS362/9. Article 12.8 of the Understanding on Rules and Procedures Governing the Settlement of Disputes (DSU) provides that the period in which a panel shall conduct its examination, from the date that the composition and terms of reference of the panel have been agreed upon until the date the final report is issued to the parties to the dispute, shall, as a general rule, not exceed six months. Article 12.9 of the DSU provides that, when a panel considers that it cannot issue its report within six months, it shall inform the Dispute Settlement Body (DSB) in writing of the reasons for the delay, together with an estimate of the period within which it will issue its report.
8. See 'US-China Draft WTO Resolution Leaked', *Managing Intellectual Property*, 10 October, 2008, at http://www.managingip.com/Article/2027904/US-China-draft-WTO-resolution-leaked-subscribers-only.html.
9. The matter that has been removed from the United States' complaint is on unavailability of criminal procedures and penalties for a person who engages in

either unauthorized reproduction or unauthorized distribution of copyrighted works. Through consultations, it has been clarified that the 'reproduction and distribution' in Article 217 of Chinese Criminal Law should be read as 'reproduction and/or distribution', which is confirmed in the Judicial Interpretation issued by the China's Supreme People's Court in April 2007.

10. The 'Interpretations of Some Issues Concerning the Concrete Application of Laws in the Handling of Criminal Cases of Infringing Intellectual Property Rights' (Interpretations I) was issued by the Chinese Supreme People's Court and the Chinese Supreme People's Procuratorate on 21 December 2004, for the first time, stipulating a specific number of pirated compact disks as the standard for imprisonment. Anyone who publishes more than 1000 copies of a written literary work, musical composition, film, television or musical work, computer software program, or other copyrighted work without the consent of the copyright owner shall be sentenced to prison or criminal detention for a fixed term of less than three years and/or be fined. On 5 April 2007, Interpretations II was released and the criminality threshold was dropped to 500 copies.

11. See USTR '2004 Report to Congress on China's WTO Compliance', 11 December 2004, at http://www.ustr.gov/assets/Document_Library/Reports_Publications/2004/asset_upload_file281_6986.pdf. Under the report, '[T]he United States made IPR enforcement its highest priority during the run-up to the April 2004 Joint Commission on Commerce and Trade (JCCT) meeting'. 'At the April 2004 JCCT meeting, China pledged that, by the end of this year, it would issue judicial interpretations that lower the value thresholds that trigger criminal investigations and prosecutions, and that apply criminal sanctions to the import, export, distribution and storage of counterfeit goods as well as to online piracy'.

12. The full text of Article 61.1 of the TRIPS Agreement is as follows: 'Members shall provide for criminal procedures and penalties to be applied at least in cases of willful trademark counterfeiting or copyright piracy on a commercial scale'.

13. For example, 'relatively large illegal income' under Article 217 of the Criminal Code refers to over 30000 RMB yuan and 'very large illegal income' over 150000 RMB yuan. See supra note 10.

14. See Hong Xue, 'Rethinking of TRIPS', International Association for the Advancement of Teaching and Research in Intellectual Property (ATRIP) Congress, 21–23 July 2008.

15. See Article 27 of Chinese Customs Intellectual Property Rights Regulations and Article 30 of the Implementing Measures. Where the confiscated infringing goods can be used for charitable purposes, customs shall transfer them to the charitable organizations; where the right-owner is willing to purchase the infringing goods, customs may sell the goods to them; where the infringing goods cannot be used for charitable purposes and the right-owner does not intend to purchase the goods, customs may auction off the goods after removing the infringing features from the goods; where it is not feasible to remove the infringing features, customs shall destroy the infringing goods.

16. It is interesting to note that the United States' claim is based on Article 46, rather than Article 59 of the TRIPS Agreement, which is more relevant to customs enforcement.

17. See the Implementing Regulations of the Copyright Law, Article 6.

18. Under the second paragraph of Article 4 of the Chinese Copyright Law, copyright owners, in exercising their copyright, shall not violate the Constitution or laws or prejudice the public interest.

19. At the beginning of 2008, thousands of sex photos of Hong Kong entertainment celebrities were posted onto the Internet. The photos were taken by

Edison Chen, a singer and actor in Hong Kong. The police quickly prohibited any transmission of the photos according to the Hong Kong Ordinance for Obscenity. Although Edison Chen later claimed his copyright for these photos under the Hong Kong Copyright Ordinance, it is believed that he would not be able to enforce his copyright against unauthorized Internet distribution anyway and, if he, in an unlikely case, got the damages, he would be liable for profiting from the illegal obscene objects. Therefore, in certain circumstances, public remedy aided by the police's investigation, confiscation and prohibition can more effectively combat illegal distribution and communication of a work.

20. Article 17 of the Berne Convention provides that '[T]he provisions of this Convention cannot in any way affect the right of the Government of each country of the Union to permit, to control, or to prohibit, by legislation or regulation, the circulation, presentation, or exhibition of any work or production in regard to which the competent authority may find it necessary to exercise that right'. Article XX of GATT provides that '[S]ubject to the requirement that such measures are not applied in a manner which would constitute a means of arbitrary or unjustifiable discrimination between countries where the same conditions prevail, or a disguised restriction on international trade, nothing in this Agreement shall be construed to prevent the adoption or enforcement by any contracting party of measures: (a) necessary to protect public morals'.

21. See 'Public Order and Chinese Copyright Enforcement', at http://worldtradelaw.typepad.com/ielpblog/2008/06/public-order-an.html.

22. See 'Doha Ministerial Declaration on TRIPS Agreement and Public Health', Doc. No. WT/MIN(01).DEC/1 (20 November 2001), at http://www.wto.org/english/thewto_e/minist_e/min01_e/mindecl_trips_e.htm.

23. The enforcement agenda includes a number of initiatives including: the Anti-Counterfeiting Trade Agreement (ACTA); World Customs Organization's Provisional Standards Employed by Customs for Uniform Rights Enforcement (SECURE); World Health Organization's International Medical Products Anti-Counterfeiting Taskforce (IMPACT); the US Chamber of Commerce's 'Coalition against Counterfeiting and Piracy Intellectual Property Enforcement Initiative: Campaign to Protect America'; the Security and Prosperity Partnership of North America; WIPO's discussions at the Advisory Committee on Enforcement; European Commission's Economic Partnership Agreements; and many bilateral and regional free trade agreements and investment treaties.

24. See 'European Parliament to Sarkozy: No "Three Strikes" Here', 10 April 2008, at http://www.eff.org/deeplinks/2008/04/european-parliament-sarkozy-no-three-strikes-here. 'Three strikes' is the proposed legislation backed by the music industry to create a class of digital outcasts, forbidden from accessing the Internet if repeatedly accused by music companies of downloading infringing content.

25. See 'Act against ACTA', IP Justice, at http://ipjustice.org/wp/campaigns/acta/.

26. See supra note 3. In the Revised Program and Budget 2008/09 (WO/PBC/13/4) of WIPO Assemblies on 12 December 2008, 'international cooperation of building respect for intellectual property', such as enforcement, is listed as one of the strategic goals. Enforcement is also labeled as a 'development activity'. See http://www.wipo.int/edocs/mdocs/govbody/en/wo_pbc_13/wo_pbc_13_4.pdf.

27. This wording is largely the result of an inter-institutional legal argument over whether the European Community has the power or 'competence' to regulate such criminal penalties in the context of the EU legal system; http://www.out-law.com/page-7920.

28. Article 51 of the TRIPS Agreement states, '[M]embers shall, in conformity with the provisions set out below, adopt procedures to enable a right-holder, who

has valid grounds for suspecting that the importation of counterfeit trademark or pirated copyright goods may take place, to lodge an application in writing with competent authorities, administrative or judicial, for the suspension by the customs authorities of the release into free circulation of such goods. Members may enable such an application to be made in respect of goods which involve other infringements of intellectual property rights, provided that the requirements of this Section are met. Members may also provide for corresponding procedures concerning the suspension by the customs authorities of the release of infringing goods destined for exportation from their territories'.

29. The caveat is shown in the case of Monsanto against Argentina concerning importation of Round-Up Ready soybeans into the European Union (EU) zone. Monsanto tried to use patents obtained in the EU to stop Argentina's exports of processed soybean meal to Europe. Soybean meal is a derivative product of soybeans while the patents cover genetic sequences within a living soy plant. According to EU Biotechnology Directive (Article 9) a gene 'should perform its functions', which is rendered impossible by the processing needed to make the soy plant into flour. But some European countries complied with Monsanto's claim and stopped imports based on the suspicion of patent infringement. See Carlos Correa, 'Abuse of IP Enforcement Procedure: Lessons from the Monsanto Case', at South Centre International Symposium on 'Examining IP Enforcement from a Development Perspective', 16 September 2008.

30. See Article 2 of Council Regulation (EC) No. 1383/2003 concerning customs action against goods suspected of infringing certain intellectual property rights and the measures to be taken against goods found to have infringed such rights, issued on 22 July 2003.

31. See supra note 30, Article 1 and Article 16.

32. Chinese Regulations on Customs Protection of Intellectual Property Rights was enacted on 26 November 2003 and entered into force as of 1 March 2004.

33. OEM means an original equipment manufacturer, referring to manufacturers who resell another company's product under their own name and branding. China, known as a world workshop, has become the largest base for the manufacture of OEM products. Once an overseas order involves an intellectual property dispute with another company, the Chinese manufacturer, irrespective of its innocence, will suffering from a ban on export of goods. See 'Fights between Two Nikes', http://www.cslawyer.cn/article/article_1738.htm.

34. See supra note 3. The WIPO officer stated in the interview, '[A] country might well be interested in prescribing border measures for export control of counterfeit trademark and pirated copyright goods regardless of the fact that only border measures to prevent the importation of such goods are mandatory under the TRIPS Agreement. Counterfeit and pirated goods are often ordered by dealers in third countries for the purpose of resale and a government might wish to place this additional burden for a number of reasons on its customs authorities, for example, in order to benefit from favorable treatment in other fields offered in bilateral trade negotiations. By the way, border measures in the form of export control are required under a number of laws including those of developing countries such as the People's Republic of China'.

35. The head of one of Britain's biggest Internet providers has criticized the music industry for demanding that he act against pirates. See 'Policing Internet "not ISP's job"', *BBC News*, 4 April, 2008, at http://news.bbc.co.uk/2/hi/uk_news/7329801.stm.

36. For example, Chinese Regulations on Protection of the Right of Communication through Information Networks, enacted in 2006, are, mutatis mutandis, the same as the DMCA on the notice-and-takedown measures.

37. The recent Microsoft 'black screen' case shows that the software users are very vulnerable when confronted with a software giant's technological measures. In October 2008, Microsoft's new version of 'Windows Genuine Advantage' in China turns a monitor screen's background black every hour if the installed software fails a validation test. Chinese Internet users have criticized what they deem to be Microsoft's violation of their right to privacy. See 'China's Internet users lash out at Microsoft's anti-piracy system', at http://www. scmagazineus.com/Chinas-internet-users-lash-out-at-Microsofts-anti-piracy-system/article/119913/.

38. The USTR stated in a report to the Congress, '[A]lthough China is not obligated under WTO rules to accede to the WIPO treaties, the United States considers these treaties to reflect international norms for providing copyright protection over the Internet'. The United States 'has urged China for some time to accede to the WIPO treaties and fully harmonize its regulations and implementing rules with them. At the April 2004 JCCT meeting, China agreed to ratify and implement the WIPO treaties as soon as possible, although it has not yet done so'. See supra note 11.

39. The UN Universal Postal Union Congress in August 2008 adopted a resolution (No. 40) that encouraged Members to identify counterfeit and pirated items in the postal network and to cooperate with the relevant national and international authorities in awareness-raising initiatives to prevent illegal circulation of counterfeit goods. World Custom Organization's SECURE draft would allow applications from private right-holders directly to customs officials (bypassing judges and other proper authorities). See 'The South strikes back against overreaching IP enforcement', *Intellectual Property Watch*, 17 September 2008, at http://www. ip-watch.org/weblog/index.php?p=1229.

40. For instance, ACTA may become a new forum to circumvent the TRIPS Agreement and WIPO negotiations entirely. World Customs Organization's Provisional Standards Employed by Customs for Uniform Rights Enforcement (SECURE) attempts to dwarf the special requirements related to border measures of the TRIPS Agreement.

41. See 45th Proposal in 'The 45 Adopted Recommendations under the WIPO Development Agenda' at http://www.wipo.int/ip-development/en/agenda/ recommendations.html. Also see the TRIPS Agreement, Article 7, the protection and enforcement of intellectual property rights should contribute to the promotion of technological innovation and to the transfer and dissemination of technology, to the mutual advantage of producers and users of technological knowledge and in a manner conducive to social and economic welfare, and to a balance of rights and obligations.

42. See supra note 39. The Revised Program and Budget 2008/09 (WO/PBC/13/4) of WIPO Assemblies on 12 December 2008 listed a new Strategic Goal to enhance international cooperation on building respect for IP. This is a broad, cross-cutting goal, which is more inclusive than the narrower concept of enforcement. It calls for a balanced approach, focusing on international cooperation where WIPO can make a difference, and conducted within the spirit of Development Agenda, 45th Proposal. WIPO's activities in support of this goal apply across all areas, including capacity building, provision of training, awareness-raising and educational programmes aimed at promoting respect for IP. See supra note 26.

43. See supra note 39.

44. This can be linked to the WIPO technical assistance. Recommendation 14 of the Development Agenda states, 'within the framework of the agreement between WIPO and the WTO, WIPO shall make available advice to developing countries and LDCs [least developed countries], on the implementation and operation of

the rights and obligations and the understanding and use of flexibilities contained in the TRIPS agreement'.

45. See Annette Kur, 'IP in Transition – Proposals for Amendment of TRIPS', at http://www.ip.mpg.de/shared/data/pdf/ipt_fuer_rom_maerz_07.pdf.

46. WIPO technical cooperation and capacity-building activities should not be limited to the implementation of TRIPS obligations, but should equally focus on preventing abuses of IPRs and on the rights provided to countries in the TRIPS Agreement, including how to make full use of the flexibilities contained in the agreement as reaffirmed by the Doha Declaration on the TRIPS Agreement and Public Health.

47. See supra note 45.

48. TRIPS Agreement, Article 40.2 states, 'nothing in this Agreement shall prevent Members from specifying in their legislation licensing practices or conditions that may in particular cases constitute an abuse of intellectual property rights having an adverse effect on competition in the relevant market. As provided above, a Member may adopt, consistently with the other provisions of this Agreement, appropriate measures to prevent or control such practices, which may include for example exclusive grantback conditions, conditions preventing challenges to validity and coercive package licensing, in the light of the relevant laws and regulations of that Member'.

49. TRIPS, Article 62.2 states, 'developed country Members shall provide incentives to enterprises and institutions in their territories for the purpose of promoting and encouraging technology transfer to least-developed country Members in order to enable them to create a sound and viable technological base'.

50. The TRIPS Agreement states the goal of protection and enforcement of intellectual property rights as to contribute to the promotion of technological innovation and to the transfer and dissemination of technology, to the mutual advantage of producers and users of technological knowledge and in a manner conducive to social and economic welfare, and to a balance of rights and obligations.

51. Berne Convention, Article 5.2 states, 'the extent of protection, as well as the means of redress afforded to the author to protect his rights, shall be governed exclusively by the laws of the country where protection is claimed'.

52. It is stated, '[I]n regard to counterfeit trademark goods, the simple removal of the trademark unlawfully affixed shall not be sufficient, other than in exceptional cases, to permit release of the goods into the channels of commerce'.

53. See supra note 27.

PART III

STRATEGIC CONSIDERATIONS TO
ADDRESS THE CHALLENGES

8. Dealing with forum shopping: some lessons from the SECURE negotiations at the World Customs Organization

Henrique Choer Moraes[1]

INTRODUCTION[2]

Forum shopping is a widely used tool in policy-making as a whole. This is no less true in the domain of international intellectual property rights (IP/IPRs), the history of the TRIPS Agreement[3] being a prominent example.[4] Despite the challenges posed to international governance by the proliferation of overlapping agendas, it is a fact that countries seek amenable venues to push their interests. Since there is no such thing as a clear-cut, stone-written division of labour among international fora, to a certain extent convenience is the rule that dictates where a given agenda is to be advanced. In this sense, forum shopping is a by-product of the 'anarchical' state that marks international politics.

Of course, some forums could arguably be regarded as being better positioned than others to host negotiations of certain issue areas. This is due to a variety of reasons ranging from institutional features – such as a specific perspective or expertise from which an organization views a given subject – to the normative *acquis* of legal instruments negotiated within the organization's framework. While this does not by itself rule out the migration of issues to alternative forums, pursuing an agenda in one organization that exhibits the features mentioned above has the added value of legitimacy.

The expansion in the scope of intellectual property rules ushered in by the advent of the TRIPS Agreement has increased the number of forums with a legitimate claim to incorporate intellectual property issues into their agendas. In light of the consequences produced by the TRIPS patent and copyright rules over, for example, public health, culture and biodiversity, the agendas of international organizations and regimes such as the WHO, UNESCO and the CBD have rearranged themselves in order to preserve their mandates from losing ground. Such movement has been accompanied by the enlargement of the range of stakeholders with an interest in following and influencing IP discussions as a whole.

This is different from 'forum shopping' given that the forums mentioned above have legitimately sought to preserve their mandates from being dented from the one-sided rationale underpinning the TRIPS regime.

Conversely, recent work of the World Customs Organization (WCO) in the area of intellectual property enforcement provides a very clear example of forum shopping: being confronted with difficulties to move forward a TRIPS-plus agenda[5] on enforcement at the WTO[6] and at WIPO,[7] developed countries have managed to set in motion an ambitious project at a forum where little, if any, attention on this issue had been devoted heretofore. In fact, the WCO has been sponsoring in recent years a politically sensitive agenda in the area of IPRs, as is evidenced by the SECURE project (Provisional Standards Employed by Customs for Uniform Rights Enforcement). IP initiatives championed by the WCO have been moving at a remarkably quick pace – and, as will be shown below, at the possible cost of eroding flexibilities that enable, inter alia, seamless trade in generic medicines and access to cultural goods. This chapter will place emphasis on an examination of the SECURE project, even if its future status (but not the TRIPS-plus agenda) has been put to question by the Secretariat of the WCO by the end of 2008. Irrespective of the prospect that lies ahead for SECURE, there are lessons to be drawn to the benefit of developing countries from the experience of the past years. These lessons are all the more important given that there are reasons to doubt the WCO will abandon its TRIPS-plus agenda altogether.

Although risking the charge of over-simplification, for the purposes of this chapter a dynamics of forum shopping in international negotiations could be superficially sketched in the following manner: (1) The strategy to forum shop flows from a certain discontent raised by the fact that a specific agenda is not moving within a given a forum as desired by a group of ('shopper') countries. (2) Once shopper countries migrate their agenda elsewhere, 'forum shopped' countries will not only have to become aware of the new situation but also organize anew their coalitions in the shopped forum. There is thus an important time component in forum shopping that could prove harmful when 'forum shopping' is used to the detriment of developing countries, in view of the difficulties they face to coordinate on short notice. (3) In a number of cases, the shopped forum can be regarded as a 'second-best' venue to pursue a given agenda, whose use is only resorted to in the face of failure to advance it in the 'well-equipped', more legitimate institution. It should therefore not be excluded that results achieved in the shopped forum be presented as a fait accompli at the forum where it has not been possible to do so originally, with a view to reverting the initial deadlock that triggered the forum shopping strategy.

Even if one considers that the SECURE project is one chapter in the broader strategy pursued by developed countries to ratchet up TRIPS enforcement provisions (Matthews, 2008; Sell, 2008), the WCO has characteristics that have made it a safe haven for advancing the TRIPS-plus enforcement agenda: from the perspective of the rules that govern the functioning of the WCO, developed countries hold prerogatives that enable them to filter decisions of the technical bodies; in addition, from the perspective of the outside world, the organization is viewed as a purely technical institution, whose discussions elicit reduced interest to policy-makers.

And yet, the WCO is the forum where a TRIPS-plus stance is being openly asserted as if this were a shared belief across its membership.[8] Instead of living up to the expected *technical* mandate of providing assistance in the implementation of the provisions enshrined in the TRIPS Agreement, the WCO thought best to endorse the *political* position according to which it is necessary to move beyond the threshold set therein. By so doing, the organization relinquished its credentials as a technical institution.

How has it been possible to get to this stage? To what extent can the WCO initiatives on IPRs undermine the positions developing countries have been able to sustain in Geneva and in other forums where legitimate and informed discussions on intellectual property rights take place? More specifically, how can the envisageable results of the work of the WCO in the field of IPRs negatively affect important instruments such as the 2001 Doha Declaration on TRIPS and Public Health? What are the challenges faced by developing countries in trying to make their views acknowledged in this scenario?

What lessons can be learned by developing countries from the experience of SECURE?

These questions are addressed below in the three sections into which the chapter is divided. The first section comprises an examination of the SECURE project and presents the documents that have been prepared within this framework, with a special emphasis on the 'SECURE Standards'. The documents that form part of the project contain many TRIPS-plus provisions and are designed to be incorporated via the technical assistance activities that the WCO is often commissioned to provide to customs administrations. This is followed by the second section, where a number of features of the WCO are identified with a view to explaining how it has been possible to swiftly move such an ambitious agenda in so short a period of time. The last section elaborates on the challenges developing countries face not only embarking on this process but also influencing its direction towards the preservation of their interests. The concluding remarks list lessons developing countries can learn from the WCO work on IPRs.

The goal of combatting piracy and counterfeiting is shared by all countries. Yet, to argue for the adoption of TRIPS-plus provisions, in particular provisions that overly increase the powers attributed to customs authorities, is a non sequitur. Be it as it may, the WCO has brandished the existence of the problem of piracy and counterfeiting to push its TRIPS-plus project. Against the compelling evidence of the harm brought about by trade in pirated and counterfeit goods, which is certainly real, it is not exactly easy to draw attention to the negative effects of the remedies proposed, which are equally real. This is what happens, for example, when one raises the question about the possible risks the measures proposed may bring to trade in generic medicines.

In a nutshell, WCO work in the area of IPRs in general – and the SECURE project in particular – is moving at the expense of informed debates. More often than not, discussions are conducted under murky or non-existing rules of procedure in an environment of poor transparency, where access to documents is restricted to a small number of actors, which includes right-holders but excludes public interest organizations and interested intergovernmental organizations. These features explain why the choice of the WCO as a shopped forum is quite original. However, they also highlight its limited legitimacy.

SECURE: A SAFE HAVEN FOR A TRIPS-PLUS AGENDA?

The SECURE project is inspired on the priorities set by the G8 countries in the area of intellectual property rights.[9] The SECURE documents originally contained a number of references to the G8 priorities, apparently as a means to accord legitimacy to the exercise the WCO was proposing to its membership.[10]

The SECURE Working Group was established by a decision of the 2007 WCO Council[11] with the purpose of replacing all the WCO's working groups responsible for IPRs.[12] Prior to that, discussions on piracy and counterfeit combat usually took place within the framework of the WCO Enforcement Committee, in whose structure an IPR Strategic Group and an IPR Task Force were entrusted to discuss the matter.

Until October 2008, the SECURE Working Group had met on four occasions. As will be explained below, the two sessions originally scheduled to take place in the first semester of 2009 have been cancelled due to the difficulties in finding consensus on the group's Terms of Reference.

At its establishment, the SECURE Working Group was tasked to *develop* 'provisional standards' on enforcement of IPRs[13] (the 'SECURE Standards' document), whose first draft, considered by the WCO members at the 2007 Council decision, was authored by the WCO Secretariat.[14] As such, it was undertaken under the label of a 'provisional' document, aimed at merely providing the *basis* for the discussions that would ensue in the Working Group.[15]

Along with the SECURE Standards, other documents have been incorporated into the Working Group agenda and have so far remained there, although until the Working Group's third meeting (April 2008) nothing other than the standards had been discussed.[16] These documents are the 'WCO Model Provisions', the 'WCO Action Plan to Fight Counterfeiting and Piracy' and the draft Terms of Reference of the Working Group.[17] While the latter document will be dealt with later in this chapter, in view of its significance as an example of the procedural originality in the conduction of business in the WCO, the other three documents will be discussed below with the purpose of underscoring how ambitious the project pushed at the WCO is when compared with the current state of discussions in this issue area in other forums. These documents highlight some

important features of the SECURE project, namely how far in the
TRIPS-plus direction are the proposed provisions.

SECURE Standards

As mentioned above, the first draft of the SECURE Standards document was prepared by the WCO Secretariat purportedly to reflect
'best practices' in force across national legislations.[18] Considering
the divergences of views expressed by members in the course of
discussions in the Working Group, it is difficult to see the proposed
standards as being 'practices' shared by many national legal systems,
let alone being their 'best' practices. This contention is all the more
confirmed by the position frequently held at the SECURE meetings by some members that the standards should be regarded as
'aspirational'. There is a conceptual difference between collecting
best practices and legislating from scratch based on aspirations. In
addition, the very idea of a best practice assumes the truthfulness of
the contention that one size fits all where lawmaking is concerned.
This assumption is not only devoid of concrete evidence in the area
of intellectual property (Choer Moraes and Brandelli, 2008) but
also erodes the flexibility provided for by Article 1.1 of the TRIPS
Agreement.[19]

The format chosen for the document apparently drew on the experience already gathered by the organization with the preparation of
standards in the field of risk analysis of consignments, within the
framework of the SAFE Working Group.[20]

The standards document is divided into three parts, as follows:
(1) IPR Legislative and Enforcement Regime Development; (2) Risk
Analysis and Intelligence Sharing; (3) Capacity Building for IPR
Enforcement and International Cooperation. As the controversies
within the Working Group focus more specially in the first part,
where a number of TRIPS-plus provisions are proposed, attention
will be devoted here exclusively to its analysis.

In general, the provisions proposed under the 'IPR Legislative
and Enforcement Regime Development' chapter of the SECURE
Standards document are drafted in language that bears little resem-
blance to the phrasing of a soft law instrument[21] – the alleged nature
of the document. Instead, the *precision*[22] of its provisions is typical of
hard law, an aspect that is confirmed by the fact that many of them
are 'should' worded.

The *rationale* of these standard provisions points clearly to a TRIPS-plus direction[23] and also to a 'one size fits all' legal framework where customs authorities enjoy over-extended powers to be exercised possibly without need for prior clearance by judicial organs.[24] One example is draft Standard No. 1,[25] according to which:

> Customs Administrations should have the legal authority to enforce IPR laws against goods which are suspected of violating IPR laws whenever such goods are deemed under national law to be under Customs control, including, but not limited to:
> - Import;
> - Export;
> - Transit;
> - Warehouses;
> - Transhipment;
> - Free zones;
> - Duty-free shops.

The draft standard above contains at least two explicitly TRIPS-plus stipulations: (1) the command for customs authorities to act in cases of IPR violations in general (by comparison, Article 51 of the TRIPS Agreement requires mandatory custom action only in cases of violation of copyrights and trademarks); (2) the widening of the situations in which customs action should take place – TRIPS requires only action in cases of import, whereas the SECURE Standards propose to cover, inter alia, the situations mentioned in the bullet points.

It could be also argued that, by implication, the draft standard above may contain another TRIPS-plus provision to the effect of enabling ex officio action by customs authorities ('Customs Administrations should have the legal authority to enforce IPR laws. . .'), a conclusion that is strengthened when the provision is read in conjunction with draft Standard 7:

> Customs Administrations should have legal authority, in accordance with relevant international agreements, to act, either at the request of the rights holder, *or upon their own initiative*, to detain or suspend the release of goods in respect of which they have acquired prima facie evidence that an intellectual property right is being infringed while protecting the legal rights of all relevant economic operators. (Emphasis added)

Aside from setting TRIPS-plus provisions, another tenet that apparently underpins the SECURE Standards is the attempt to shift the focal point for interaction with the allegedly affected private party, from the judicial bodies to the customs authorities – a shift that will ultimately amount to sliding the decisional authority from the judge to the customs official. For example, if we take Article 51 of the TRIPS Agreement,[26] it stands out that the intention of the negotiators was that customs action should be the *result* of an application lodged before the 'competent authorities, administrative or judicial'.[27] It should be noted that the TRIPS provision leaves countries with the *choice* to define who is to be understood as the 'competent authority' (a category under which 'customs authorities' *could* be included). In contrast, draft Standard 4, quoted below, seems to undermine the flexibility foreseen in TRIPS given that its wording could be construed as *requiring* (instead of *allowing*) applications to be submitted directly to customs administrations, without any mention whatsoever at the need for previous judicial order:

> With respect to requests from rights holders for Customs intervention, Customs Administrations should develop standardized application forms requesting information consisting of basic, standard data at a cost not exceeding the costs of the processing of the application.

In case they are adopted by national legislations, the three draft standards mentioned above could mean in practice that customs authorities in, for example, a developing country would be empowered to seize a given consignment on the charge of patent infringement, without the need for a previous judicial order. Such seizure would probably be grounded on an application submitted directly to customs authorities by the alleged aggrieved party, who would also provide evidence to this effect. This leads to a set of questions that, unless duly addressed, risk turning the concrete implementation of the standards into barriers to trade of legitimate goods.

Suppose the request for customs action is grounded on a claim of patent infringement related to a pharmaceutical product. Action in this case would require at least prima facie information that requires expertise from many areas other than customs alone. For example, in order to assess the validity of the claim for seizure of the pharmaceutical product, it would be necessary to define, inter alia, (1) whether the patent is effectively valid in the territory where customs holds jurisdiction (it would have to be defined, for instance, if the patent is sub judice or even in the public domain); (2) whether the imported product has been purchased abroad from the patent-holder (in which case it would be necessary to examine whether the country where customs holds jurisdiction provides for a rule of international exhaustion of patents); (3) whether the pharmaceutical product in question is being imported under a research exemption clause that might be present in the national legislation (in which case the assessment of a prima facie violation would not be enough to substantiate a claim for seizure). All these issues require an expert opinion, whose absence could turn the seizure into a trade barrier if the operation is conducted exclusively by customs.

An issue of particular concern in this respect is the highly technical, but necessary, distinction that should be drawn between *generic* and *fake* medicines.[28] There is a risk that customs officials rely exclusively on the information provided by the complaining party, without time to afford the importer the opportunity to present a defence. The consequences, especially in the field of importation of generic medicines, could be significant in view of the blockages to their legitimate entry into a given market. This question has barely been discussed at the WCO and yet it is a possible side-effect of the standards proposed for adoption.[29] Another area where there are concerns as to the need for expert assessment is that related to seizures of goods circumventing technological protection measures (TPMs) and Digital Rights Management (DRM), which is discussed below in the subsection on the 'WCO Model Provisions'.

Even if customs authorities limit their activity in this respect to retaining the consignment until the importing party presents evidence in its defence, the shift in the burden of proof towards the importer could stimulate abusive applications.

An additional aspect that deserves to be highlighted is the overlapping of the SECURE Standards with the border measures provisions envisaged in the negotiations of the Anti-Counterfeiting Trade Agreement (ACTA), sponsored by the G8 countries. Although the draft negotiating text of ACTA was not publicly available at the time this chapter was written, a discussion paper made known through the Internet[30] gives an idea of how much the SECURE project borrows from the political objectives of the main champions of the ACTA negotiations. In many instances, the very language employed by the SECURE Standards is similar to that presented in the discussion paper.

*Table 8.1   Border measures discussed in ACTA linked to SECURE
Standards*

ACTA – Issues Relating to Border Measures	SECURE Standards
Ex officio authority for customs authorities to suspend import, export and transhipment of suspected IPR-infringing goods	Standards 1 and 7
Procedures for right-holders to initiate suspension by customs authorities of import, export and transhipment of suspected IPR-infringing goods	Standards 3, 4 and 5
Measures to ensure the seizure and destruction of IPR-infringing goods	Standard 10
Allocation of liability for storage and destruction fees between the importer/exporter and the right-holder, and/or the appropriate government agency, so as not to place unreasonable burdens on right-holders	Standard 11
Authority to impose deterrent penalties	Standard 12
Measures to ensure that goods are not released into channels of commerce without right-holder permission in cases where the goods have been determined by the competent authorities to be infringing IPRs	Standard 10

In Table 8.1 are examples of border measures being discussed in the framework of the ACTA, linked to the corresponding SECURE provisions.

WCO Model Provisions[31]

A second instrument on the SECURE agenda are the 'WCO Model Provisions', whose intent is to provide national authorities with recommendations for the implementation of border measures aimed at the protection of intellectual property rights.

The degree of precision of the model provisions is undeniably that of mandatory legislation. There is no clarity, however, as to how the WCO Model Provisions are related to the SECURE Standards.

Although the WCO Model Provisions have been on the agenda of the SECURE Working Group, the document has not been discussed in this forum.[32]

The Model Provisions represent another example of how far

beyond its mandate the WCO intends to go in a TRIPS-plus direction. To begin with, the document assumes that the TRIPS Agreement is insufficient and that it is necessary to grant 'certain powers and measures that go beyond the minimum requirement set forth in the TRIPs Agreement'. Its Introduction states:

> WTO membership requires Governments to implement Special Border Measures consistent with a prescribed minimum standard as defined in the Agreement on Trade-Related Aspects of Intellectual Property Rights (the TRIPs Agreement). *The experience of customs administrations in numerous countries has indicated, however, that only by granting certain powers and measures that go beyond the minimum requirement set forth in the TRIPs Agreement,* Governments can provide an effective and efficient level of IPR protection and enforcement at their borders. (Emphasis added)

In line with this reasoning, the Model Provisions contain TRIPS-plus articles, some of which in a not so evident manner. One example is the proposal to introduce the obligation to enforce technological protection measures (TPMs) and Digital Rights Management (DRM) through their incorporation into national law via customs legislations. This is achieved by engineering the definition of the 'goods' subject to customs action:

> Goods Infringing Intellectual Property Rights shall mean:
>   . . .
> *For the purposes of this law goods protected with copyright or related rights with respect to which the rights management information they may incorporate has been removed, altered, or added without the right-holders' authorization shall be deemed to be goods infringing the said intellectual property rights.* (Emphasis added)

The explanatory note to this model provision is eloquent: it shows how misplaced a forum the WCO is to host discussions on substantive and sensitive issues such as TPMs and DRM. At the same time, it draws the attention to how vigilant developing countries should be with respect to what is presented as a 'model' of legislation:

> Although the TRIPs Agreement does not oblige Member States to protect technical measures used by right-holders, the 1996 WIPO Treaties (the WIPO Copyright Treaty [WCT] and the WIPO Performances and Phonograms Treaty [WPPT]) require that Contracting Parties make available adequate legal protection and effective legal remedies to protect technologies used by right-holders. An essential element of adequate

protection and effective remedies is legal protection against devices that circumvent technological measures. *It is therefore only natural that border measures be extended to cover also devices the primary purposes of which is to defeat such technologies used by right holders to protect their intellectual property*. (Emphasis added)

The provision above recognizes its TRIPS-plus nature when it is admitted that there is no obligation in the agreement to protect TPMs and DRM. Yet, it seeks to misconstrue the international legal framework by claiming that such an obligation is required by the WIPO treaties. It nevertheless omits the fact that the latter treaties have been ratified only by a non-representative number of countries (67 for the WCT and 66 for the WPPT[33]). Other misguiding aspects of the explanation provided by the WCO are the assumptions that (1) 'an essential element of adequate protection and effective remedies is legal protection against devices that circumvent techno-logical measures' and that (2) it would *naturally* follow that border measures should be extended to cover TPMs and DRM.

And yet, if one looks at the discussions on copyright at WIPO it would show clearly how sensitive is the issue of TPMs and DRM, not only for developing countries, but in developed countries as well. Suffice it to be recalled that one of the major concerns voiced in this respect deals with the prerogatives TPMs/DRM ascribe to right-holders to define unilaterally what is considered a fair use of copyrights, in particular, the cases in which copyright exceptions and limitations can be enjoyed.[34]

In addition, considering that the majority of WCO members are not signatories to the WIPO treaties mentioned by the Model Provisions, implementation into national legislation of a provision such as the one above would constitute a clear case of 'backdoor' legislation.

Another question that should be highlighted about customs activities in the area of copyright is that concerning the protection of privacy, in particular at which point exactly to draw the line with respect to the prerogatives enjoyed by customs.

Finally, the technical complexity of the questions raised by the existence of TPMs/DRM into a given product as well as the legal status accorded to such devices require that decisions on a possible seizure of goods in this condition take into account the assessments of experts from many fields other than customs alone. Otherwise, there would be, also here, a risk of creating a barrier to trade in legal goods and also possible cases where privacy rights may be eroded.

WCO Action Plan to Fight Counterfeiting and Piracy

The 'Action Plan' was prepared by the WCO Secretariat and so far has not been discussed by the SECURE Working Group, albeit being on its agenda since the outset. The document compiles a series of activities envisaged by the WCO in its work in the field of the fight against piracy and counterfeiting.

One of the main chapters of the Action Plan deals with Improving Legislative Provisions, in which most of the envisaged actions are entrusted to the SECURE Working Group along with the WCO Secretariat. One point worthy of attention is that foreseen under Action No. 8: 'Study whether applicable sanctions set forth in national law are sufficient and appropriate'. According to the scheme organized by the WCO Secretariat, this activity would be the responsibility of 'all WCO members' on a 'permanent' basis.

What exactly is contemplated by such an activity? To submit a given state's national legislation to deliberation and evaluation by 'all WCO members'? Would that not amount to the same as submitting said national legislation to the multilateral scrutiny of all members of the WCO? And to what end?

In case a WCO member understands that the national legislation of another member does not provide enough IPR protection ('sufficient and appropriate'), can the former raise its concerns on this issue at the WCO? Or would not the WTO be the forum to resort to if a state understands the legislation of a third state not to provide 'sufficient and appropriate' sanctions? In the latter case, doesn't the complaining member have to comply with a number of conditions set out by WTO rules in order to submit a national legislation to the scrutiny of the competent organs of that organization?

In this case, is the WCO not intending to establish an ad hoc tribunal of national legislations where members can freely criticize other members' legislations without having to bear the burden of litigation?

Viewed in conjunction with the SECURE standards, the Action Plan puts into question the claim that the standards are voluntary. If the action mentioned above is taken as an example, it is not difficult to assume the pressure that could be put on members to sign in to the standards if its national legislation was considered insufficient and inappropriate.

***

The reach of the proposals contained in the documents above does not reflect the level of consensus currently existing in the international discussions on intellectual property enforcement. As a matter of fact, it far exceeds this level.

The agenda put forward in Brussels could hardly have a chance of success in Geneva. The next section seeks to identify the reasons that possibly explain the 'decoupling' of the WCO from the forums with competence on intellectual property matters. A glance at some aspects of the functioning of the WCO can help clarify the reasons for the same.

WHY IS IT A CASE OF FORUM SHOPPING? THE SECURE PROJECT VIEWED FROM THE CONTEXT OF THE FUNCTIONING OF THE WCO

Following the establishment of the SECURE Working Group by the 2007 Council session, the WCO Secretariat estimated that the documents in the SECURE package should be ripe for approval at the 2008 Council meeting,[35] after the three meetings scheduled for the inter-sessional period. Considering the exceedingly TRIPS-plus provisions and initiatives foreseen in the SECURE documents, along with the contentiousness of debates of the same nature at the WTO and at WIPO, the ease with which the Secretariat forecast the closing of the exercise is a sign of a great confidence to deliver.

This is evidence of the considerable ascendancy the WCO Secretariat exerts over the intergovernmental process. It reveals, in turn, that the Secretariat enjoys a great deal of latitude to engineer initiatives and solutions. This is mostly due to the lack of clear rules on many procedural areas and, where rules exist, to their remarkable malleability.

Thus, countries pushing the SECURE package found a very unique and favourable forum to advance their claims. One additional reason for it is that developed countries can count on the many institutional mechanisms that shield the activities under way at the WCO from dissonant voices and ensure limited transparency to the outside world, in stark contrast to the majority of international organizations.

These issues are elaborated below, by means of a look at the institutional arrangements that govern the functioning of the organization.

They can provide inputs to answer the following question: How has the WCO managed to advance an agenda that the proponents have been unable to move forward in Geneva?

Institutional Aspects of the Decision-making Process

During the three meetings held following the 2007 Council decision that decided on the launching of the SECURE project, the SECURE Working Group discussed substantive issues on the document containing the standards. Despite that, the Working Group's Terms of Reference have never been adopted. At least as late as the fourth session (October 2008), they remained a draft. This exemplifies the wide array of procedural challenges that need to be addressed in order to ensure transparent, balanced and informed – in short, legitimate – discussions.

The composition of the SECURE Working Group is also telling: member states and representatives of the private sector, predominantly from right-holders, act on the same footing, presenting proposals and commenting on each other's positions. This feature is not worthy of criticism were it not for the fact that, conversely, admission of public interest organizations, public or private, is made difficult. The South Centre, an intergovernmental organization, was admitted to the third session but there are indications that it will not be accredited for the next meetings. Other public interest organizations report having never received a response from the Secretariat to their request for accreditation.

Access to relevant documents also merits being highlighted. Access to working documents is conditioned upon the possession of a password. On the other hand, the few working documents available on the WCO website about the SECURE project normally do not reflect the current status of debates. This prevents public scrutiny of the activities carried out therein.

On the top of that, documents are 'protected' by a copyright notice on behalf of the WCO. Therefore, 'requests and inquiries concerning translation, reproduction and adaptation rights' should be submitted to the Secretariat. Irrespective of the existence of a legal basis for such a measure, it would be debatable whether it could override copyright exceptions.

Democratic decision-making process in the WCO is somewhat complicated by the existence of the Policy Commission, a body that sits between the technical bodies and the summit body, the Council. Most, if not all, of the main issues to be discussed at the Council are first deliberated by the Policy Commission. And most, if not all, of the issues decided by the Council are based on recommendations by the Policy Commission.

The peculiar mark is that the Policy Commission is not open for participation by the entire membership. The body is composed of: (1) the Chair of the Council (as Chair of the Commission); (2) the six Vice-Chairs of the Council, each of whom shall represent one of the WCO's six regions; (3) in an ex officio capacity, for no more than two years immediately following the year during which they ceased to hold office as Chair of the Council, former Chairs of the Council who are still serving in their national customs administrations; (4) 17 members elected by the Council in accordance with the following distribution as between the six regions established by Council Decision No. 283:

- one member from the East and Southern Africa region;
- seven members from the Europe region;
- four members from the Far East, South and South East Asia, Australasia and the Pacific Islands region;
- one member from the North of Africa, Near and Middle East region;
- three members from the South America, North America, Central America and the Caribbean region;
- one member from the West and Central Africa region;

As observers, there are seats for the member on whose territory the Council has its headquarters and to any member that is not a member of the Policy Commission and is to host a session of the Commission held elsewhere than at the headquarters of the Council.

In application of the rules in place, the members of the Policy Commission in the period June 2008–June 2009 were the following: New Zealand, Argentina, Ireland, Korea, Morocco, Mozambique, Senegal, France, Japan, Nigeria, Norway, Russian Federation, Rwanda, Saudi Arabia, Slovenia, United Kingdom, United States, Canada, China, Germany, Malaysia, Mexico, Spain and Thailand. Belgium and Gabon acted as observers.

The distribution of seats is also worthy of a specific mention: South, Central and North America are entitled to three seats. Yet, the entire

North American subcontinent is represented in the Commission. On the other hand, only Argentina held a seat on behalf of the rest of the region during the 2008–09 period. Of course, this is in part a result of the arrangements entered into by the regional group. But the rules above also have an influence in ensuring the lack of balance in the composition: for example, while the entire American continent has three seats, the Europe region was allotted seven seats, which represents, by itself, almost a third of the entire composition of the Commission.

In theory, all countries are represented in the Commission albeit indirectly through their regional representatives. Now, even acknowledging that the regional representative is in a position to convey to the Commission the concerns or proposals originating from one regional member, this is not the same as having the latter member directly defending its interests in plenary. To make things more difficult, in case a proposal by a country non-member to the Policy Commission is rejected in this forum (or accompanied by a 'recommendation' not to be adopted), this country will have to afford the political burden of opening the discussions at the Council session.

Of the G8 countries, only Italy was not a member of the Policy Commission during the period described above. Of the 24 members of the Commission (observers excluded), 12 are also members of the OECD. This gives an idea of the influence developed countries have on this body. If one considers in addition that the Policy Commission is tasked to turn the inputs from the technical bodies into recommendations to the Council, it comes as small wonder that developed countries hold a 'filter' mechanism in their hands.

But the filter exercised by the Policy Commission is a remedy of last resort. Prior to that, the Secretariat itself has prerogatives that enable it to influence the decision-making process. This results essentially from the lack of clear rules on certain procedural steps to be taken, from which the Secretariat extracts influential power.

A good example of the exercise of influential power by the Secretariat is provided by the recent history of the SECURE Working Group. After the three sessions held from June 2007 to April 2008, no consensus had been reached in order to allow for the SECURE Standards to be finalized. The document remained open for further changes, including for changes intended for those standards that had not received comments, as the Working Group did not decide to undertake an 'early harvest' of the work. In fact, it is often claimed by developing countries such as Brazil that 'nothing is agreed until everything is agreed'.[36] Yet, there are no clear rules as to the procedure to be followed for the preparation of the documents that are meant to be considered by the Policy Commission. It is not clear whether the Secretariat can draw its own conclusions as to the state of play and submit a document prepared accordingly to the Commission, absent prior approval by the member states.

Unfortunately, this is exactly what happened in the interval between the third meeting of the SECURE Working Group and the June 2008 Policy Commission session. Contrary to at least the assessment of a part of the membership as to the current status of the standards, the Secretariat authored a document ('Report of SECURE Working Group')[37] whereby it was stated that 'the SECURE Working Group had reached consensus on an updated version of the Provisional SECURE Standards, except for three Standards'. Following the presentation of the three 'non-consensual' provisions, the Secretariat's document contained language whereby it was suggested that the SECURE Working Group had requested the Policy Commission to recommend the Council to adopt a decision on this matter.[38] But this issue had never been raised in the Working Group nor has it at any time decided to seek a political decision on the matter.

Members of the SECURE Working Group have not been consulted during the preparation of the document. As a matter of fact, they were presented this document only a couple of days prior to the 2008 Council session.

Examples such as this call urgently for increased transparency and member-driven processes at the WCO, or else balanced and legitimate discussions are put in peril. The haphazard manner with which work is sometimes conducted is a mark that has been perceived in the functioning of the WCO, which should be addressed.

***

These aspects of the functioning of the WCO account for it being regarded as a convenient destination for proponents of a TRIPS-plus agenda: it is insulated from other forums where discussions on intellectual property are held in an informed manner; access to documents is difficult; accreditation of public interest organizations is not as easy as that of right-holders; finally, the Secretariat enjoys a significant degree of unaccountability in the production of documents that will serve as the basis for the decision-making process. On the top of all that, developed countries hold the upper hand in the body entrusted with outlining the decisions that are forwarded to the Council for final decision.

For developing countries, these features have translated into a host of major difficulties, from the virtual surprise of seeing the WCO pushing an ambitious TRIPS-plus agenda – and the time required to coordinate an appropriate reaction – to unexpectedly unfavourable measures in the conduction of business. This adds to the traditional limitations imposed on developing countries, in particular the scarcity of human resources.

The next section examines the effects of the SECURE project, as a forum shopping initiative, over policy-making by developing countries.

DEALING WITH SECURE FROM A DEVELOPING COUNTRY PERSPECTIVE

At least since the process that led to the 2001 Doha Declaration on TRIPS and Public Health, developing countries have perceived the existence of common concerns in the area of intellectual property. More importantly, they have been able to translate these concerns into political action.

While in the early stages of this coordinated policy-making process attention was focused more emphatically on health issues, over time the joint action generated positive externalities that have enabled developing countries to work together on other areas also potentially affected by the increasing pressure to steer international negotiations in a TRIPS-plus direction. This move is illustrated by two initiatives worthy of notice: the incorporation of a 'Development Agenda' into WIPO and the proposal to amend the TRIPS Agreement in order to make it compatible with the Convention on Biological Diversity, a proposal co-sponsored by a group of developing countries exceeding half of the entire membership of the WTO.

Further to these initiatives, other examples of developing country coordinated action on areas potentially affected by the expansion of IP norms could include the discussion of the effects of intellectual property rights on public health innovation, within the framework of the WHO, as well as the signing of the Convention on Cultural Diversity at UNESCO.

The positive externalities that emerged from the coordinated action can be partially ascribed to a learning process in which developing countries as well as public interest organizations became cognizant of the concrete impact of the intellectual property provisions enshrined in the TRIPS Agreement. The learning experience also contributed to assessing better the possible implications of the TRIPS-plus agendas pushed by developed countries since the mid-1990s, whose paramount examples are the 'patent agenda' and the 'digital agenda' at WIPO. By then, developing countries' delegates in Geneva as well as their colleagues in the corresponding capitals were increasingly aware of the political dimension of intellectual property negotiations.

The forums mentioned above could arguably be regarded as *political* and, until recently, it could be said that intellectual property negotiating agendas were to a certain extent confined to forums of this nature. Compared with this backdrop, the WCO is a new frontier: for the first time a politically sensitive agenda is embraced by an organization so far viewed as essentially technical.

From a developing country perspective what is relevant to observe about the SECURE project is how challenging it is to muster support amongst developing countries in this unexpected scenario. Different from the situation described above regarding political forums, developing country policy-making in the case of SECURE requires triggering a joint learning process anew. What is even more challenging, ensuring coherence between positions in Geneva and in Brussels entails very particular coordination efforts at the domestic level: as opposed to the cases of the *political* forums, where coordination involved more often than not only political actors, this time around positions have to be fine-tuned with customs administrations at home.

This process brings to the fore a new geometry that needs to be duly grasped by developing countries in order to turn the defence of their interests into effective action. Developing countries can certainly benefit from what has already been done in Geneva, but, among other factors, it takes time to translate this into action in Brussels.

These questions are addressed below in two parts. First, an overview of the difficulties faced so far by developing countries in the SECURE process is presented. This is followed by the challenges that lie ahead and the possible questions to which developing countries' attention could be directed with a view to influencing the results of SECURE.

Salient Difficulties Faced by Developing Countries, as Shown by the Example of the Work Concerning SECURE

The fact that the launching of the SECURE initiative met limited or no opposition at the 2007 Council session does not mean that this project reflects a shared sentiment by the entire membership, including developing countries. It means, more likely, that not everyone was fully aware of what was being proposed. In the case of developing countries more specifically, it probably means also that they were not represented in plenary by the people in their governments who hold expertise on IP. And this for a simple reason: anyone who cares to look at the agenda of the 2007 Council will not find an item called 'SECURE Standards' or any name suggesting its discussion, let alone its approval. What is more, the document that provided the basis for the discussions (the 'Provisional' version prepared by the Secretariat) will not be found among the documents available for the Council session either. It is to be found only in the agenda of the 57th Policy Commission session, which took place in Brussels from 25 June to 27 June 2007 – that is, three days before the Council session. But even here an interesting fact is to be highlighted: according to the information provided on the WCO website, the standards document itself was posted on the Policy Commission site on 6 June, that is, 19 days before the Policy Commission started. This is relevant when one takes into account that it was the first time *ever* that this draft document was made available to members.[39]

The basis for the Council decision on the item concerning SECURE was then produced by the 57th Policy Commission. Considering that the Policy Commission comprises only a fraction of the membership (24 states), those members who did not participate in the 57th session – that is, the majority of the 174 members – were only informed of what was to be the basis for the Council decision the day before the Council session began.

In this situation it was very difficult for countries to prepare themselves for the 2007 Council discussion on the item concerning SECURE. This is all the more the case for developing countries.

If one considers the 19-day period during which countries were aware of the content of the draft SECURE Standards before the

Council session, it is virtually impossible to conceive that developing countries had the time not only to coordinate at their domestic
levels but also among themselves in order to take an informed
position on this item. Viewed in this light, it does not come as a
contradiction that although developing countries were represented
at the discussions of the item on SECURE during the 2007 Council
session, many of them raised concerns with respect to this very
project only at a later stage. It is also not surprising that the number
of developing countries doing so is increasing.

Developing countries' participation in such an arcane process
is aggravated by key difficulties that they would anyway confront.
These difficulties concern shortages of staffing in Brussels as well
as the challenge of coping with the time it takes for coordination
among themselves and at the domestic level.

There is also another potential difficulty developing countries may
face when trying to establish their position regarding SECURE:
by and large, the WCO agenda is followed by representatives from
customs agencies and not by their foreign affairs or trade counterparts in the government. And this is justified by the fact that the
WCO has been seen, at least until the introduction of the SECURE
agenda, as dealing with purely customs issues. Concerns expressed
to customs by other government agencies about the ongoing activities of the SECURE Working Group give rise to an interplay at the
domestic level that could be time-consuming and, in some cases,
defy the coherence in terms of the positions upheld in Geneva and
in Brussels.

Despite all these challenges, the balance of developing country
participation within the SECURE Working Group reveals that
some of their concerns have been reflected in the discussions and also
that developing countries have managed to stress how sensitive the
issue of IPRs can be.

However, there remain a number of issues that need to be
addressed if developing countries' interests are to be safeguarded.
These questions are dealt with below.

**What Have Developing Countries Done So Far in the SECURE
Process? What Efforts Could Be Scaled Up?**

Much needs to be done in order to ensure balanced work within the
SECURE Group. (1) On the procedural level, issues such as the lack

of transparency and uncertain rules should be addressed. Unclear or non-existent rules deprive members of their prerogative to steer the process. Other important procedural questions include the need for public access to SECURE documents (which means addressing the copyright protection imposed over working documents and the need for a password to access working documents) and also the process for admission of observers. (2) As far as the substance is concerned, the discussion of the standards would stand to gain from being more informed, especially to the benefit of developing countries.

The entire membership would benefit from more in-depth discussions about the implications of each proposed standard – not only to assess their efficiency vis-à-vis the goals they were conceived to achieve but also to examine their pros and cons from a broader perspective. These discussions could be undertaken with the help of stakeholders with varied backgrounds.

As shown above, until the 2007 Council session, the process that led to the launching of SECURE was led almost exclusively by a handful of developed countries and by the WCO Secretariat. It was not until the initiative was already in motion that developing countries began to take a more active part and express their concerns with respect to the direction SECURE was originally designed to take.

It is a fact that developing countries' concerns were initially triggered at the substantive provisions of the draft SECURE Standards document, and not at the procedural-systemic questions. But this is basically due to the unusual order the work was arranged by the champions of SECURE.

Although the first meeting of the SECURE Working Group (October 2007) saw some divergences among members, it focuses more on differences on the implementation level of the draft standards than on the concept itself of the entire project. At the second session (February 2008), Brazil raised its concerns with respect to the TRIPS-plus push behind the SECURE project. Brazil also cautioned that a TRIPS-plus discussion was unsuited to the mandate of the WCO and that there existed forums with competence to undertake these discussions. In order to safeguard the positions developing countries have been sustaining in Geneva for quite some time, Brazil then proposed a blanket provision (by then termed 'Standard 0') whereby the standards should not undermine the flexibilities accorded by relevant international agreements, in particular the TRIPS Agreement. In addition, seeking to effectively reflect the purported voluntary nature of the document, Brazil requested the replacement of the 'shoulds' with 'mays' throughout the operative part of the standards. Both proposals met resistance by a couple of developed countries and were left between square brackets for the subsequent meeting, which took place in April 2008.

During the third meeting, the number of developing countries with an active role in the session was visibly larger. Not only Brazil, but also Argentina, Ecuador, Mexico and China voiced concerns with both the substance and the process that were being imposed at the meeting. While the former 'Standard 0' was adopted, other standards ended the meeting between square brackets. The issue of lack of agreed Terms of Reference was also raised by developing countries. In sum, at the closing of the third meeting, nothing had been finalized and a number of questions remained pending.

In the interval between the third meeting and the period of the summit bodies' meetings (Policy Commission and the Council), developing countries have also had to react to a document prepared exclusively by the Secretariat under the name of 'Report of SECURE Working Group'[40] in which the state of play of that time was presented as one where consensus had been reached by the Working Group. At the Policy Commission and at the 2008 Council sessions, the views sustained by developing countries were upheld and it was decided that further work was needed.

The fourth meeting was held in October 2008, during which the draft Terms of Reference were discussed for the first time. Also with a view to this session, Brazil and Argentina submitted the document 'Ensuring Transparency, Legitimacy and a Member-driven Process in the SECURE Working Group', whose main purpose was to address the procedural irregularities verified so far in the conduction of the entire process. The fourth session did not come up with an agreed response to these questions.

Following the difficulty in bridging the gap between developing and developed countries after the fourth meeting, the Secretariat proposed to 'set aside' the discussions on the SECURE Standards and recommended the establishment of a new group to deal with IPR matters. This proposal has been submitted, and approved, by the 24 members of the Policy Commission that met in Buenos Aires, on 9 and 10 December 2008.

According to the proposal adopted in Buenos Aires, the Secretariat will be in charge of drafting the Terms of Reference for the new group. The draft will be 'finalized' by the 24 members of the Policy Commission before it is submitted for adoption, one day later, at the 2009 Council session. In other words, no change in the decision-making procedure has been undertaken at the WCO.

This will, of course, put to the test once again developing countries's capabilities of coordinating on short notice, since it is expected that they will only be provided the text they should discuss a day before the Council meeting.

CONCLUSIONS

Although spurred by the concrete challenges posed by counterfeiting and piracy, the solution proposed by the SECURE project, in particular by the SECURE Standards, risks overshooting its target as it may threaten, among a host of other objects, the legal trade in generic medicines. This is done, for example, by including patent infringements among those cases for which customs authorities would be empowered to act. There is no sign that the group that may be established to replace SECURE will move in a different direction.

Issues such as the possible barriers that might ensue over trade in generic medicines should be raised and discussed at the WCO, ideally with a more balanced representation (that is, not only right-holders) and with the presence of experts on intellectual property rights. Informed and balanced discussions should be a condition for the work of the organization in the field of IPR.

With hindsight, it is clear that the participation of developing countries in the WCO has been growing since the second meeting of the SECURE Working Group in February 2008. The increased participation of developing countries in the process results chiefly from a network action that occurs in Brussels, Geneva and in the capitals. This is coupled with a growing number of awareness-raising activities by which delegates and capital-based officials are alerted to the overall consequences of the SECURE project as proposed.

On the other hand, legitimate decision-making is defied by a number of institutional devices existing at the WCO, the most prominent being the composition of the Policy Commission, which is not only a faint representation of the membership but is also dominated by developed countries.

Whatever new group might be created at the WCO to discuss and propose measures on the IP sector, its mandate should reflect what is the object of consensus across the membership. The challenge by piracy and counterfeiting is real and there are ways to constructively address them from a customs perspective, as long as it respects the mandate of the WCO as well as the flexibilities provided for in the applicable legal framework. Solutions should be found that do not affect negatively legitimate trade.

In sum, some lessons can be drawn by developing countries from the work carried out so far at the WCO, as follows:

1.   TRIPS-plus strategies pushed by developed countries are moving from the stage of substantive norm-setting to the drafting of implementation-level standards or to the provision of TRIPS-plus technical assistance. This leads to a change in the interlocutors that developed countries will approach in developing countries: while beforehand negotiations were pursued by diplomats, the dialogue seems to be currently undertaken with customs officials, police officers, patent examiners and so on, under the label 'technical' dialogues or the like.

2.   Developing countries' interests risk being eroded at 'second-best' forums, in which it is normally not expected to see emerge negotiations of a politically sensitive nature. In this context, developing countries will stand to gain by operating in network. Specifically where IP is concerned, it is important to bring aboard developing countries' delegates in Geneva so that discussions on these second-best forums can be followed in tandem with the work in Geneva, so as to ensure coherence.

3.   Negotiations pursued at 'second-best' forums may require strengthened domestic coordination within developing countries, in order to ensure coherence on their external actions. This can prove challenging especially in cases where the 'second-best' forums are normally viewd as 'purely technical'.

4.   The work of the WCO in the area of IPRs should be submitted to increased accountability and scrutiny from public opinion. It is thus important to engage in awareness-raising activities with a focus on public interest organizations, as well as parts of the private sector currently not represented at the WCO, such as generic manufacturers.

NOTES

1. The opinions in the text are the author's alone and do not necessarily reflect the positions of the Brazilian government. E-mail: hcmoraes@braseuropa.be.
2. Quotations of texts originating from reports of World Customs Organization (WCO) meetings have been omitted in view of the fact that the organization claims copyright over them. While the very claim is debatable, let alone its extension over scientific articles, the author preferred not to quote excerpts of said documents. This is without prejudice to the precise references of where relevant passages are to be found in these documents.
3. 'Agreement on Trade-Related Aspects of Intellectual Property Rights', Agreement Establishing the World Trade Organization, Annex 1C, Legal Instruments. *Results of the Uruguay Round*, vol. 31, *International Legal Materials* **33** (81) (Marrakesh: 15 April, 1994).
4. The push to incorporate intellectual property rights within the scope of the Uruguay Round of negotiations (thereby depriving WIPO [World Intellectual Property Organization] of its prerogative as the only standard-setting institution in this field) is recognized as a result of, among other factors, the 'disillusionment' of the private sectors in the United States with WIPO, which was later followed by their counterparts in Europe and Japan. See Drahos (2002, p. 110).
5. To the effects of this chapter, a 'TRIPS-plus' agenda refers to a number of proposals that seek to increase the protection accorded to right-holders in excess of the level set by the WTO TRIPS Agreement. More often than not, these proposals come at the detriment of the normative flexibilities that allow states to pursue many policies of public interest, for example, in the areas of public health, access to culture and incentives to research. Proposals that ultimately target inscribing TRIPS-plus commitments in this sense have traditionally met resistance by developing countries, who depend by and large on policies put in place by their governments in order to satisfy societal goals.
6. See, for example, the communication by the European Communities 'Enforcement of Intellectual Property Rights' (IP/C/W/448, 9 June 2005), followed by other communications of a similar nature. The proposal to discuss the issue raised by the European proposal (also supported by other developed countries) has met criticism from a great number of WTO members who have concerns with a TRIPS-plus discussion on this matter.
7. At WIPO, the Advisory Committee on Enforcement (ACE) does not have a mandate to set normative standards of whatever nature.
8. One example is the assumption contained in the WCO IPR Model Provisions that it is necessary to go beyond the TRIPS Agreement in order to 'provide an effective and efficient level of IPR protection and enforcement at their borders'.
9. The main thrust leading to the upgrading of the status of piracy and counterfeit combat within WCO's agenda seems to have resulted from a statement delivered by the United Kingdom during the 2005 Council session (Document No. SC0066E1a, paragraph 266). Two months later, in September 2005, the G8 summit that took place under the British chair in Gleneagles placed emphasis on the reduction of piracy and counterfeiting through, inter alia, the promotion of laws, regulations and/or procedures to strengthen effective IPR enforcement. As early as December 2005, the WCO Policy Commission decided to request the drafting of standards on this matter to the Secretariat (Document No. SP0202E1, paragraph 170).
10. The version of the SECURE Standards that was publicly available until June 2008 (the first draft, dated June 2007, first paragraph), mentions that 'Countering

IPR infringements was a priority on the G8 agenda (United Kingdom 2005, Russia 2006, Germany 2007). In addition to health, safety and tax revenue concerns, the G8 has recognized that product innovation and entrepreneurial inventiveness are also casualties of unchecked IPR infringement'. The G8 is in fact the only international forum mentioned in this paragraph, where the justification for the existence of SECURE is presented. See: http://www.wcoomd.org/files/1.%20Public%20files/PDFandDocuments/Enforcement/SECURE_E.pdf.

11. Report of 2007 Council session (Document No. SC0082E1a, paragraph 139).
12. Report of the 57th session of the Policy Commission (June 2007, Document No. SP0250E1b, paragraph 156).
13. Report of 2007 Council session (Document No. SC0082E1a, paragraph 135).
14. The Secretariat's authorship of the first draft of the SECURE Standards stems clearly from the Report of 2007 Council session (Document No. SC0082E1a, paragraph 135).
15. During the 2007 Council session, the Secretary General of the WCO recognized this fact by stating his hope that the definitive standards would come into existence in a few years' time (Report of 2007 Council session (Document No. SC0082E1a, paragraph 137)). The decision by the 2007 Council meant that members signalled their intention to accept the provisional document as a basis to start discussions. It would be far-fetched to see in the 2007 Council decision an outright agreement with the content of the standards. Such a conclusion would be denied by the wide-ranging controversies that have pervaded the discussions of the standards ever since the first meeting of the Working Group.
16. The draft Terms of Reference have been discussed for the first time at the fourth meeting of the SECURE Working Group (October 2008).
17. Other documents/programmes mentioned at the WCO website are the following 'WCO Risk Management Guidelines for More Effective Controls', 'IPR Diagnostic Survey', 'WCO IPR E-Learning Module' (http://www.wcoomd.org/home_wco_topics_epoverviewboxes_epwcostrategyiprsecure.htm). These issues have not been discussed by the SECURE Working Group.
18. Report of the 57th session of the Policy Commission, June 2007 (Document No. SP0250E1b, paragraph 143).
19. 'Members shall be free to determine the appropriate method of implementing the provisions of this Agreement within their own legal system and practice'.
20. Report of 2007 Council session (Document No. SC0082E1a, paragraph 133). The SAFE Working Group is entrusted with preparing standards in the area of risk analysis for, inter alia, inspections of consignments.
21. Although the alleged nature of the standards is voluntary, the fact that its provisions are drafted in a mandatory language may have legal consequences as interpretative tools that could, for example, be borrowed by dispute settlement bodies requested to solve cases brought before them that concern IP enforcement.
22. The term 'precision' is used here in the sense suggested by Keohane et al. (2000, p. 417): 'Precision means that the rules unambiguously define the conduct they require, authorize or proscribe'.
23. A thorough examination of the draft standards vis-à-vis the obligations from the TRIPS Agreement can be found in Li (2008b).
24. Countries who have an interest in incorporating TRIPS-plus provisions into their legislations should be able to do so. The concern raised by the activities proposed at the WCO lies in the fact that it can ultimately sweep away this possibility, by constraining countries to adopt, from a top–bottom, 'one-size-fits-all' approach, what the organization will label as a 'best practice' (a concept that excludes different practices as not being as appropriate).

25. This draft version of Standard 1, as well the other draft standards quoted below, were discussed during the third meeting of the SECURE Working Group (April 2008).
26. 'Members shall, in conformity with the provisions set out below, adopt procedures [footnote omitted] to enable a right-holder, who has valid grounds for suspecting that the importation of counterfeit trademark or pirated copyright goods [footnote omitted] may take place, to lodge an application in writing with competent authorities, administrative or judicial, for the suspension by the customs authorities of the release into free circulation of such goods'.
27. Article 51 makes a difference between, on the one side, *the competent authorities, administrative or judicial* and, on the other, *the customs authorities*: while the former receive the applications, the latter comply with whatever decision is taken by the 'competent authorities', including the suspension of the release into free circulation of the goods.
28. This issue has been raised by the European Parliament in a Draft Report on the Impact of Counterfeiting on International Trade (Committee on International Trade, 26 June 2008): 'a distinction needs to be drawn between generic medicines, the circulation of and trading in which should be encouraged, both in the EU and in developing countries, and counterfeit [sic] medicines'. The private sector in developing countries has already realized the serious impacts that might emerge from a possible 'overempowerment' of customs authorities beyond their area of expected expertise. The Vice-Chair of the Brazilian Association of the Fine Chemistry, Biotechnology and its Specialties (ABIFINA) has voiced concerns with respect to the work of the SECURE (Oliveira, 2008). The Indian generics industry is also concerned with the proposed SECURE standards ('Indian drug firms wary of global customs norms' (Mathew, 2008)).
29. This is already a reality for generic producers who choose to stop in transit at European ports, where many of their shipments are retained on the charge of carrying counterfeit drugs. See 'Shipments seizure: India's drug makers may avoid EU route: problematic definitions of counterfeit drugs may be leading to misinterpretation of patent laws', Livemint.com, 12 December 2008. Available at http://www.livemint.com/2008/12/12000018/Shipments-seizure-India8217. html; accessed 20 January 2009.
30. http://wikileaks.org/leak/acta-proposal-2007.pdf, accessed 18 December 2008.
31. The version of the document retrieved from the WCO members-only website is not protected by copyright.
32. For this reason, during the second session of SECURE (February 2008), the Brazilian delegation has made clear that the document does not have Brazil's approval. See report of the second meeting of the SECURE Working Group (Document No. LS0007E, Annex II). During the fourth meeting (October 2008), Brazil requested clarification from the Secretariat as to whether the current version of the Model Provisions had been submitted for approval by the membership. The answer provided was that a 1995 Council decision approved a version of the document prepared, then, with a view to helping countries to implement the TRIPS Agreement. That 1995 decision would be the ground for the subsequent updatings, including the current version of 2001. Brazil challenged the 'blank cheque' explanation and presented its view that this document was deprived of any approval by the membership.
33. WIPO Copyright Treaty, *International Legal Materials* **36**, 65 (Geneva: 20 December 1996); WIPO Performances and Phonograms Treaty, *International Legal Materials* **36**, 76 (Geneva: 20 December 1996). The number of parties to each instrument is provided according to information contained in the WIPO website (www.wipo.int) on 15 September 2008.

34. The tension underlying this question is portrayed, for example, in Garret (2006).
35. Report of the first session of the SECURE Working Group (Document No. LS0004E1, paragraph 27).
36. See report of the third meeting of the SECURE Working Group (Document No. LS0008E1a, paragraph 18).
37. Document No. SP0269E1a.
38. Id., paragraph 9.
39. During the February 2007 session of the Enforcement Committee, references were made to instruments with 'customs norms' and 'standards', apparently prepared by the Secretariat (Document No. EC0205E1, paragraph 127), which could be the origin of the 'Provisional' version of the SECURE Standards. However, there was no suggestion by then that the text as discussed in the June 2007 Policy Commission already existed. In fact, the document that served as a basis for the discussion of this issue during the June 2007 Policy Commission mentions that it resulted from consultations and discussions held at the December 2006 session of the Policy Commission, at the February 2007 session of the Enforcement Committee and at the IPR Strategic Group meeting in March 2007 (footnote to page 1 of Document No. SP0241E1a). This information confirms that the document was prepared having in view the 57th session of the Policy Commission.
40. See note 36.

9. Ensuring the benefits of intellectual property rights to development: a competition policy perspective

Yusong Chen[1]

BACKGROUND: GLOBAL PROLIFERATION OF INTELLECTUAL PROPERTY AND CHALLENGES FOR DEVELOPING COUNTRIES

The past several decades have seen a significant proliferation of intellectual property rights (IPRs) across the world. Among these developments, a concrete step was the conclusion of the WTO TRIPS Agreement,[2] which has substantially increased global IPR protection levels in the following ways: (1) for the first time, it provides comprehensive harmonized minimum standards for almost all kinds of IPRs, and extends IPR obligations for many developing countries (Finger and Schuler, 1999); (2) it stipulates, also for the first time in international treaties, extensive enforcement obligations for all WTO Members; (3) it incorporates an effective dispute settlement system within the WTO framework.

The requirements for a high level of IPR protection in the TRIPS Agreement have brought enormous challenges for developing countries. They are very sceptical that high incentives would bring technologies and innovations quickly and automatically (Sakakibara and Branstetter, 2001). In fact, fostering domestic innovation and creativity is a long-term process and depends on various local conditions,[3] which may not exist in many developing countries (UNCTAD, 1996). At the same time, developing countries may suffer seriously from huge social costs arising from IPRs.

Perhaps the most significant challenge for developing countries is that sometimes protection of IPRs may also lead to barriers for innovation and development. It should be pointed out that patents, copyrights, trademarks, industrial designs, and so on are private rights owned by right-holders participating in market competition and pursuing economic benefits to the maximum possible extent. Certain practices of right-holders could generate anticompetitive behaviour that may have a negative impact on consumers and prejudice national economic development. For example, patent pools or cross-licence arrangements of transnational corporations (TNCs) may prevent competitors from accessing essential technologies and restrain new innovations;[4] exclusive dealings, tying arrangements or excessive pricing may bring harm to downstream industries and consumers.[5] Developing countries are vulnerable to this kind of abusive use of IPRs (Tom and Newberg, 1997). Most developing countries are highly dependent on the transfer of technology from developed countries. Restrictive practices imposed by TNCs may raise extensive barriers of transfer of technology to developing countries.[6]

This chapter will first examine the practices of developed countries in coping with the anti-competitive aspects of IPRs; then it will analyse activities in international forums in this regard and explore the policy space available to states under the relevant international conventions. In the light of this analysis, the chapter will provide some practical policy suggestions for developing countries.

The central theme of this chapter is that IPR protection should not be pursued in isolation from competition policy. Developing countries need to formulate and enforce domestic regulations to eliminate negative impacts of the monopolistic private rights conferred by the grant of IPRs, so as to ensure to the largest extent the benefits of IPRs in terms of their development objectives.

BALANCING INTELLECTUAL PROPERTY RIGHTS AND PUBLIC AND SOCIAL INTERESTS: APPROACHES OF DEVELOPED COUNTRIES

Most developed countries adopted competition/antitrust laws as countermeasures against abuse of IPRs. Their experiences could be useful for developing countries to formulate their own policies to control the negative effects of abuse of IPRs.

The United States

Antitrust regulations against abuse of IPRs have been implemented in the United States for a considerable period. During the 1970s, the US antitrust authorities used to have a restrictive view of the monopolistic nature of IPRs. The well-known 'Nine No-No's' illustrated per se rules for licensing practices (Wilson, 1970; Pate, 2007).[7] Since the 1980s, under the influence of the economic thinking of the 'Chicago school', the agencies have gradually changed their minds and applied a more tolerant view towards the exercise of IPRs.[8]

On 6 April 1995, the US Department of Justice (DOJ) and the Federal Trade Commission (FTC) issued the 'Antitrust Guidelines for the Licensing of Intellectual Property', which formed a landmark in the development of antitrust policy concerning intellectual property.[9] The guidelines are based on three core principles: (1) for the purpose of antitrust analysis, the US antitrust agencies regard intellectual property as being essentially comparable to any other form of property; (2) the antitrust agencies do not presume that intellectual property creates market power in the antitrust context; and (3) the antitrust agencies recognize that intellectual property licensing allows firms to combine complementary factors of production and is generally procompetitive.[10]

The guidelines state that 'the intellectual property laws and the antitrust laws share the common purpose of promoting innovation and enhancing consumer welfare'. The US antitrust agencies 'apply the same general antitrust principles to conduct involving intellectual property that they apply to conduct involving any other form of tangible or intangible property'. In this regard, in the vast majority of cases, the US antitrust agencies evaluate restraints in intellectual property licensing arrangements under the *rule of reason*. And if the 'nature and necessary effect' of a restraint are 'so plainly anticompetitive', then it should be treated as unlawful per se. Among the restraints that have been held per se unlawful are naked price-fixing, output restraints, market division among horizontal competitors, as well as certain group boycotts and resale price maintenance.[11]

Following the guidelines, a Task Force of the DOJ made three recommendations in October 2004 with regard to antitrust enforcement: (1) support the rights of intellectual property owners to decide independently whether to license their technology to others;

(2) encourage trade associations and other business organizations seeking to establish industry standards for the prevention of intellectual property theft to use the Justice Department's business review procedure for guidance regarding antitrust enforcement concerns; and (3) continue to promote international cooperation and principled agreement between nations on the proper application of antitrust laws to intellectual property rights.[12]

Currently, the US authorities primarily focus on specific anticompetitive actions of intellectual property right-holders as judged by their effect on markets and consumer welfare. At the same time, the agencies also try to make their analysis objective, predictable and transparent (DOJ and FTC, 2007).

European Community

Articles 81 and 82 of the EC Treaty [Treaty Establishing European Community] constitute the basis of European Community competition policy in relation to private undertakings. While enforcing these provisions and other related secondary legislations, the European Commission and the European Court of Justice (ECJ) had progressively developed a set of principles and rules for regulating various aspects of the exercise of IPRs (Anderman, 1998).

Generally, the European authorities draw a distinction between the *existence* of IPRs and their *exercise*.[13] It is stated that these rights can only be exercised to protect the 'specific subject matter' of the property concerned. In this context, Article 81 has been used to regulate the abusive conduct of individual right-holders, including refusal to deal, refusal to license, tie-ins, and so on. Article 82 and the block exemption regulation mainly focus on terms of bilateral technology transfer agreements. Furthermore, the competition rules for IPRs also extend to joint ventures, mergers and acquisition. With respect to remedies, the competition rules on IPRs appear to be rather stringent and ambitious compared with antitrust rules in the United States.[14]

On 27 April 2004, the European Commission enacted Commission Regulation No. 772/2004 on the Application of Article 81(3) of the Treaty to Categories of Technology Transfer Agreements.[15] It also released on the same date 'Commission's Guidelines on the Application of Article 81 EC to Technology Transfer Agreements'. As the most important legislative works in this area, the new

Regulation and the Guidelines abandon the previous formalistic approach, expand the scope of regulation and offer greater flexibilities. These changes reflect the present philosophy of the Commission that most licence agreements do not restrict competition and create pro-competition efficiencies (Kjøelbye and Peeperkorn, 2007).

Japan

The Anti-Monopoly Act (AMA) of Japan was enacted in 1947, which established a general framework of competition policy. Article 21 of the AMA provides that, 'The provisions of this Act shall not apply to such acts recognizable as the exercise of rights under the Copyright Act, the Patent Act, the Utility Model Act, the Design Act, or the Trademark Act'.[16] This means that the Anti-Monopoly Act is applicable to restrictions in relation to the use of technology that is essentially not considered to be the exercise of IPRs.[17]

In 1968, Japan's Fair Trade Commission published the 'Antimonopoly Act Guidelines for International Licensing Agreements', aiming to regulate 'unfair' provisions in licensing agreements.[18] The guidelines were revised in 1989 and 1999 and apply to both domestic and international agreements.[19] The 1999 guidelines, which include detailed analysis of a wide range of conceivable clauses in licensing agreements, appear to shift away from the formalistic approach of the 1989 version and to a certain extent adopt the rule of reason approach (Heath, 2007).

The most recent policy instrument enacted was the 'Guidelines for the Use of Intellectual Property under the Anti-Monopoly Act', issued by the Fair Trade Commission on 28 September 2007, which is designed to provide more clarity on the opinions underlying the AMA in relation to IPRs.[20] The new guidelines extend the scope of the AMA to all intellectual properties related to technology, and provide for 'a comprehensive consideration of the content of the restrictions' in order to evaluate whether or not restrictions in relation to the use of technology lessens competition in a market.[21]

A Few Observations

Competition policy is as equally essential as IPR protection in developed countries to promote research and development (R&D)

and encourage innovations. Experiences of the developed economies show that competition policies contributed substantially to
achieving efficiencies and ensuring public interests while enforcing
IPRs.

The philosophy of competition law has been profoundly changed
by the Chicago School since the 1990s. Now more and more governments believe that only the minimum extent of intervention is needed
and the market will regulate itself. In this regard, the principle of
rule of reason or similar analysis is accepted by many competition
authorities. However, this approach of rule of reason leaves more
discretion to competition authorities, and also may create some
uncertainties in the enforcement of competition policy (Barton,
1997).

It could also be seen that, in addition to the basic competition
legislations, competition authorities tend to issue some guidelines
regarding IPRs in order to further elaborate policies. While including detailed analysis and various examples, these guidelines are defi-
nitely helpful to improve the transparency and predictability of the
competition policy.

INTEGRATING COMPETITION POLICY AND INTELLECTUAL PROPERTY: EXPLORING POLICY SPACES IN INTERNATIONAL TREATIES

Competition policy and IPRs are as integrated as two sides of a
coin. Most international IPR conventions incorporate competition
regulations. And today, from WIPO to WTO, competition issues are
widely discussed at international forums.

Traditions of Limitations and Exceptions in International Intellectual Property Conventions and Treaties

Almost all international IPR conventions provide certain inherent
limitations and exceptions on the rights conferred, particularly on
competition aspects. Some examples can be seen in the following:

- Paris Convention: Article 5A(2) specifically provides that
  each country shall have the right to take legislative measures

providing for the grant of compulsory licences to prevent the abuses that might result from the exercise of the exclusive rights conferred by the patent. Article 10*bis* also provides regulations against unfair competition.[22]

- Berne Convention: Article 17 of the Berne Convention articulates that provisions of the convention can in no way affect the right of the government to regulate. Limitations and exceptions to established rights are also provided for or permitted under the convention.[23]

- Rome Convention: Article 15(2) of the Rome Convention stipulates that, 'any Contracting State may, in its domestic laws and regulations, provide for the same kinds of limitations with regard to the protection of performers, producers of phonograms and broadcasting organizations, as it provides for, in its domestic laws and regulations, in connection with the protection of copyright in literary and artistic works'.[24]

- Brussels Convention: Article 7 states that the convention shall in no way be interpreted as limiting the right of any contracting state to apply its domestic law in order to prevent abuses of monopoly.[25]

In fact, these provisions are so broad that governments could have substantial policy spaces to implement their national competition policies with regard to IPRs.[26]

International Efforts to Harmonize Competition Rules Relating to IPRs

The issue of competition policy vis-à-vis IPRs was detected by the founding fathers of the world trading system during the 1940s. Chapter V of the Havana Charter (1948) contained articles on the obligations of Members to address restrictive business practices and provided for the creation of an international framework and procedure to investigate such practices.[27] The following restrictive practices of IPRs were specifically listed in the Havana Charter:

(f) extending the use of rights under patents, trade marks or copyrights granted by any Member to matters which, according to its laws and regulations, are not within the scope of such grants, or to products or conditions of production, use or sale of which are likewise not the subject of such grants.[28]

The issues pertaining to competition and measures to deal with restrictive business practices were also raised in the GATT Uruguay Round negotiations. Although there is no multilateral agreement on trade and competition policy, the issue is very much present in many of the provisions of the existing WTO agreements (Kennedy, 2001).[29]

There has been much comprehensive work carried out at UNCTAD since the 1960s on restrictive business practices, when UNCTAD started to negotiate a Code of Conduct on the Transfer of Technology (Roffe, 1998). UNCTAD had discussed the text of this code until 1985 and the text submitted by the President of the Conference during its sixth session specified 14 types of restrictive practices from which countries making technology transactions should refrain.[30] This work did not conclude due to divergence among countries. In 1980, the UN General Assembly adopted the 'Set of Multilaterally Agreed Equitable Principles and Rules for the Control of Restrictive Business Practices', and it also provides rules for the control of anticompetitive practices and a framework for cooperation at the international level.

Another important attempt to promote the competition rules of IPRs was made by the OECD since the 1970s.[31] The OECD Competition Committee met regularly to exchange views and experience on the relationship between competition policy and IPRs.

In addition, national competition authorities also benefitted from enhanced cooperation by participating in other formal/informal international forums. For example, the International Competition Network (ICN) has provided an informal international network of public and private antitrust experts that seeks to promote best practices and facilitate soft convergence in antitrust enforcement, and it has convened working groups on various issues, including IPRs.[32]

Current Competition-related Provisions in the WTO TRIPS Agreement

The TRIPs Agreement, while stipulating rather strong minimum standards of protection for IPRs, incorporates a number of provisions that provide considerable policy space for WTO Members to formulate domestic regulations to ensure the proper use of the exclusive rights of IPRs (UNCTAD and ICTSD, 2005). This could be seen from several aspects:

First, the TRIPS Agreement generally recognizes WTO Members' right to adopt appropriate measures to prevent the abuse of intellectual property rights. Article 8.2 sets out the general principle that 'Appropriate measures, provided that they are consistent with the provisions of this Agreement, may be needed to prevent the abuse of intellectual property rights by right-holders or the resort to practices which unreasonably restrain trade or adversely affect the international transfer of technology'.[33]

Second, Section 8 of the TRIPS Agreement is particularly focused on 'Control of Anti-Competitive Practices in Contractual Licenses'.[34] Article 40.1 provides that Members agree that some licensing practices or conditions pertaining to intellectual property rights that restrain competition may have adverse effects on trade and may impede the transfer and dissemination of technology

Article 40.2 further emphasizes that 'Nothing in this Agreement shall prevent Members from specifying in their legislation licensing practices or conditions that may in particular cases constitute an abuse of intellectual property rights having an adverse effect on competition in the relevant market'. It also specifies three examples of potentially abusive licensing practices, namely, (1) exclusive grant-back conditions; (2) conditions preventing challenges to validity, and (3) coercive package licensing. In this regard, WTO Members are entitled to adopt, provided they are consistent with other provisions of the Agreement, appropriate measures to prevent or control anticompetitive practices.

Third, the TRIPS Agreement provides for a consultation and discovery procedure when a WTO Member has cause to believe that an IPR owner of another Member is violating antitrust laws and regulations.[35]

Fourth, explicitly regarding compulsory licensing, the TRIPS Agreement also specially attends to measures taken to address anticompetitive practices.[36]

Perspectives on the Work in WIPO and WTO

Development issues have been discussed intensely in the WIPO meetings in recent years. In October 2007, the WIPO General Assembly adopted a set of 45 recommendations to enhance the development dimension of its activities, and established a Committee on Development and Intellectual Property (CDIP) aiming to implement this Development Agenda.[37] Competition policy issues are expressly addressed in the Agenda:

- Promote measures that will help countries deal with IP-related anticompetitive practices, by providing technical cooperation to developing countries, especially LDCs, at their request, in order to better understand the interface between intellectual property rights and competition policies.[38]
- The WIPO Secretariat, without prejudice to the outcome of Member States' considerations, should address in its working documents for norm-setting activities, as appropriate and as directed by Member States, issues such as links between IP and competition.[39]
- To consider how to better promote pro-competitive intellectual property licensing practices, particularly with a view to fostering creativity, innovation and the transfer and dissemination of technology to interested countries, in particular developing countries and LDCs.[40]
- To have within the WIPO opportunities for exchange of national and regional experiences and information on the links between IP rights and competition policies.[41]

During the first two sessions of CDIP in 2008, detailed discussions were conducted on the effective implementation of these recommendations.[42] It could be seen that, although there is still a long way to go to implement all the recommendations in WIPO's future work, developing countries would benefit from this process.

As for the forum of WTO,[43] it could be seen that, due to the highly controversial positions of WTO Members, the WTO General Council decided in July 2004 that the issue of the interaction between trade and competition policy would no longer form part of the Doha Work Programme[44] and therefore that no work towards negotiations on any of these issues will take place within the WTO during the Doha Round. It seems that the issue of competition policy will not come back to the multilateral negotiations very soon (Anderson and Wager, 2006).[45]

INTEGRATING COMPETITION POLICY AND INTELLECTUAL PROPERTY: POLICY RECOMMENDATIONS FOR DEVELOPING COUNTRIES

Developed countries are major beneficiaries of the higher standards of IPR protection and developing countries are major losers (McCalman, 2001).[46] To ensure the benefits of IPR protection, it is essential for developing countries to take concrete steps to strike a proper balance between the need to protect and stimulate innovation and research, the need for transfer of technology, the interest of consumers and the needs of national economic development.

Adopt a Pro-competitive Intellectual Property Policy

A pro-competitive IPR policy means to integrate checks and balances in national IP legislations and enforcement systems. Article 1.1 of the TRIPS Agreement firmly declares that 'Members shall be free to determine the appropriate method of implementing the provisions of this Agreement within their own legal system and practice'. Both the TRIPS Agreement and other international IPR conventions contain various checks and balances of IPRs, such as fair use under copyright, the disclosure requirement and the limited term of patents. Therefore it is important for developing countries to fully explore these flexibilities and adopt a pro-competitive IPR policy (Correa, 2001).

Adopt National Competition Legislation Against Abuse of IPRs

Developing countries are mostly users, consumers and licensees of IPRs,[47] and they should accord greater importance on formulation and legislation of competition policy vis-à-vis IPRs. As a sword of Damocles for utilization of IPRs, competition legislation is fundamental to ensuring that IPRs will contribute to national economic development, innovative activities and transfer of technology. Moreover, it is also important for competition authorities of developing countries to enhance their cooperation with domestic intellectual property authorities with a view to improving their mutual understanding and developing appropriate national IP policies.

Enhance Enforcement of National Competition Policy Vis-à-vis IPRs

Developing countries should make every effort to enforce competition policy in order to achieve a proper balance between right-holders' interests and social and economic welfare. The relationship between intellectual property and competition is rather complex, especially with the infusion of economic principles into antitrust analysis. In this regard, competition authorities have to develop the capability to distinguish various forms of IP practices and their potential impact on static and dynamic competition. Moreover, as the most effective remedy to curb some blatant forms of anticompetitive activities, developing countries should maintain compulsory licensing mechanisms as explicitly provided in the TRIPS Agreement.

Improve the Capacity of Developing Countries in Utilization of Competition Policy

Capacity building and technical assistance are important for many developing countries facing difficulties in effective enforcement competition policy regarding IPRs. It seems that application of competition policy has not been given considerable attention in technical assistance programmes so far. In this regard, 'Developed countries and international institutions that provide assistance for the development of IPR regimes in developing countries should provide such assistance in concert with the development of appropriate competition policies and institutions' (CIPR, 2002). In fact, technical assistance has been carried out by a number of international organizations, such as WTO, WIPO, UNCTAD and South Centre,[48] but more attention should be attached on the competition aspects.

Improve International Cooperation in Dealing with Transnational Issues

International cooperation against transnational cartels and abuse of dominant position of IPRs is also crucial for developing countries. It seems that the current international cooperation regime on competition issues is not so efficient. One option is to further improve the mechanism as provided in Article 40 of the TRIPS Agreement for cooperation among WTO Members. On the other hand, various arrangements of cooperation among competition authorities in the regional trade agreements (RTAs) should also be encouraged (Brusick et al., 2005).

Reconsider International Harmonization of IPR Competition Rules

Past experience showed difficulties in negotiating an international agreement for substantive competition rules. Some developing countries believe that, given the freedom presently available under the TRIPS Agreement on competition policy, it may not be prudent to enter the stage of negotiations on competition issues.[49] There is also a fear among some others that such negotiations may discipline the use of these measures more than the TRIPS Agreement does, and use analogies from developed Members such as the United States and European Community (Watal, 2001).

However, it should be noted that the harmonization of competition rules will nevertheless benefit all the countries since it will contribute to reducing international anticompetitive practices of TNCs. Developing Members may benefit from strengthened competition rules on IPRs in the international market. In this regard, some multilateral soft law guidelines could be considered instead of a set of uniform rules, so that developing countries could maintain their policy autonomy. And as the issue of competition anyway appears in many international legislative processes and related work,[50] developing countries should enhance their cooperation in international norm-setting forums, like WIPO or WTO, to promote an integration of competition regulations governing the exercise of IPRs.

CONCLUSIONS

Developing countries are facing continuous pressures from developed countries today for accepting and enforcing levels of protection of IPRs, which are much higher than they are obligated to provide. The United States has incorporated a wide range of TRIPS-plus provisions in its Bilateral Investment Treaties (BITs) and free trade agreements (FTAs), which has substantially increased levels of protection of almost all kinds of IPRs (Fink and Reichenmiller, 2005). Since 2005, a number of developed countries started to negotiate a new Anti-Counterfeit Trade Agreement (ACTA), aiming to further elevate levels of protection and enhance the enforcement of IPRs (USTR, 2007; Biadgleng and Tellez, 2008b).

Competition policy is indeed the most important and most effective weapon for developing countries to ensure an appropriate balance between protection of IPRs and other social and public interests. Developing countries should accord great importance to the competition aspect while providing IPR protection, so as to ensure that benefits of the IP system are available to developing countries. The WIPO Treaties and the WTO TRIPS Agreement provide enough policy space in this regard for formulating and implementing competition policy for controlling abuse of IPRs. Developing countries should seek to explore this option.

Although the competition issue has been now removed from the Doha Development Agenda, some substantive work may still be explored under the WTO TRIPS Agreement. It is also important to enhance technical assistance to developing countries and improve international cooperation on the competition issues at regional and international levels to address transnational concerns.

NOTES

1. The views expressed here belong to the author only, and do not necessarily represent those of the government of China. E-mail: yusong.ch@gmail.com.
2. World Trade Organization, Agreement on Trade-Related Aspects of Intellectual Property Rights, http://www.wto.org/english/docs_e/legal_e/legal_e.htm, accessed 10 September 2008.
3. These local conditions could include, for example, local technology bases, national infrastructures for research and development, human and financial resources, and so on.
4. For example, during the 1990s, Koninklijke Philips Electronics, N.V., Sony Corp. and Pioneer Electronic Corp. of Japan formed a patent pool for DVD-Video and DVD-ROM standards, licensing 210 patents. This constituted substantial barriers for companies from developing countries to access these technologies.
5. See, for example, the price of Microsoft's Vista in the Philippines was set at S$340.95 (US$216.92) for the Home Basic version, even much higher than that sold in the United States (US$199). Jeremy Reimer, 'Vista too expensive for developing countries, says analyst', at http://arstechnica.com/news.ars/post/20070506-vista-too-expensive-for-developing-countries-says-analyst.html, accessed 27 December 2008.
6. This could be seen from the discussions of the WTO Working Group on Trade and Transfer of Technology (WGTTT). The WGTTT was established by the Ministers in Doha, aiming to examine 'the relationship between trade and transfer of technology', and 'any possible recommendations on steps that might be

taken within the mandate of the WTO to increase flows of technology to developing countries'. See, for example, 'Report of the Working Group on Trade and Transfer of Technology to the General Council', WT/WGTTT/5, 14 July 2003; 'Technology Transfer – the Canadian Experience', WT/WGTTT/2, 9 October 2002.

7. This was summarized in a speech in 1970 by Bruce Wilson. These practices included: (1) mandatory package licensing; (2) tying of unpatented supplies to the licensing of patented products; (3) compulsory assignment of grant-backs; (4) vertical distribution restraints, such as post-sale restraints on resale by purchasers; (5) compulsory payment of royalties of amounts unrelated to the sales of the patented product; (6) restrictions on the licensee's freedom to deal in products or services outside the scope of the patent; (7) grants to the licensee of veto power over further licenses; (8) restraints in sales of unpatented products made by a patented process; and (9) minimum price maintenance.

8. The Chicago School is normally known as an economic school of thought that embraces an economic efficiency orientation in antitrust rules and emphasizes reliance on economic theory in antitrust enforcement.

9. See, 'Antitrust Guidelines for the Licensing of Intellectual Property (1995)', www.usdoj.gov, accessed 31 October 2008.

10. Id.

11. Id.

12. Id.

13. For example, in an earlier case, the ECJ stated that: 'Although a patent confers on its holder a special protection at national level, it does not follow that the exercise of the rights thus conferred implies the presence together of all three elements in question. It could only do so if the use of the patent were to degenerate into an abuse of the abovementioned protection'. See, Case 24/67 *Parke & Davis* v. *Probel* [English special edition 1968] ECR 55. See also, 'On the Relationship between the Trade-Related Aspects of Intellectual Property Rights and Competition Policy, and Between Investment and Competition Policy', Communication from the European Community and its Member States, WT/WGTCP/W/99, 25 September 1998, para. 26.

14. This could probably be seen from the *Microsoft* Case (2004).

15. The regulation entered into force on 1 May 2004 and will expire on 30 April 2014. The regulation repealed the previous legislation in this area, that is, Commission Regulation No. 240/96 of 31 January 1996 on the Application of Article 85(3) of the Treaty to Certain Categories of Technology Transfer Agreements.

16. See, Article 21, Act on Prohibition of Private Monopolization and Maintenance of Fair Trade (Act No. 54 of 14 April 1947, as amended), www.jftc.go.jp, accessed 9 November 2008.

17. In other words, if any business activity that may seem to be an exercise of a right is found to deviate from or run counter to the purposes of the intellectual property system, then it cannot be 'recognizable as the exercise of the right' under aforesaid Section 21.

18. The 1968 guidelines provided a short 'blacklist' of prohibited licensing provisions and also a 'white list' of expressly permitted practices. It could be seen that, since the 1968 guidelines applied solely to international licences, it was criticized as disfavouring non-Japanese licensors during the period when Japanese industry was licensing (that is, importing) a great deal of foreign technology (Harris, 2002). There have been two other guidelines on this issue: 'Guidelines Concerning Joint Research and Development' (20 April 1993), 'Guidelines Concerning Distribution Systems and Business Practices' (11 July 1991). See, WTO, Working Group on the Interaction between Trade and Competition

Policy, Communication from Japan, No. WT/WGTCP/W/106, 27 October 1998.

19. See, 'Guidelines for Patent and Know-How Licensing Agreements under the Anti-Monopoly Act', 1999, http://www.jftc.go.jp/e-page/guideli/patent99.htm, accessed 15 November 2008.

20. The guidelines are available online at http://www.jftc.go.jp/e-page/legislation/index.html, accessed 20 November 2008. These guidelines supersede the 1999 guidelines.

21. Elements considered in this analysis include 'how it is imposed, the use of the technology in the business activity and its influence on it, whether or not the entities in relation to the restrictions are competitors, their market positions (such as market share and rank), the overall competitive conditions (such as the number of competitors of the entities concerned, the degree of market concentration, the characteristics and the degree of differentiation of the products involved, distribution channels and difficulties in market entry) of the markets, whether or not there are any justifiable grounds for imposing the restrictions, as well as the effects on incentives of research, development and licensing'. See, ibid.

22. Since 1980, negotiations were hosted by WIPO with a view to elaborating and improving these articles. However, the revision conference over a 15-year period failed to come to an agreement and no new act to the Paris Convention was adopted. This may also be one of the reasons why the United States proposed the inclusion of intellectual property matters in the negotiations of the Uruguay Round of the GATT.

23. See, Berne Convention for the Protection of Literary and Artistic Works.

24. See, International Convention for the Protection of Performers, Producers of Phonograms and Broadcasting Organizations, Rome, 26 October 1961.

25. See, Convention Relating to the Distribution of Programme-Carrying Signals Transmitted by Satellite 1974.

26. However, attempts could be seen from developed countries to eliminate certain exemptions in international IP conventions in order to further elevate the level of protection. For instance, while most countries allow farmers and other traditional breeders to be exempted from the provisions of UPOV (Union for the Protection of New Varieties of Plants) as long as they do not indulge in branded commercial transactions of the varieties, UPOV 1991 has tightened the monopolies of plant variety breeder rights by substantially removing these exemptions to farmers.

27. Final Act of the United Nations Conference on Trade and Employment: Havana Charter for an International Trade Organization, held at Havana, Cuba, 1948, Chapter V, Article 46–Article 54.

28. Id.

29. For instance, Article XVII of GATT, Article VIII and IX of GATS, Article 9 of the TRIMS Agreement and also provisions in the TRIPS Agreement. For a detailed discussion, see Kennedy (2001).

30. Those practices included, (1) grant-back provisions; (2) challenges to validity; (3) exclusive dealing; (4) restrictions on research; (5) restrictions on use of personnel; (6) price-fixing; (7) restrictions on adaptations; (8) exclusive sales or representation agreements; (9) tying arrangements; (10) export restrictions; (11) patent pooling or cross-licensing agreements and other arrangements; (12) restrictions on publicity; (13) payments and other obligations after expiration of industrial property rights; (14) restrictions after expiration of arrangements.

31. The OCED Guidelines for Multinational Enterprises, in Chapter IX on Competition, provide that 'enterprises should, within the framework of applicable laws and regulations, conduct their activities in a competitive manner',

http://www.oecd.org/document/28/0,3343,en_2649_34889_2397532_1_1_1_1,00
.html, accessed 10 October 2008.

32. The ICN can be reached at http://www.internationalcompetitionnetwork.org/, accessed 6 December 2008.

33. Though certain phrases, such as 'consistent with the provisions of this Agreement', 'abuse of intellectual property rights', 'unreasonably restrain trade', 'adversely affect the international transfer of technology', have not been tested in the WTO dispute cases, however, it is understood that Article 8.2 is a 'policy statement that explains the rationale for measures taken under Article 30, 31 and 40', and in fact the TRIPS Agreement does not place significant limitations for WTO Members to take measures to control anticompetitive practices (Fox, 1996; Gervais, 2003; Abbott, 2005).

34. Some other provisions of the TRIPS Agreement could also be seen as competition-related, for example, Article 6 'Exhaustion', Article 13 'Limitations and Exceptions', Article 17 'Exception', Article 30 'Exceptions to Rights Conferred', and so on.

35. Although this provision was not used frequently so far, it has for the first time established an international cooperation regime for all WTO Members in coping with transnational anticompetitive practices.

36. Article 31(k) stipulates that 'Members are not obliged to apply the conditions set forth in subparagraphs (b) and (f) where such use is permitted to remedy a practice determined after judicial or administrative process to be anti-competitive. The need to correct anti-competitive practices may be taken into account in determining the amount of remuneration in such cases. Competent authorities shall have the authority to refuse termination of authorization if and when the conditions which led to such authorization are likely to recur'.

37. The 45 recommendations adopted are divided into six clusters, namely: Cluster A: Technical Assistance and Capacity Building; Cluster B: Norm-setting, Flexibilities, Public Policy and Public Domain; Cluster C: Technology Transfer, Information and Communication Technology (ICT) and Access to Knowledge; Cluster D: Assessments, Evaluation and Impact Studies; Cluster E: Institutional Matters Including Mandate and Governance; and Cluster F: Others. These include 19 recommendations for immediate implementation by WIPO (including Recommendation 7) and 26 for which the CDIP is required to develop a work programme. See, http://www.wipo.int/ip-development/en/agenda/recommendations.html, accessed 15 September 2008.

38. Recommendation 7, Cluster A.
39. Recommendation 22, Cluster B.
40. Recommendation 23, Cluster B.
41. Recommendation 32, Cluster C.
42. See, WIPO documents, CDIP/1/4 and CDIP/2/4, at www.wipo.org, accessed 15 December 2008.

43. WTO Members agreed in 1996 at the Singapore Ministerial Conference to establish a Working Group on Trade and Competition Policy (WGTCP). The issue of IPRs was also one of the core subjects discussed within this WGTCP, though no consensus was achieved. Developing countries were concerned about excessive protection of IPRs in the TRIPS Agreement, while developed countries opposed any dilution of the protection, and felt that the competition provisions contained in the TRIPS Agreement were sufficient. See, for example, 'Report (1998) of the Working Group on the Interaction between Trade and Competition Policy to the General Council', WT/WGTCP/2, 8 December 1998. A number of WTO Members provided written submissions on this issue, for example, the European Community and its Member States (WT/WGTCP/W/99), the United

States (WT/WGTCP/W/101), New Zealand (WT/WGTCP/W/103), Hong Kong, China (WT/WGTCP/W/104), Korea (WT/WGTCP/W/105), Japan (WT/WGTCP/W/106), and Turkey (WT/WGTCP/W/113).

44. Together with the issue of investment, and transparency in government procurement.

45. It seems that since 2004, competition policy was not the focus of WTO Members. And it also has not been raised by Members in the review of the TRIPS Agreement. For the consultation procedures under Articles 40.3 and 40.4, it seems no case has been reported.

46. For instance, the United States is the major beneficiary that gains nearly $4.5 billion from the TRIPS Agreement.

47. According to a UNDP report, developed countries hold nearly 97 per cent of all patents worldwide (UNDP, 1999).

48. Some of the work that has been done can be seen from the notifications under the WTO TRIPS Agreement, for example, for the work in 2007, see, IP/C/W/494, IP/C/W/495 and the addendums.

49. That is the reason why some developing countries opposing the 'Singapore Issues' and are also reluctant to negotiate competition rules in the FTA negotiations.

50. In this regard, an example is the issue of patent and standard-setting. One or more patent-holders can 'hold up' licensees by waiting until participants are locked into the standard, then charging an 'excessive' royalty for patents that cover the standard. Therefore, it is important to include certain compulsory disclosure requirements before the standard is set.

10. Towards a development approach on IP enforcement: conclusions and strategic recommendations

Xuan Li and Carlos M. Correa

The TRIPS Agreement introduced for the first time a wide set of international minimum standards on IPRs. The proponents of the agreement consciously complemented the standards on the availability of IPRs with detailed rules on preliminary and permanent injunctions, border measures, damages and other enforcement issues that were absent in previous international agreements on IPRs. Given the complexity of the matter and the great variation in enforcement measures in national laws, the TRIPS rules define the objectives that such measures are intended to reach, rather than the specific means to be used to that end. This realistic approach (it would have been impossible to obtain consensus on more detailed enforcement standards) left WTO Member States considerable leeway to maintain or adopt new enforcement measures in accordance with the peculiarities of their legal systems.

The implementation of the TRIPS enforcement standards required extensive changes in the legislation of many countries, particularly in developing countries as those standards largely reflected the interests and policies applied in the advanced countries.

Any legal mechanism for protection of rights and the realization of their attendant obligations must be backed by an effective enforcement regime. This fundamental rationale behind legal enforcement of substantive rights and obligations is also applicable to enforcement of intellectual property (IP) rights. However, all states have the right to frame their own legal systems of IP protection and enforcement within the minimum international legal framework under the TRIPS

Agreement. The TRIPS lays down the basic conditions that must be complied with by all the Member States of the WTO. As mentioned, it also provided states with some flexibilities to define their IP enforcement systems. An effective system of enforcement against any act of IP infringement must be made available by Member States, in accordance with the provisions of Part III of TRIPS. States must make available civil judicial and administrative proceedings for IP enforcement that meet the standards of fair and equitable procedures, based on reasoned decisions backed by evidence and the availability of judicial review. However, the TRIPS Agreement does not require states to make available special systems of IP enforcement (such as special IP courts or tribunals with special powers and procedures) distinct from their general system of law enforcement.

For the purposes of TRIPS compliance, it is sufficient that the general law enforcement system of the state satisfies the standards of due process for IP enforcement laid down in TRIPS, and empowers the judiciary to provide remedies like injunction, compensatory damages, disposal of infringed products or services outside the channels of commerce, and so on, as well as take provisional measures where appropriate in accordance with Article 50. It should be noted, in particular, that the TRIPS Agreement does not require states to provide criminal procedures and penalties for IP enforcement except in cases of *willful trademark counterfeiting or copyright piracy on a commercial scale* (Article 61). Moreover, special provisions regarding border measures are also to be made available to right-holders with regard to counterfeit trademark or pirated copyright goods only. Under Article 51, right-holders may apply to competent judicial or administrative authorities to suspend the release of such goods into circulation, and customs authorities may also be empowered to suspend the release of infringing goods destined for *exportation* from their territories. Members *may*, but are not bound to, extend these procedures to other fields of IP infringement. However, even these special procedures must satisfy due process requirements laid down in Articles 52 to 60. In sum, the TRIPS Agreement requires states to make available effective civil judicial and administrative procedures of IP enforcement, which may be made available through the normal systems of law enforcement in the state. Criminal enforcement and special border measures must be available for willful trademark counterfeiting or copyright piracy only.

Soon after the adoption of the TRIPS Agreement, however,

a number of initiatives were launched in the United States and Europe in order to further strengthen the IP enforcement standards. A main motivation behind these initiatives was the perception by some industries (notably pharmaceuticals, music, cinematographic, software) about the persistence and, in some instances, growth of counterfeiting and piracy. Characterized as a *global* rather than a domestic problem, they were successful in mobilizing their governments and some international organizations (such as WIPO and WCO) in seeking the expansion of IP enforcement standards beyond what was required by the TRIPS Agreement. In doing so, the interested industries and governments have stretched the concept of 'counterfeiting and piracy' so as to include IPR infringements that do not relate to trademark imitation and unauthorized reproduction of copyrighted works.

The main avenues for the expansion of TRIPS-plus IP enforcement measures have included:

- adoption of new treaties on copyright and performers' rights;
- developed countries' programs to combat IP infringement domestically and in foreign countries;
- technical assistance to and training of officials from developing countries by developed countries' agencies;
- requirements imposed on countries acceding the WTO;
- free trade and other bilateral agreements;
- initiatives at international forums, such as WTO, WIPO, WCO and UPU.

The IP enforcement has also included a challenge to IP enforcement measures before the WTO through a tenuous interpretation of the TRIPS provisions in Part III (see Chapter 7) and the negotiation of a TRIPS-plus international treaty on the matter – the Anti-Counterfeiting Trade Agreement (ACTA) – in a non-transparent and non-participatory manner that notably overlooks the interests of developing countries.

Developing countries have historically played a limited role in the establishment of the multilateral intellectual property rules. Rather, they have reluctantly adopted the rules that mainly suit the economic interests of developed countries. Despite the important concessions already made by developing countries in the area of IP enforcement under the TRIPS Agreement, they are currently under strong pressure to further increase their efforts at the national level to effectively enforce intellectual property rights. These demands seem to overlook the cost of the required actions, the different priorities that exist in developing countries regarding the use of public funds (health and education would normally be regarded as more urgent than IP enforcement) and the crucial fact that IPRs are *private rights* and, hence, the burden and cost of their enforcement is to be borne by the right-holder, not the public at large.

The analysis contained in the book suggests that the TRIPS plus-agenda on IP enforcement pursued by developed countries is marked by the following three characteristics:

1. Expansion of the concept of counterfeiting as applicable to all kinds of IP infringement, thereby magnifying the extent of the problem. In addition, methodologically flawed economic assessments of the losses generated by counterfeiting contribute to create a deep misconception about the nature and extent of IP infringement.

2. Forum-shifting to non-IP and non-trade international organizations such as the WHO, WCO, UPU, where attempts are made to develop standards and model laws on counterfeit medical products, expanded authority of national customs authorities to apply an extended understanding of counterfeiting and piracy to prevent the release of any allegedly IP-infringed good into the channels of commerce. Going beyond the requirement of the TRIPS Agreement, this approach seeks to enable customs authorities to seize the infringed products not only when they are imported, but also when they are meant for export or are in transit, and to empower such authorities to detain goods suspected of infringing *any* IPRs. This approach creates an undue burden on the customs authorities who do not have the wherewithal to determine, for instance, whether a product infringes a patent, and may lead to abuses by right-holders.

     The current strategy of promoting IP enforcement negotiations bears some similarities with that used by them 14 years ago when pushing for incorporation of TRIPS into the WTO rule system, but also has some new features. What is common in both is that they all used the tactic of forum shopping. At that time, the approach of shopping was to establish the link between WIPO and WTO. By incorporating the relatively weak WIPO treaties into the WTO, which has a relatively stronger power of enforcement, the interest groups concerned wanted to standardize, legalize and internationalize their policy objectives. The difference is that the current strategy of IP promotion by developed countries is a multi-pronged offensive at regional, global and bilateral levels at the same time, as reflected by attempts to craft new IP enforcement laws and standards (voluntary or factual). Once accomplished, they would encourage the adoption of these standards in other forums, with the purpose of eventually turning them into mandatory arrangements.

3. Shifting the burden of IP enforcement from right-holders to the state and the defendant. The state is expected to act as the defender of the right-holders' interests and enforce the same by policing against any act of IP infringement. A manifestation of this is the expectation that developing countries should provide criminal enforcement proceeding for all acts of IP infringement, and take suo motu administrative action against suspected acts of IP infringement, without regard to most of the due process requirements laid down in TRIPS. This will entail significant financial burden on the law enforcement system of the developing countries and also amount to denial of principles of due process and natural justice in IP enforcement procedures.

In sum, the IP enforcement offensive focuses almost exclusively on the interests of right-holders, and overlooks their obligations towards other stakeholders. Such an approach disturbs the balance between rights and obligations that needs to be maintained in IP laws under the requirements of the TRIPS Agreement.

In various chapters, this book analyzes and explains the main elements of the current discourse on IP enforcement. It identifies the challenges faced by governments and provides information and guidance about the strategies that may be adopted to design enforcement rules and procedures consistent with local legal systems and the realization of the development objectives. Such challenges include: (1) how to maintain an effective IP enforcement regime when state resources are scarce and need to be allocated to other development priorities; (2) how to balance the right-holders' and public interest in the IP system; and (3) how to prevent the abuse of IPRs by right-holders, through the misuse of IP enforcement procedures. The book may assist governments in addressing these challenges and in devising appropriate national policies and legislations on IP enforcement. IP regimes are policy tools that should be functional to the promotion of innovation and social and economic development. The fundamental principle of IP enforcement should be based on optimal IP theory and serve the purpose of maximizing national interests. Through assessing the impact of current rules on national economies, the rules should be measured and amended constantly to minimize their deviation from socially optimal targets and provide guidance to the formulation of national IP enforcement policies. As stressed in Chapter 9, developing an appropriate framework for IP enforcement requires, inter alia, the implementation of competition policies that protect public interests against abuses of IPRs.

Bibliography

Abbott, Frederick M. (2000), 'TRIPS in Seattle: the not-so-surprising failure and the future of the TRIPS Agenda', *Berkeley Journal of International Law*, **18** (1), 165–79.

Abbott, Frederick M. (2005), 'Are the Competition Rules in the WTO Agreement on Trade-Related Aspects of Intellectual Property Rights Adequate?', in Ernst-Ulrich Petersmann (ed.), *Reforming the World Trade System: Legitimacy, Efficiency, and Democratic Governance*, Oxford: Oxford University Press, pp. 317–34.

Abraham, John (2002), 'The Political Economy of Medicines Regulation in Britain', in H. Lawton Smith (ed.), *The Regulation of Science and Technology*, Basingstoke, UK: Palgrave, pp. 221–63.

Anderman, Steven D. (1998), *EC Competition Law and Intellectual Property Rights: The Regulation of Innovation*, Oxford: Clarendon Press.

Anderson, Robert D. and Hannu Wager (2006), 'Human rights, development and the WTO: the cases of intellectual property and competition policy', *Journal of International Economic Law*, **9** (3), 707–47.

Apostolopoulos, Haris (2007), 'Anti-competitive abuse of IP rights and compulsory licensing through the international dimension of the TRIPS Agreement and the Stockholm proposal for its amendment', *Richmond Journal of Global Law & Business*, **6** (3), 265–82.

Ariyanuntaka, Vichai (2005), *Enforcement of Intellectual Property Rights under TRIPS: A Case Study of Thailand*, available at: http://www.us-asean.org/us-thai-fta/IPR_study.pdf; accessed 20 January 2009.

Asian Development Bank (2002), 'Technical Assistance (Financed by the Japan Special Fund) to the People's Republic of China for Enforcement of World Trade Organization Rules by the Judicial System', TAR:PRC 36199, available at: http://www.adb.org/Documents/TARs/PRC/36199-PRC-TAR.pdf; accessed 20 January 2009.

'Australian draft report casts doubt on piracy stats', 10 November 2006, available at: http://www.afterdawn.com/news/archive/8110. cfm; accessed 20 January 2009.

Australian Government (2007), 'An International Proposal for a Plurilateral Anti-Counterfeiting Trade Agreement (ACTA)', *Department of Foreign Affairs and Trade Discussion Paper*, available at: http://www.dfat.gov.au/trade/acta/discussion-paper.html; accessed 7 November 2008.

Barton, J. (1997), 'The balance between intellectual property rights and competition: paradigms in the information sector', *European Competition Law Review*, 7, 440–45.

Beckerman-Rodau, Andrew (2007), 'The Supreme Court engages in judicial activism in interpreting the Patent Law in *eBay, Inc.* v. *MercExchange, L.L.C.*', *Tulane Journal of Technology & Intellectual Property*, **10** (1), 165–210.

Benson, Eric E. and Danielle M. White (2008), 'Using apportionment to rein in the Georgia Pacific factors', *Columbia Science and Technology Law Review*, **9**, 1.

Bently, L. and B. Sherman (2004), *Intellectual Property*, 2nd edn, Oxford: Oxford University Press.

Berne Convention for the Protection of Literary and Artistic Works (1886), available at: http://www.wipo.int/treaties/en/ip/berne/trtdocs_wo001.html; accessed 19 January 2009.

Biadgleng, Ermias T. and Viviana Muñoz Tellez (2008a), 'The Changing Structure and Governance of Intellectual Property Enforcement', *Research Papers*, No. 15, Geneva: South Centre, available online at: http://www.southcentre.org/index.php?option=com_content&task=view&id=614&Itemid=1; accessed 14 December 2008.

Biadgleng, Ermias.T. and Viviana Muñoz Tellez (2008b), 'The International IP Enforcement Landscape from a Developing Country Perspective', *South Centre Research Paper*, No. 15, available at: http://www.southcentre.org/index.php?option=com_docman&task=doc_download&gid=353&Itemid=69; accessed 10 December 2008.

Blakeney, Michael (2005), *Guidebook on Enforcement of Intellectual Property Rights*, available at: http://www.delpak.ec.europa.eu/WHATSNEW/Guidelines.pdf; accessed 20 January 2009.

Blenko, Walter J. Jr. (1990), 'The doctrine of equivalents in patent infringement', *JOM*, **42** (5), 59, available at: http://www.tms.

org/pubs/journals/JOM/matters/matters-9005.html; accessed 20 January 2009.

Boiron, P. and G. Tulquois (2008), 'Three strikes and out' (July/ August 2008), *Copyright World*, Issue No. 182 (July/August 2008), 16–17.

Bosworth, Derek (2006), 'Counterfeiting and Piracy: The State of the Art', paper presented at Intellectual Property in the New Millennium Seminar, Oxford Intellectual Property Research Centre, St. Peter's College, 9 May 2006, available at: http://www.oiprc.ox.ac.uk/EJWP0606.pdf; accessed 20 January 2009.

Brusick, Philippe, Ana Maria Alvarez and Lucian Cernat (2005) (eds), *Competition Provisions in Regional Trade Agreements: How to Assure Development Gains*, New York and Geneva: UNCTAD.

Burk, Dan L. and Mark A. Lemley (2003), 'Policy levers in patent law', *Virginia Law Review*, **89** (7), 1575–696.

Business Software Alliance (BSA) (2005), *Second Annual BSA and IDC Global Software Piracy Study*, available at: http://w3.bsa.org/ globalstudy//upload/2005-Global-Study-English.pdf; accessed 20 January 2009.

Carroll, Michael W. (2006), 'One for all: the problem of uniformity cost in intellectual property law', *American University Law Review*, **55** (4), 845–900.

Carroll, Michael W. (2007), 'Patent injunctions and the problem of uniformity cost', *Michigan Telecommunications and Technology Law Review*, **13** (2), 421–44.

Centre for Economics and Business Research (CEBR) (2002), *Counting Counterfeits: Defining a Method to Collect, Analyse and Compare Data on Counterfeiting and Piracy in the Single Market*, Final Report for the European Commission, Directorate-General Single Market.

China National Intellectual Property Protection Working Group (2007), *Digest of Intellectual Property for Leaders*, China: Remin Publisher.

Choer Moraes, Henrique and Otávio Brandelli (2008), 'The Development Agenda: Context and Origins', in Neil Netanel (ed.), *The Development Agenda: Global Intellectual Property and Developing Countries*, Oxford: Oxford University Press, pp. 33–49.

Coco, R. (2008), 'Antitrust liability for refusal to license intellectual property: a comparative analysis and the international setting', *Marquette Intellectual Property Law Review*, **12** (1), 1–48.

Commission for Intellectual Property Rights (CIPR) (2002), *Integrating Intellectual Property Rights and Development Policy: Final Report*, London, UK: Commission on for Intellectual Property Rights.

Commission on Intellectual Property Rights, Innovation and Public Health (CIPIH) (2006), *Report on Intellectual Property Rights, Innovation and Public Health*, Geneva: World Health Organization.

Cornish, William R. (1999), *Intellectual Property*, 4th edn, London: Sweet & Maxwell.

Cornish, William and David Llewelyn (2007), *Intellectual Property: Patents, Copyright, Trade Marks and Allied Rights*, London: Sweet & Maxwell.

Correa, Carlos M. (2000), *Intellectual Property Rights, the WTO and Developing Countries: The TRIPS Agreement and Policy Options*, London: Zed Books, Third World Network.

Correa, Carlos M. (2001), 'Pro-competitive measures under the TRIPS Agreement to promote technology diffusion in developing countries', *The Journal of World Intellectual Property*, **4** (4), 481–96.

Correa, Carlos (2006), 'La disputa sobre soja transgénica. *Monsanto* vs. *Argentina*', in *Le Monde Diplomatique/El Dipló*.

Correa, Carlos (2007), *Trade-Related Aspects of Intellectual Property Rights*, Oxford: Oxford University Press.

Correa, Carlos (forthcoming 2009), *The New Offensive for the Enforcement of Intellectual Property Rights and the Interests of Developing Countries*, ICTSD Programme on Intellectual Property and Sustainable Development.

Correa, Carlos M. and Sisule F. Musungu (2002), 'The WIPO Patent Agenda: The Risks for Developing Countries', *T.R.A.D.E Working Papers*, No. 12, Geneva: South Centre.

Dannay, Richard (2008), 'Copyright injunctions and fair use: enter *eBay* – four-factor fatigue or four-factor freedom?', *Journal of Copyright Society of the U.S.A.*, **55** (2008), 459.

DaSilva, Russell J. (1980), 'Droit moral and amoral copyright: a comparison of artists' rights in France and the United States', *Bulletin of the Copyright Society*, **28**, 1.

Delich, V. and López, A. (2008), *The Political Economy of High-tech*

Commodities: the Successful and Litigious Case of the Genetically Modified Soy in Argentina, Geneva: United Nations/UNCTAD Virtual Institute.

Devereaux, C., R.Z. Lawrence and M.D. Watkins (2006), *Case Studies in US Trade Negotiation*. Vol. 2: *Resolving Disputes*, Washington, DC: Institute for International Economics.

'Discussion Paper on a Possible Anti-Counterfeiting Trade Agreement' (leaked draft 2008), p. 3, available at: http://ipjustice.org/wp/wp-content/uploads/ACTA-discussion-paper-1.pdf; accessed 30 November 2008.

Drahos, Peter (1996), *A Philosophy of Intellectual Property*, Dartmouth: Applied Legal Philosophy Series.

Drahos, Peter (2002), 'Developing Countries and International Intellectual Property Standard Setting', *Study Papers*, No. 8, London: Commission for Intellectual Property Rights.

Drahos, Peter and John Braithwaite (2003), *Information Feudalism – Who Owns the Knowledge Economy?*, New York: New Press.

Drahos, Peter and John Braithwaite (2004), 'Who Owns the Knowledge Economy? Political Organising Behind TRIPS', *Corner House*, Briefing No. 32, available at: http://www.thecornerhouse.org.uk/pdf/briefing/32trips.pdf; accessed 20 January 2009.

Dratler, Jay (1994), *Licensing of Intellectual Property*, New York: Law Journal Press.

Dreyfuss, Rochelle C. (2009), 'Resolving Patent Disputes in a Global Economy', in Toshiko Takenaka (ed.), *Patent Law and Theory: A Handbook of Contemporary Research*, Cheltenham, UK and Northampton, MA, USA: Edward Elgar, forthcoming.

Dutfield, Graham and Sisule F. Musungu (2003), 'Multilateral Agreements and a TRIPS-plus World: The World Intellectual Property Organization', *TRIPS Issue Papers*, No. 3, QUNO Geneva, and QIAP Ottawa.

EC (2005), *European Commission Directorate General for Trade: Strategy for the Enforcement of IPR in Third Countries*, available at: http://trade.ec.europa.eu/doclib/docs/2005/april/tradoc_122636.pdf; accessed 20 January 2009.

Economides, Nicholas and William N. Herbert (2008), 'Patents and antitrust: application to adjacent markets', *Journal on Telecommunications & High Technology Law*, **6** (2008): 460–68.

Ellis, Douglas, John Jarosz, Michael Chapman and Oliver L. Scott (2008), 'The economic implications (and uncertainties) of obtaining permanent injunctive relief after *eBay* v. *MercExchange'*, *Federal Circuit Bar Journal*, **17** (4), 437–73.

EPA (2008), Economic Partnership Agreement between the CARIFORUM States, of the one Part, and the European Community and its Member States, of the other Part, available at: http://www.normangirvan.info/wp-content/uploads/2008/10/epa_text_15th_october08_final.pdf; accessed 20 January 2009.

Epstein, Richard A. (2008), 'Introduction to the Italian edition of Overdose', *Cumberland Law Review*, **38** (1), 227.

EU (2005), 'Strategy for the Enforcement of Intellectual Property Rights in Third Countries', *Official Journal of the European Union*, 2005/C 129/03, available at: http://eur-lex.europa.eu/LexUriServ/LexUriServ.do?uri=OJ:C:2005:129:0003:0016:EN:PDF; accessed 20 January 2009.

European Parliament (2007), *On the Amended Proposal for a Directive of the European Parliament and of the Council on Criminal Measures Aimed at Ensuring the Enforcement of Intellectual Property Rights* (COM(2006)0168 – C6-0233/2005 – 2005/0127(COD)), Committee on Legal Affairs, available at: http://www.europarl.europa.eu/sides/getDoc.do?Type=REPORT&Reference=A6-2007-0073&language=EN; accessed 20 January 2009.

European Scrutiny Committee (2006), *Criminal Measures to Enforce Intellectual Property Rights*, 31st Report, available at: http://www.ipo.gov.uk/scrutinyreport.pdf; accessed 20 January 2009.

Farrell, Joseph and Robert P. Merges (2004), 'Incentives to challenge and defend patents: why litigation won't reliably fix patent office errors and why administrative patent review might help', *Berkeley Technology Law Journal*, **19** (3), 943–70.

Faunce, T.A. (2007), 'Reference pricing for pharmaceuticals: is the Australia-United States Free Trade Agreement affecting Australia's pharmaceutical benefits scheme?', *Medical Journal of Australia*, **187** (1), 1–3.

Finger, Michael J. and Philip Schuler (1999), 'Implementation of Uruguay Round Commitments: The Development Challenge', *World Bank, Policy Research Working Paper*, No. WPS2215.

Fink, Carsten and Patrick Reichenmiller (2005), 'Tightening TRIPS: Intellectual Property Provisions of U.S. Free Trade Agreements', in Richard Newfarmer (ed.), *Trade, Doha, and Development: A Window into the Issues*, The World Bank, pp. 285–300.

Fox, Eleanor M. (1996), 'Trade, competition, and intellectual property – TRIPS and its antitrust counterparts', *Vanderbilt Journal of Transnational Law*, **29**, 481–506.

Franzosi, Mario (1996), 'La teoría degli equivalenti', in *Il Brevetto: Quale Tutela?*, Milan: Giuffré.

G8 (2008), *Report of Discussions, G8 Intellectual Property Experts' Group Meeting*, available at: http://www.mofa.go.jp/policy/economy/summit/2008/doc/pdf/0708_02_en.pdf; accessed 20 January 2009.

Gad, Mohammed O. (2008), 'TRIPS Dispute Settlement and Developing Country Interests', in Carlos M. Correa and Abdulqawi A. Yusuf (eds), *Intellectual Property and International Trade: The Trips Agreement*, 2nd edn, The Hague: Walters Kluwer, pp. 355–63.

Garret, Nic (2006), 'Automated Rights Management Systems and Copyright Limitations and Exceptions', available at: http://www.wipo.int/edocs/mdocs/copyright/en/sccr_14/sccr_14_5.pdf; accessed 17 December 2008.

Geiger, Christophe (2007), 'Copyright and the freedom to create, a fragile balance', *International Review of Intellectual Property and Competition Law*, **38** (6), 707–22.

Geiger, Christophe (2008), 'Die Schranken des Urheberrechts als Instrumente der Innovationsförderung – Freie Gedanken zur Ausschliesslichkeit im Urheberrecht', *Gewerblicher Rechtsschutz und Urheberrecht – Internationaler Teil*, **57** (6), pp. 459–467.

Geist, Michael (2008), 'Public left out of anti-counterfeiting trade talks', *The Star*, available at: http://www.thestar.com/Business/article/468267; accessed 20 January 2009.

Gervais, Daniel (2003), *The TRIPS Agreement – Drafting History and Analysis*, 2nd edn, London: Sweet & Maxwell.

Gervais, Daniel J. (2007), *Intellectual Property, Trade and Development: Strategies to Optimize Economic Development in a TRIPS-plus Era*, Oxford: Oxford University Press.

Grosse Ruse-Khan, Henning (2008a), 'Proportionality and Balancing within the Objectives of Intellectual Property Protection', in P. Torremanns (ed.), *Intellectual Property and Human Rights*, London: Kluwer Law International, pp. 161–94.

Grosse Ruse-Khan, Henning (2008b), 'A Comparative Analysis of Policy Space in WTO Law', *Max Planck Papers on Intellectual Property, Competition & Tax Law Research Paper*, No. 08-02, available at: http://papers.ssrn.com/sol3/papers.cfm?abstract_id=1309526; accessed 20 January 2009.

Harris, H.S. Jr. (2002), 'Competition law and patent protection in Japan: a half-century of progress, a new millennium of challenges', *Columbia Journal of Asian Law*, **16**, 71–140.

Heath, Christopher (2007), 'The Interface between Competition Law and Intellectual Property in Japan', in Steven D. Anderman (ed.), *The Interface Between Intellectual Property Rights and Competition Policy*, Cambridge: Cambridge University Press, pp. 250–311.

Holman, Christopher M. (2007), 'Do reverse payments settlements violate the antitrust laws?', *Santa Clara Computer & High Technology Law Journal*, **23** (3), 489–588.

Holzmann, Richard T. (1995), *Infringement of the United States Patent Right: A Guide for Executives and Attorneys*, Westport, CT: Greenwood Publishing Group.

Hugenholtz, P.B. and Lucie Guibault (2002), *Study on the Conditions Applicable to Contracts Relating to Intellectual Property in the European Union*, Amsterdam: IVIR, available at: http://www.ivir.nl/publications/other/final-report2002.pdf; accessed 29 September 2008.

Isaacs, Davida H. (2007), 'Not all property is created equal: why modern courts resist applying the takings clause to patents, and why they are right to do so', *George Mason Law Review*, **15** (1), 1–44.

Keller, Eric (2008), 'Time-varying compulsory license: facilitating license negotiation for efficient post-verdict patent infringement', *Texas Intellectual Property Law Journal*, **16** (3), 434.

Kennedy, Kevin (2001), *Competition Law and the World Trade Organization: The Limits of Multilateralism*, London: Sweet & Maxwell Limited.

Keohane, Robert O., Kenneth Abbott, Andrew Moravcsik, Anne-Marie Slaughter and Duncan Snidal (2000), 'The concept of legalization', *International Organization*, **54** (3), 401–19, available at: http://www.princeton.edu/~amoravcs/library/concept.pdf; accessed 17 December 2008.

Khan, Zorina (2002), 'Study Paper 1a: Intellectual Property and Economic Development: Lessons from American and European History', available at: http://www.iprcommission.org/graphic/documents/study_papers.htm; accessed 14 December 2008.

Kjøelbye, Lars and Luc Peeperkorn (2007), 'The New Technology Transfer Block Exemption Regulation and Guidelines', in

Claus Dieter Ehlermann and Isabela Atanasiu (eds), *European Competition Law Annual 2005: The Interaction between Competition Law and Intellectual Property Law*, Oxford and Portland, OR: Hart Publishing, pp. 161–209.

Kumar, Nagesh (2002), 'Study Paper 1b: Intellectual Property Rights, Technology and Economic Development: Experiences of Asian Countries', available at: http://www.iprcommission.org/graphic/documents/study_papers.htm; accessed 14 December 2008.

Lemley, Mark A. (2008), 'Are universities patent trolls?', *Fordham Intellectual Property Media & Entertainment Law Journal*, **18** (3), 611–32.

Lemley, Mark A. and Carl Shapiro (2007), 'Patent holdup and royalty stacking', *Texas Law Review*, **85** (7), 1991–2050.

Li, Xuan (2008a), 'Ten common misunderstandings about the enforcement of intellectual property rights', *South Bulletin*, Issue 9.

Li, Xuan (2008b), 'SECURE: a critical analysis and call for action', *South Bulletin*, Issue No. 15, 16 May 2008.

Li, X. (2008c), 'Return to sender – TRIPS-plus enforcement attempts by the World Customs Organization through the Universal Postal Congress', *South Bulletin*, Issue No. 21, 16 August 2008, available at: http://www.southcentre.org/index.php?option=com_content&task&id&Itemid=105; accessed 14 December 2008.

Locklear, Fred (2004), 'IDC says piracy loss figure is misleading', available at: http://arstechnica.com/news.ars/post/20040719-4008.html; accessed 20 January 2009.

Mantilla, Galo Pico (2007), *Criminal Measures for Enforcement of Intellectual Property Rights – Sanctions in the ANDEAN Community*, Advisory Committee on Enforcement, Fourth Session Geneva, WIPO, WIPO/ACE/4/5, available at: http://www.wipo.int/edocs/mdocs/enforcement/en/wipo_ace_4/wipo_ace_4_5.pdf; accessed 20 January 2009.

Maskus, Keith E. (1998), 'The role of intellectual property rights in encouraging foreign direct investment and technology transfer', *Duke Journal of Comparative & International Law*, **9** (1), 109–61.

Maskus, Keith E. (2000), *Intellectual Property Rights in the Global Economy*, Washington, DC: Institute for International Economics.

Maskus, Keith E. and Jerome H. Reichman (2005), 'The Globalization of Private Knowledge Goods and the Privatization of Global Public Foods', in Keith E. Maskus and Jerome H. Reichman (eds), *International Public Goods and Transfer of Technology Under a Globalized Intellectual Property Regime*, Cambridge: Cambridge University Press, pp. 1–69.

Mathew, Joe C. (2008), 'Indian drug firms wary of global customs norms', *Business Standard*, New Delhi, 12 June 2008.

Matthews, Duncan (2002), *Globalizing Intellectual Property Rights: The TRIPS Agreement*, London: Routledge.

Matthews, Duncan (2008), 'The Fight Against Counterfeiting and Piracy in the Bilateral Trade Agreements of the EU', *European Parliament Briefing Paper*, available at: http://www.europarl.europa.eu/activities/committees/studies/download.do?file=21459; accessed 17 December 2008.

May, Christopher and Susan Sell (2005), *Intellectual Property Rights: A Critical History*, Boulder, CO: Lynne Rienner.

McCalman, Phillip (2005), 'Reaping what you sow: an empirical analysis of international patent harmonization', *Journal of International Economics*, 55, 161–86.

McCullagh, D. (2008), 'RIAA, MPAA resume lobbying push to expand copyright law', *CNet News*, 11 September 2008.

McDermott, E. (2008), 'Kerala becomes first Indian state to issue IP policy', *Managing Intellectual Property Rights – Weekly News*, 14 July 2008.

Narendranath, K. (2008), 'WTO fake drug definition hitting India?', *The Economic Times*, New Delhi 5 August 2008.

Nielsen, Carol M. and Michael R. Samardzija (2007), 'Compulsory patent licensing: is it a viable solution in the United States?', *Michigan Telecommunications & Technology Law Review*, 13 (2), 509–40.

OECD (2007), *The Economic Impact of Counterfeiting and Piracy*, available at: http://www.oecd.org/dataoecd/13/12/38707619.pdf; accessed 20 January 2009.

Okediji, Ruth L. (2006), 'The International Copyright System', *ICTSD Issue Paper*, No.15, Geneva: ICTSD.

Oliveira, Nelson Brasil de (2008), 'Separando o joio do trigo', São Paulo, Brazil: O Estado de São Paulo, 10 September 2008. Available at http://www.abifina.org.br/noticias.asp?secao=20&noticia=688; accessed 17 December 2008.

Ollier, P. (2008), 'Philippines announces IP enforcement strategy',

Managing Intellectual Property Rights, Weekly News, 3 July, 2008.

Paris Convention for the Protection of Industrial Property (1883), available at: http://www.wipo.int/treaties/en/ip/paris/trtdocs_ wo020.html; accessed 19 January 2009.

Parliament of Australia (2006), *Review of Technological Protection Measures Exceptions Canberra: the Parliament of the Commonwealth of Australia*, available at: http://www.aph.gov. au/HOUSE/committee/laca/protection/report/fullreport.pdf; accessed 30 September 2008.

Pate, R.H. (2007), 'Competition and Intellectual Property in the US: Licensing Freedom and the Limits of Antitrust', in Claus Dieter Ehlermann and Isabela Atanasiu (eds), *European Competition Law Annual 2005: The Interaction between Competition Law and Intellectual Property Law*, Oxford and Portland, OR: Hart Publishing, pp. 49–58.

Patry, William F. (2008), *Patry on Copyright* 6, Thomson Reuters/ West, online edition.

Peterson, B. (2008), 'Injunctive relief in a post *eBay* world', *Berkeley Technology Law Journal*, **23** (2), 192–218.

Prakash-Canjels, Gauri and Kristen Hamilton (2008), 'United States: implication of *eBay* for noncompetes, other entities', *Law360* (2 September 2008).

Reichman, Jerome H. (2008a), 'Nurturing a Transnational System of Innovation', in I. Govaere and H. Ullrich (eds), *Intellectual Property, Public Policy, and International Trade*, Brussels: Peter Lang International.

Reichman, Jerome H. (2008b), 'Universal Minimum Standards of Intellectual Property Protection under the TRIPS Component of the WTO Agreement', in *Intellectual Property and International Trade*, Brussels: Peter Lang Publishers.

Reichman, Jerome H. and Catherine Hasenzahl (2003), 'Non-Voluntary Licensing of Patented Inventions: Historical Perspective, Legal Framework Under TRIPS, and an Overview of the Practice in Canada and the United States of America', *UNCTAD-ICTSD Project on IPRs and Sustainable Development Series Issue Paper*, No. 5.

Robertson, Mark D. (2008), 'Sparing Internet radio from the real threat of the hypothetical marketplace', *Vanderbilt Journal of Entertainment & Technology Law*, **10** (3), 543–52.

Robin, Marie-Monique (2008), 'Le monde selon Monsanto. De la dioxine aux OGM, une multinationale qui vous veut du bien', *La Découverte-Arte Editions*, Paris, 274–90.

Robinson, William C. (1890), *The Law of Patents for Useful Inventions*, Boston: Little, Brown.

Roffe, Pedro (1998), 'Control of Anti-competitive Practices in Contractual Licences under the TRIPS Agreement', in Carlos M. Correa and Abdulqawi A. Yusuf (eds), *Intellectual Property and International Trade: the TRIPS Agreement*, London: Kluwer Law International, pp. 261–96.

Roffe, Pedro (2008), 'Bringing Minimum Intellectual Property Standards into Agriculture: The Agreement on Trade-Related Aspects of Intellectual Property Rights (TRIPS)', IDRC, available at: http://www.idrc.ca/en/ev-119947-201-1-DO_TOPIC.html; accessed 20 January 2009.

Roughton, Ashley (2008), *Intellectual Property Rights*, in Peter Roth QC and Vivien Rose (eds), *Bellamy & Child European Community Law of Competition*, 6th edition, Oxford: Oxford University Press.

Russian Federation (2004), 'Enforcement: Criminal, Administrative, Border Measures and Civil Law Remedies and Procedures in the Russian Federation', 2004/ IPEG1/045, Agenda Item: 6 (6) (iii) (e-2), Intellectual Property Experts' Group Meeting Beijing, People's Republic of China 20–21 April 2004.

Ryan, David F. (2008), 'Patent Jurisprudence After *Quanta* and *eBay*: is the Supreme Court Moving the Patent Clause to Article III?', unpublished draft 28 July 2008.

Sag, Matthew and Kurt Rohde (2007), 'Patent reform and differential impact', *Minnesota Journal of Law, Science & Technology*, **8** (1), 1–93.

Sakakibara, M. and Lee Branstetter (2001), 'Do stronger patents induce more innovations? Evidence from the 1988 Japanese Patent Law reform', *RAND Journal of Economics*, **32** (1), 77–110.

Santilli, Marina (1997), 'United States moral rights developments in European perspective', *Marquette Intellectual Property Law Review*, **1**, 89–108.

Sarnoff, Joshua D. (2007), '*Bio* v. *DC* and the new need to eliminate federal patent law preemption of state and local price and product regulation', *Patently-O Patent Law Journal*, 31–2.

Sarnoff, Joshua D. (2008), '*Bilcare, KSR*, presumptions of validity, preliminary relief, and obviousness in patent law', *Cardozo Arts & Entertainment Law Journal*, **25** (3), 995–1058.

Schoenhard, Paul (2008), 'Who took my IP? – defending the availability of injunctive relief for patent owners', *Texas Intellectual Property Law Journal*, **16** (2008), 196.

Sell, Susan (2008), 'The Global IP Upward Ratchet, Anti-Counterfeiting and Piracy Enforcement Efforts: The State of Play', *Occasional Papers*, No. 1, Geneva: IQsensato.

Sindico, Francesco (2005), 'The GMO Dispute before the WTO: Legal Implications for the Trade and Environment Debate', *FEEM Fondazione Eni Enrico Mattei Research Paper Series*, Working Paper No. 11.06, available at: http://papers.ssrn.com/sol3/papers.cfm?abstract_id=655061; accessed 15 November 2008.

South Centre (2008), 'Who Should Bear the IP Enforcement Cost?', *Policy Brief*, No. 12.

South Centre and CIEL (2008), 'The International Medical Products Anti-Counterfeiting Taskforce (IMPACT): Is the WHO on the Right Track?', *IP Quarterly Update*, Issue No. 3, pp. 1–14.

Statement by the Development Manager of Monsanto Argentina, *Newspaper La Nación*, March 6 2006, Section 2, p. 3.

Sterk, Stewart E. (2008), 'Property rules, liability rules, and uncertainty about property rights', *Michigan Law Review*, **106** (7), 1285–336.

Stiefel, Aron (2008),'Two years since *eBay*: the impact on permanent injunctive relief in patent cases', *Patent, Trademark & Copyright Journal*, **76** (1867), 62 (BNA).

Story, Joseph (1870), *Commentaries on Equity Jurisprudence as Administered in England and America*, Isaac F. Redfield (ed.) (10th edn), Boston: Little Brown.

Sweney, M. (2008), 'Illegal downloaders to get warning letter in government clampdown', *The Guardian* (24 July 2008).

Tom, Williard K. and Joshua A. Newberg (1997), 'Antitrust and intellectual property: from separate spheres to unified field', *Antitrust Law Journal*, **66**, 167–230.

Trebilcock, Michael J. and Robert Howse (2005), *The Regulation of International Trade*, 3rd edn, London: Routledge.

UNCTAD (1996), *The TRIPS Agreement and Developing Countries*, UN Doc. No. 96/II/D/10, 1996.

UNCTAD (2007), *The Least Developed Country Report 2007 – Knowledge, Technological Learning and Innovation for Development*, Geneva: UNCTAD.

UNCTAD and ICTSD (2005), *Resource Book on TRIPS and Development*, Cambridge: Cambridge University Press, available at: iprsonline.org/unctadictsd/ResourceBookIndex.htm; accessed 29 September 2008.

UNDP (1999), *Human Development Report.*

United States Patent and Trademark Office (2008), *Manual of Patent Examining Procedure (MPEP)* (8th edn).

US Department of Justice and Federal Trade Commission (DOJ and FTC) (2007), *Antitrust Enforcement and Intellectual Property Rights: Promoting Innovation and Competition*, available at: April 2007, http://www.ftc.gov/bc/tech/property/reports.htm; accessed 21 September 2008.

USTR (2007), 'Ambassador Schwab Announces US Will Seek New Trade Agreement to Fight Fakes', USTR Press Release, 23 October 2007, available at: http://www.ustr.gov/Document_Library/ Press_Releases/2007/October/Ambassador_Schwab_Announces_ US_Will_Seek_New_Trade_Agreement_to_Fight_Fakes.html; accessed 5 October 2008.

USTR (2008), *National Trade Estimate Report on Foreign Trade Barriers*, p. 24, available at: http://www.ustr.gov/assets/Document_ Library/Reports_Publications/2008/2008_NTE_Report/asset_ upload_file365_14652.pdf; accessed 5 December 2008.

Vernon, John A., Joseph H. Golec and W. Keener Hughen (2006), 'The economics of pharmaceutical price regulation and importation: refocusing the debate', *American Journal of Law & Medicine*, **32** (2), 175–92.

Vrins, Olivier and Marius Schneider (2006), *Enforcement of Intellectual Property Rights through Border Measures, Law and Practice in the EU*, Oxford: Oxford University Press.

Watal, Jayashree (2001), *Intellectual Property Rights in the WTO and Developing Countries*, London: Kluwer Law International.

Wechkin, John M. (1995), 'Drug price regulation and compulsory licensing for pharmaceutical patents: the New Zealand connection', *Pacific Rim Law & Policy Journal*, **5** (1), 237–60.

Wegner, Harold C. (2008), 'Post-*eBay* Compulsory Licenses: TRIPS Standards', paper prepared for the 41st World Congress of the Association Internationale pour la Protection de la Propriété

Intellectuelle, Boston 6–11 September 2008, available at: http://
www.aippiboston.org/en/phpincludes/program/workshops/
twelve/pdfs/WS_XII_Wegner.pdf; accessed 24 January 2009.

Whitaker, Leroy (1974), 'Compulsory licensing – another nail in the
coffin', *American Patent Law Association Quarterly Journal*, **2** (1),
165–8.

WHO (1992), *Counterfeit Drugs: Report of a Joint WHO/IFPMA
Workshop*, WHO/DMP/CFD/92, 1–3 April, Geneva.

WHO (2006), *Counterfeit Medicines*, available at: http://www.who.
int/mediacentre/factsheets/fs275/en/; accessed 20 January 2009.

Wilson, Bruce B. (1970), 'Patent and Know-How License Agreements:
Field of Use, Territorial, Price and Quantity Restrictions',
Address before the Fourth New England Antitrust Conference, 6
November 1970.

WIPO (1999), 'The Role of the Government Authorities in the
Enforcement of Intellectual Property Rights', WIPO Workshop on
the Enforcement of Intellectual Property Rights for Judges, WIPO/
IPR/JU/BEY/99/5B, available at: http://www.wipo.int/edocs/
mdocs/sme/en/wipo_ipr_ju_bey_99/wipo_ipr_ju_bey_99_5b.pdf;
accessed 20 January 2009.

WIPO (2003), *Intellectual Property: A Powerful Tool for Economic
Growth*, available at: http://www.wipo.int/export/sites/www/
freepublications/en/intproperty/888/wipo_pub_888_1.pdf; accessed 20 January 2009.

World Bank (2001), *Global Economic Prospects and the Developing
Countries*, Washington, DC: World Bank.

Xue, H. (2005), 'Between the hammer and the block: China's intellectual property rights in the network age', *University of Ottawa
Law & Technology Journal*, **2** (2), 291–314.

Xue, H. (2007), 'Les Fleurs du Mal: a critique of the legal transplant
in Chinese Internet copyright protection', *Rutgers Computer and
Technology Law Journal*, **34** (1), 173–84.

Appendix: about the South Centre

The South Centre, with headquarters in Geneva, is an intergovernmental organization and think tank of developing countries established by an intergovernmental treaty that came into force on 31 July 1995. It currently has 50 Member Countries.

The Centre has grown out of the work and experience of the South Commission and its follow-up mechanism, and from recognition of the need for enhanced South–South cooperation. The Report of the South Commission emphasized that the South is not well organized at the global level and has thus not been effective in mobilizing its considerable combined expertise and experience, nor its bargaining power.

The South Centre meets the need for analysis of development problems and experience, and provides intellectual and policy support required by developing countries for collective and individual action, particularly in the international arena. The Innovation, Access to Knowledge and Intellectual Property Programme (IAKP) is one of three major institutional pillars of the Centre. The mission of the IAKP is to contribute to the development, coordinated use and improvement of the capacity of developing countries and their institutions to integrate the development dimension into their innovation, access to knowledge and intellectual property policies.

The objective of the IAKP is to ensure that global, regional and national rules facilitate the generation of knowledge, goods and services in key areas such as health, industry and agriculture and that such knowledge, goods and services are available and affordable for all.

For more information, visit the South Centre website at http://www.southcentre.org (English, French and Spanish).

Index